Preparing Your Son for Every Man's Battle

STEPHEN ARTERBURN
FRED STOEKER
WITH MIKE YORKEY

Preparing Your Son for
Every Man's
Battle

Honest Conversations About Sexual Integrity

WaterBrook
PRESS

PREPARING YOUR SON FOR EVERY MAN'S BATTLE
PUBLISHED BY WATERBROOK PRESS
12265 Oracle Boulevard, Suite 200
Colorado Springs, CO 80921

All Scripture quotations, unless otherwise indicated, are taken from the Holy Bible, New International Version®. NIV®. Copyright © 1973, 1978, 1984 by International Bible Society. Used by permission of Zondervan Publishing House. All rights reserved. Scripture quotations marked (KJV) are taken from the King James Version. Scripture quotations marked (MSG) are taken from The Message by Eugene H. Peterson. Copyright © 1993, 1994, 1995, 1996, 2000, 2001, 2002. Used by permission of NavPress Publishing Group. All rights reserved. Scripture quotations marked (NASB) are taken from the New American Standard Bible®. © Copyright The Lockman Foundation 1960, 1962, 1963, 1968, 1971, 1972, 1973, 1975, 1977, 1995. Used by permission. (www.Lockman.org). Scripture quotations marked (NKJV) are taken from the New King James Version®. Copyright © 1982 by Thomas Nelson Inc. Used by permission. All rights reserved. Scripture quotations marked (NLT) are taken from the Holy Bible, New Living Translation, copyright © 1996. Used by permission of Tyndale House Publishers Inc., Wheaton, Illinois 60189. All rights reserved. Scripture quotations marked (RSV) are taken from the Revised Standard Version of the Bible, copyright © 1952 [2nd edition, 1971] by the Division of Christian Education of the National Council of the Churches of Christ in the USA. Used by permission. All rights reserved. Scripture quotations marked (TLB) are taken from The Living Bible, copyright © 1971. Used by permission of Tyndale House Publishers Inc., Wheaton, Illinois 60189. All rights reserved.

Italics in Scripture quotations reflect the authors' added emphasis.

Names and facts from stories contained in this book have been changed, but the emotional and sexual struggles portrayed are true stories as related to the authors through personal interviews, letters, or e-mails.

Trade Paperback ISBN 978-0-307-45856-8
eBook ISBN 978-0-307-55275-4

Published in association with the literary agency of Alive Communications Inc., 7680 Goddard Street, Suite 200, Colorado Springs, CO 80920, www.alivecommunications.com.

Published in the United States by WaterBrook Multnomah, an imprint of the Crown Publishing Group, a division of Penguin Random House LLC, New York.

WATERBROOK and its deer colophon are registered trademarks of Penguin Random House LLC.

Library of Congress Cataloging-in-Publication Data
Arterburn, Stephen, 1953–
     Preparing your son for every man's battle : honest conversations about sexual integrity / Stephen Arterburn, Fred Stoeker with Mike Yorkey.—1st ed.
       p. cm.
   1. Sex—Religious aspects—Christianity. 2. Sex instruction for teenagers—Religious aspects—Christianity. 3. Teenage boys—Religious life. 4. Christian teenagers—Religious life. 5. Fathers and sons—Religious aspects— Christianity. 6. Parent and teenager—Religious aspects—Christianity. I. Stoeker, Fred. II. Yorkey, Mike. III. Title.
   BT708.A755 2003
   241'.66—dc21 2003013622

Printed in the United States of America
2015

10 9 8 7

SPECIAL SALES
Most WaterBrook Multnomah books are available at special quantity discounts when purchased in bulk by corporations, organizations, and special-interest groups. Custom imprinting or excerpting can also be done to fit special needs. For information, please e-mail SpecialMarkets@WaterBrookMultnomah.com or call 1-800-603-7051.

contents

Foreword by Stephen Arterburn ix
Acknowledgments xiii

book 1: for dad (or single mom)

Introduction 3
1   Stepping Through the Crack in the Door 11
2   The First Half Is Still the First Half 16
3   Diving Deep 27
4   The Swapping Place 34
5   "You Go First, Dad" 43
6   Doing Book 49
7   Rules of the Game 59
8   Outside the Swapping Place 74
9   Running All the Way 80
10 The Spiritual Inheritance 91

book 2: for son and dad

Introduction 111

Part 1: Changes 119

1   The Planet "Pupiter" 121
2   What Does Making Love Mean? 128
3   When Girls Enter the Picture 132
4   What's Happening 138
5   Does Everyone Else Know More Than I Do? 143
6   The Ps in the Pod 149
7   Flip Sides 154

8   My Story 163

9   The Eyes Have It 172

10   Manly Eyes. 180

11   Self-Control 187

Part 2: The Birth of a Man 195

12   My Story: The Sequel 197

13   Sloppy Promises 205

14   What's Independence? 210

15   We Aren't Perfect 217

16   Normal or Warped? 223

17   Who Loves Ya? 233

18   The Trap 240

19   Treat Her Like a Sister 246

20   Date Away 256

21   Are You Ready for Your Number to Be Called? 264

foreword

(by Stephen Arterburn)

When I was in junior high, I felt like a loser. That was a very tough time for me, just as it is for most young people today. My daily goal was to not humiliate myself or look like the awkward, uncomfortable, pimply young man that I was. If I could get through a day of not saying something stupid or stumbling or having my voice crack in midsentence, then it was a good day. Even on my best days, though, I felt like a loser, and on one never-to-be-forgotten, very bad day, I definitely *was* one.

The horrific day started out on the massive turf of Kyle Field in College Station, Texas, home of the Texas Aggies. Somehow I had landed on our school's track team, and we were in town to compete in a big track meet. All morning my stomach was filled with butterflies, moths, bees, bats, and everything else that flutters. In the simple terms of my mother, I was a nervous wreck.

All morning I watched our team's embarrassment grow as my fears intensified. The shot-putters could not put, and they looked pretty shot. The pole-vaulters were all pole and little vault. The high-jumpers wore lead boots. We were pathetic. But worse than that, each dismal event drew us closer to the 440 relay, where I suspected I would become the focal point of all the earth's negative attention.

I was the anchor, the one who is supposed to be the fastest runner. That I was the anchor still amazes me to this day and shows just how pitiful we were. I was full of dread that I'd grip the baton, only to lose the race in a dead heat at the finish line. Playing the final moments over and over again in my head, I envisioned a last monumental push to the tape that would not be enough to win, whereupon I would collapse from exhaustion in the humiliation of defeat. This was my worst nightmare, but it did not happen. Instead, something far worse than my worst nightmare was about to unfold.

Our moment had finally come, and when the gun fired, I jumped as if I had been shot. Six runners burst from the blocks, and for about three glorious seconds, all looked evenly matched. But as each sprinter shifted into his highest gear, the grand humiliation began to build. Our first runner looked like he was jogging! Mister Slow Mo just could not get the glue off his shoes, and by the time he passed the baton, the other teams were halfway to the third leg of the race.

It kept getting worse. My teammates seemed drugged as I pleaded from my post, helplessly leaping, yelling, and flinging my arms, urging on the slowest, deaf relay team ever known to man.

Swoosh! My heart sank as the first runner blitzed by me. Then another swoosh, and then a third, fourth, and a fifth. Then I waited…and waited…and waited. "Come on! Come on!" I shouted to our third runner, but he was still so far away he could not hear me. Still, I pleaded on, jiggling and grimacing until he finally stretched that baton toward my right hand. Snatching it, I turned my face resolutely toward the finish line only to see five rear ends break the tape just as I began.

So there I was, running all alone in what seemed like a two-hour dash to the finish. There would be no final, last-second lunge. I was given the baton too late to do anything but humiliate myself. I can still hear the laughter roaring as I finished the relay alone, and I can still see the fingers pointing at Loser Boy on display. I certainly didn't get through *that* day without embarrassing myself. I vowed that I would never run in the Dunce Bowl again, and I never did.

But while it was my last footrace, it was certainly not my last humiliation. The "passing of the baton too late" became the metaphor for my life. Every father passes a baton to his son in the generational relay, and my dad was no exception. He had stuffed that baton with Christian truths and moral principals, and he believed I would carry it well and build upon the heritage he'd built.

But there was a problem—he passed it off too late. By the time he thought I was ready to receive it, much of my race was over, and the agony of defeat was already rooted in place. My old-fashioned Texan father thought you became a man at age twenty-one, but he was sadly mistaken. The perils in our race toward manhood come much earlier than twenty-one years of age, and a late baton pass eliminates any real chance of winning.

Passing the baton is what *Preparing Your Son for Every Man's Battle* is all about. Your son needs the baton now. While a young man might have his first sexual experience at the age of sixteen or eighteen, he is developing thoughts and attitudes about that first sexual experience at the age of eleven or twelve. His preparation must begin and his questions must be answered during the early legs of the race to instill the confidence, integrity, and purity necessary to run well in the latter legs. We are thrilled with the opportunity to be your assistant coaches in this race.

You have to be careful, though. You may want to do more than hand your son the baton that your father passed to you. Unless you are one of the rare and fortunate men of our day, that baton you received was probably cracked and stained. If you have not done some serious work on your own character and have not allowed God to repair your soul, that baton is probably in no better shape than when it was handed to you. If you feel you need to do some work in that area, we hope you will seek out the other books in the Every Man series written just for you. Do you want to pass off something to your kids that far exceeds what you received from your father? Fred and I do. If you have that same desire, we think you are on the right track.

The effective father must pass along a baton that teaches his son how to delay gratification, take responsibility, and connect deeply with others, including God. When this happens, his son will become a man of character, someone who knows who he is, and someone who is ready to make a difference in fulfilling God's mission for his life.

We have developed this book because we want to see the pattern of our lives reversed. We were equipped too late to be the young men that God would have loved for us to be, but it is not too late for your son. The book you are holding in your hands is the evidence that you want something better for him. We want that for your son too, and we stand with you as you stretch the baton his way. May God bless you as you run!

acknowledgments

Thanks to Steve Arterburn, an empathetic man who knows how to walk in another's shoes and who knows how to walk his talk.

Thanks to Mike Yorkey. God was with us. Rogers and Hammerstein never had it so good!

Thanks to Gary Meyer and Dave Roe, men who understand the times and are raising boys to be real men in the face of it all.

Thanks to Gary Rosberg. I love you like a brother, and I honor your work, but mostly I just plain, downright like you. Thanks for being you.

Thanks to Lt. Vicki Cluney and Pastor Ray and Joyce Henderson for your ceaseless prayer for my ministry, and thanks to Pastor Roger and Liz Sieh and your intercessors in Reinbeck. When told of this book, you invited me to join you for intercession one bright autumn Tuesday. What a morning! You marched out before me that day and have covered my flanks throughout the course of this battle. Then, when the battle was darkest, you stood up and carried me home. Your love for God and your perseverance bring tears to my eyes. One thing I know...your Father hears your every cry.

Blessings to Jasen, Laura, Rebecca, and Michael. The stories of your lives are the stuff of legend to me. Your wisdom always stops me in my tracks, and I'm far better for having known you. God sees your sacrifices...He will personally reward you.

Brenda, your kiss is still on my list of the best things in life. But your spiritual growth this past year has been nothing short of spectacular. You are lovelier than I've ever known you. Oh, that we could marry and live another life together! The moment I laid eyes on you was my finest moment, and our wedding was my finest hour. May God's glory ever rest on your brow, my sweet!   —*Fred Stoeker*

Thank you, Fred Stoeker! Your wisdom from God is changing lives all over the world. I am blessed to be your partner.   —*Stephen Arterburn*

Preparing Your Son for Every Man's Battle

Book I

for dad
(or single mom)

I saw Ben not long ago on a bright, crisp autumn Thursday in Iowa. Ben is a business client of mine from Mason City. I see Ben exactly once a year when he places his annual order with me. Our actual business takes but a minute or two, and then we're off to talking about more important things—kids and boats and golf, topics that middle-aged Midwestern fathers like to talk about.

When Ben inquired about my son Jasen, his eyes lit up when I told him that my oldest child was enjoying his freshmen year at Iowa State University, which happened to be Ben's alma mater. "How 'bout those Cyclones?" Ben asked, proud that *his* football team was having a banner season.

We jabbered on about Iowa State football and the big game coming up on the weekend. "Yeah, I'm taking my son Derek down to see the Texas Tech game on Saturday," Ben said. "I usually go down to Ames for one game each year, and I really like the atmosphere of those 6:00 P.M. games, with the crisp, autumn air and popcorn under the lights. And what a great match-up this year too! Oughta be a wild one!"

"I'll say," I offered. "With Tech's offense averaging forty points a game, the 'Clones should have a real track meet on their hands."

"Yep, they always put on a good show down there," Ben said. "My son's really looking forward to the game. He's in eighth grade now, you know. You have one in junior high too, don't you?"

"Correct. She's in eighth grade too. Ah, junior high! Weird times, dontcha think?"

That casual comment struck a chord with Ben, who used my comment to shift the conversation in a different direction "You know, Fred, you're *so* right about that. It's funny," he mused. "I've always felt close to my kids. But now, with

Derek in junior high, I can't really read him any more. Well, some days I can, like I'm reading his mail, but there are many days that I look at him and I just can't read him at all."

I chuckled. It seems as our children age, it is *our* sight that diminishes! This hardly seems fair, since there will never be a time when we need our insight to be sharper. Our parenting trek enters our own personal "final frontier" when adolescence arrives. But unlike television's *Star Trek,* we must boldly go where *many* have gone before—the teenage years! As *Toy Story*'s Buzz Lightyear might say, "To their puberty...and beyond!"

And though you may have trouble reading adolescents as you're warping your way into uncharted space, it doesn't take a rocket scientist to read one thing loud and clear: Your teen needs you in the captain's chair on this voyage. Your kids need your input, your leadership, your heritage, and stories from your youth. They need to hear from you immediately, because many teens bounce into adolescence having no idea what hit them. When that happens, they feel...*desperate.*

Trouble is, too often they remain desperate. They don't get our input because our subspace communications with our kids have failed.

Why is that? Is it because they've changed so much as they've moved into adolescence and have become harder to read, jamming communication?

Nope. These changes are just a normal, glorious part of God's plans for our kids' growth into adulthood. That's why our teens aren't the problem. The real problem lies with our *sins* as fathers.

You heard me right. Among fathers, what is the most common sin in this world? If you've read our first book, *Every Man's Battle,* you might suspect I'd name sexual impurity as our number one transgression. If we were playing *Family Feud,* there's no doubt that sexual sin would rank as one of the top three answers. But what is the number one most common sin of the fathers?

The answer is: failing to make the hand-off.

What do I mean by hand-off? For those of you who grew up in Antarctica, the hand-off is a football term for when the quarterback hands the football to the running back, hoping that he'll escape the clutches of the defensive linemen and break free for a long run. The hand-off is a great metaphor for what we'll be discussing throughout the rest of this book, and it's all laid out here in Scripture:

Fix these words of mine in your hearts and minds; tie them as symbols on your hands and bind them on your foreheads. Teach them to your children, talking about them when you sit at home and when you walk along the road, when you lie down and when you get up. (Deuteronomy 11:18-19)

JUST HALF A MINUTE

How's your ball-handling? Do you feel like you are—or have been—successfully handing the ball to your son?

It's our belief that too many parents are fumbling away their chances to make a successful hand-off. Recent studies have replicated what earlier studies reported years ago: Fathers are not interacting with their children. When fathers were wired with recording devices and sent home to tape their interactions with their kids at night, the average American father spent about thirty seconds in direct conversation with his children. Thirty seconds! Little is happening as we sit, walk, lie down, and get up in our homes.

Bart Starr, quarterback of the Green Bay Packers dynasty of the sixties, believed that one of his most important responsibilities was the hand-off, an aspect of the game that few football fans notice. Starr practiced for *years* placing the ball into the runner's hands at just the right spot, at just the right time, with the same precision and pressure. Why? To insure that his running backs could fulfill *their* roles too. The responsibility for the hand-off lay with the quarterback, never with the running back.

I quarterbacked my high-school team for three seasons, and I worked extra snaps after practice to perfect the proper hand-off. Like Bart Starr, I was determined that no player on my team would ever wonder if he was going to get the ball when and where he should.

My days of gridiron glory are long past. But, in a sense, the art of the hand-off has never been more critical for me. Why is that? Because I have an eleven-year-old son on my team, ready to run for daylight, and I'm responsible for getting him the ball.

We've huddled up, and Michael's play has been called—adolescence is upon him. The ball of truth has been snapped, and as the quarterback and leader of my team, I must get the ball into Michael's hands. God is opening holes in the offensive line of life for him to safely pass through. But if I'm sloppy with the hand-off or a split second late, the gap in the line may close, stacking him up at the line of scrimmage until an enemy wave overwhelms him.

But how do I *accomplish* this hand-off? What do I tell my son about how his transition from boy to man is going to go? How do I tell him all that I've learned from God, my pastors, and my mentors? What do I tell him about *my* mistakes and what I've learned from them? Most difficult of all, *when* do I tell him? Life is just so doggone busy.

Beneath the roar in the stadium of life, the crush of school performances, swim meets, and piano recitals, how can I even be sure that Michael is hearing my signals? If you are remotely like those average fathers who interact just thirty seconds a day, you can be sure he isn't. It's not because *he* has hearing problems; it's because you aren't talking enough.

You haven't had much practice making that hand-off. You've got to get talking. For now, beginning in junior high and through early high school, our boys really want to hear from us. So many things are confusing them, and so many things are new.

When my firstborn son, Jasen, was eleven years old, I stumbled onto a process that opened my life to Jasen and gave him a steady voice that he could hear and understand as he entered this strange, strange world of puberty and adolescence. I got him the ball.

Jasen is in college now, charging through the opposing lines on the field of life, the ball of truth safely tucked under his lanky arm. As he runs for daylight, a lump comes to my throat as I whisper a line from a favorite song: "Godspeed, dear runner. Carry it home!" I know Jasen will not fumble.

What about your little runner? It's tough for a man to talk to his son about sexual issues. To raise the subject fights against that time-honored code that almost every male we've known has followed, which is called the Sexual Code of Silence. The code states that it's okay to joke about sex or even lie about it, but other than that, it's your solemn duty—as a male—to keep silent whenever a *serious* discussion about sex takes place.

Everyone seems determined not to talk about the eight-hundred-pound gorilla sitting in the middle of the living room. Maybe it is too embarrassing, but it doesn't help that we adults often have a fuzzy picture of what healthy sex is all about. If we're confused, imagine what is going on in the heads of our pubescent sons! They must be walking around in a twisting, swirling fog.

Even the best fathers we know fear discussing the topic. They can't bring themselves to convey the truths they long to share with their sons. My friend Kenny, a father of three, once told me, "I remember when I was in high school and my father and I were driving home from a fishing trip in southern Missouri. I noticed his hands tightening their grip on the steering wheel, and then he said it: 'Son, you're getting older. Do you have any questions about girls?'

"And in my great wisdom at age fifteen, I emphatically said, 'No!' And nothing else was said about the topic the whole trip. In fact, the subject was never brought up again. I didn't know anything then, and I'm still learning years later. What a loss," Kenny concluded.

Without a decent "How to Talk to Your Son About Sex" example set by our dads—and with the Code of Silence hanging heavy like ankle weights as you prepare to walk down this path—most of us haven't a clue about where to start this discussion.

What should I say to my precious boy?

How much do I tell him?

Do I talk about dating?

Do we discuss touching girls where they shouldn't be touched?

Do I have to talk about masturbation?

Do I tell him about my own sins in high school and college? That might strengthen him, but it might weaken him too. How do I know?

Arghh!

Our fears and our inadequacies urge us to think of "the talk" as a one-time event, a towering mountain that must be scaled as quickly as possible. Mustering up the courage to begin climbing is difficult enough, but if our sons say they don't have any questions, we're happy never to leave base camp, saying, "Okay, but if you ever do want to talk about it, let me know." We instinctively know that those questions will never arise again, so we are only too happy to kick back and watch the sun settle behind the horizon. But look again at Kenny's words.

"What a loss," he said. We cannot do that to our sons.

That's why Stephen Arterburn and I have decided on a two-books-in-one approach to this topic. Book 1 is for parents only and teaches an easy, easy way for you to approach any topic with your sons (and daughters, too), including sex. It involves reading through books with your kids, and while that thought may evoke unpleasant images of a class at school, nothing I do with my kids is more fun or pleasant.

More important, as you read along together, you'll get to interject your thoughts and your stories and your growing-up advice and your values, completing that call from God that has, for so many of us, been largely ignored in the crush of life.

Many of us men find it difficult to connect deeply with our kids, because our own fathers did not do so with us, and it doesn't seem to come naturally. Book 1 will teach you how to build bridges of connection with your kids. We want you to learn how to teach sexual truth to your sons, but we also want you to learn how to connect with any young human being in general, whether boy or girl. With this goal in mind, I'll be sharing stories of going through books with both my sons and daughters to give you a good feel for the process.

Book 2 gives you a chance to put what you've just learned into practice. This portion of the book is divided into two parts that provide timely, age-appropriate material about sex to read through with your son. We'll help you jump-start gripping discussions with your young man, teaching you *how* to say things and *when* to say things. Part 1 is for eleven- and twelve-year-old sons who are approaching the outer boundaries of puberty but are still largely sexually unaware. Part 2 is for thirteen- to fifteen-year-old sons clearly within the grasp of puberty or heading out the other side. You'll find that sharing this information is easy and fun and may be the most enriching thing you'll ever do with your son.

Okay, I saw that flicker of doubt come across your face. I know what you're thinking because I'm a guy too, remember? Maybe you're the typical overcommitted, somewhat hesitant, little-bit-guilty dad who knows he should do something about this adolescent sex stuff with his boy. Perhaps you've picked up this book and skimmed the contents, and now you're thinking, *Wow, this looks like quite a bit of prep work to do this with Johnny. Maybe I better find a different book.*

Don't worry. Only a small portion of Book 2 involves any sort of prep work. Yes, I could have given you fewer chapters, but I prayed long and hard about what I believe God wanted me to write here. I'm confident that the Lord wants this to be far more than a "here's how to talk to your son about sex" type of book. He wants to change the way you communicate with your son on *every* topic, not just the birds and the bees. He wants you and your son to be tight, and you will be tighter after you go through this book with him. *Preparing Your Son for Every Man's Battle* will affect your relationship with your son forever, and your ability to communicate with each other will never be the same.

I also believe this book can alter your son's Christian destiny. When we wrote *Every Man's Battle* and *Every Young Man's Battle*, we wanted to help free those who had already fallen into sexual sin. With *Preparing Your Son for Every Man's Battle,* our goal is to keep young men from falling into sexual sin and wasting years spinning their wheels in the slime of sexual impurity. As his father, you are his first line of defense against sexual impurity, and it is your responsibility to teach him what you know. We'll help you do that.

In line with our goal to keep them from falling, we will be less graphic in our word pictures than we were in *Every Young Man's Battle,* allowing you to teach your son at his own level. We also will not discuss masturbation in this book, since we don't want to add new temptations to the lives of the young men who haven't yet discovered the practice. You can bring it up on your own if you choose. If you find during your discussions that your son is already up to his neck in this quagmire, you might pick up a copy of *Every Young Man's Battle,* where we cover the topic exhaustively.

BUT WHAT IF DAD'S NOT HOME?

Many boys grow up in homes without fathers. I did. My parents divorced when I was eleven years old, and though Dad continued to live in the same town, the divorce blew a gap in our relationship that he could never quite bridge when trying to share the truths of human sexuality with me. If you are not living with your children—for whatever reason—I believe this book will help you bridge that gap, providing a great, healthy interface through which to pass these truths.

If you are a single mom, then you've come to the right place. You'll be able to easily use this book with your son as well. Single moms find it especially daunting to talk to a son about male sexuality. It has to be really hard, but as the only parent on duty, it's up to you, and we're here to stand behind you and encourage you to give it a shot.

Since you, as a single mother, aren't male and can't share the male point of view from stories of your own life, we will be transparent about our teen years and our father years so that you will have stories to share with your son.

Relax in the fact that we are targeting boys in the eleven- through fifteen-year-old age group. That doesn't mean *Preparing Your Son* wouldn't be useful to older teens, but we give you the age range to inform you that this book will be less sexually graphic than *Every Man's Battle* and *Every Young Man's Battle*. That should make it somewhat easier for you as a single mom.

In conclusion, our teens need to hear from us. And we need to hear from them. When that happens, relationships are deepened.

Let's chart a deeper course with them and see what we'll find.

So...ready to get started?

stepping through the crack in the door

I stood silently in the dark upper hallway, frozen by fear as I peered intently into the light slipping through the crack of Jasen's bedroom door. He sat in the middle of the floor, focused tightly on the Game Boy he was playing. I knew something he didn't…a man with wild, desperate eyes was quietly sneaking up behind him to shatter his peaceful evening.

That man would be me, his father.

Oh, he is having so much fun…I won't disturb him now. I'll come by tomorrow night instead, I reasoned to myself. That sounded like the best course of action. So good, in fact, that I'd followed that line of reasoning four nights in a row already.

Dallying in the darkness, I realized that sooner or later I was going to have to make my move. Just how many times could I sneak up the hallway, peek into his room, only to slip back down the stairs into the warmth of the family room without making a sound? And besides, just what was I going to do about that faint but unmistakable odor following me with every step? I smelled a sissy lurking about. Yes, that's right. Me again. Would I ever go into Jasen's room and have our talk?

I was scared—a big, fat yellow-bellied chicken. How do you discuss puberty with an eleven-year-old boy? I sure didn't know how, and I wasn't too anxious to learn, either. But I knew I was going to give it a try sooner or later. I had to.

I thought back to what had happened a year before on a clear, warm summer night. Forty-four guys climbed wearily onto a bus one midnight, and we rolled in the darkness toward Boulder, Colorado, for a stadium-style two-day Christian seminar.

Greg Laurie opened the seminar that Friday evening with a salvation message. While I'd been saved years ago, I was still struggling with some deep issues regarding my relationship with a dominant father. I'd been praying that God would give me some answers during the trip out west, but I figured I'd have to wait for some speaker the next day to deliver the goods. Not some hip preacher from Southern California doing an altar call before a packed house at Folsom Field on the campus of the University of Colorado.

But Greg quoted Revelation 3:20 as one of his texts that night: "Here I am! I stand at the door and knock. If anyone hears my voice and opens the door, I will come in and eat with him, and he with me." And then, while referencing this verse, he made a simple statement in the middle of his talk that just blew me away. "God just wants to put His arm around you and have a steak with you," he said. In that moment, God's revelation hit me like a comet.

God wants to put His arm around me and cut into a juicy steak with me? You're probably scratching your head and thinking, *What gives? What's the big deal with that?* All I can tell you is that when that sentence was mixed with God's power into my spirit, years of pain, agony, and frustration over my dad began to crumble and melt away instantly. My heavenly Father saw me as His son, and He didn't care a whit about what I achieved or what I did or if I were successful. All He really wanted was a relationship with me, a chance to just sit down with me, put an arm around me, and have a barbecue steak with me. I didn't have to prove myself. I had real value already.

And you know what? From that moment, it seemed like every other one of my significant relationships changed too. As far as I was concerned, the seminar could have ended right there with Greg Laurie's talk, and it would have been well worth the long bus ride across six hundred miles of farmland and open range.

But one of the most electric, emotional experiences of my life happened the very next night. As the strains of the last worship song echoed off and died against the Rocky Mountains that shadowed over us, the host introduced the next speaker,

Dr. James Dobson, the president and founder of Focus on the Family. I knew that Dr. Dobson accepted only one or two public speaking invitations a year, so I knew what I was about to receive would be a special gift. But I had no idea how special.

As the sun fell deeply behind the jagged mountains and the darkness of the night settled in, James Dobson stepped onto the stage. Fifty-two thousand men stood and cheered for upward of ten minutes—I'd never seen anything like it. My emotions flooded over every bank. I suddenly realized in that moment that nearly everything I knew about being a husband and a father had come from James Dobson. It was as if my own cherished grandfather had stepped out on stage, a grandfather who had taught me everything he knew because he loved me so. I was beaming, cheering wildly, yet tears of pride just poured from my eyes. What a moment.

Dr. Dobson was funny, poignant, and wise with his words, but I'll never forget his final statement: "God only gives us so many times to go fishing with our kids...so don't miss a one of them. Thank you." He smiled to thunderous applause, and then he disappeared behind the stage.

I was still basking in the glow of that conference a week or so later as I poked through the aisles at a Christian bookstore. I stumbled across James Dobson's pocket paperback *Preparing for Adolescence,* and remembering that special weekend, I picked it up and thumbed through it. The book had been a classic since its release fifteen years before, and though I thought I had read everything Dr. Dobson had written, somehow I'd still never gotten to this book. I bought a copy and took it with me on a flight to Dallas the next day. A short, captivating read, *Preparing for Adolescence* was easily finished on the return flight home.

Closing the book, I quietly laid it on the tray table and shut my eyes. I was pumped. *What a great book this would be to read with Jasen someday!* I bought him his own copy so that we could go through the book together when it was time for me to explain puberty and the "facts of life."

One great night in Boulder and one great read on a plane...and nearly a year passed until I figured that it was time for me to follow through on my great idea. That's when my troubles in the hallway began, the botched nights stacking up on each other. Up the stairs, up the hall, down the hall, down the stairs, over and over again.

And now tonight, for the fifth night running, I stood in the dark hallway, sweat beading my brow and moist fingers gripping two small books. My heart was pounding, and my mind was racing. Would I go in?

Dr. Dobson's voice seemed to be whispering, "Go on in! Your son needs you!" Jesus' voice seemed to whisper, "Haven't I asked you to train up this precious little boy? I'm counting on you, my friend." In my other ear, though, I listened to the whispers of doubt. I also knew that if I didn't follow through, my wife, Brenda, would only shudder and mercifully say, "Did you chicken out again?"

"Yeah, I'm afraid so."

"I don't blame you. I wouldn't want to do it."

At least your intentions are good, I said to myself.

But in the end, good intentions didn't turn the tide for me. It was my nose that tipped the scales in that dimly lit moment. I couldn't stand that sissy smell in my nostrils. *It's now or never. I'm going in!*

With my shaky courage covering my solid trepidation, I marched right into Jasen's room. Slightly startled, Jasen looked up from his game. With a smile, I handed him his copy of the book, expecting a deep, resigned sigh as it dawned on him that Dad was enacting another "plan."

Settling down onto his bed, I opened my copy and said, "Jasen, I know this might feel a little uncomfortable, but you will soon be entering a very interesting period of development."

"Oh yeah?" he responded. "I've heard of that. It's called perverty, right?"

With much effort, I suppressed a laugh. "Well, it's actually called *puberty,* Son." I paused and then chuckled. "But actually, your word might be a better fit, come to think of it." Out of the mouths of babes, you know?

Pushing ahead, I proceeded, "Anyway, puberty is going to be bringing a lot of physical changes in you. You know how Uncle Brent is always tickling you and checking for 'grass' under your arms? Well, the grass is about to start sprouting. And you'll be getting a beard, and you'll have to start shaving like me, if you can believe it."

His eyes lit up at that one.

"But there will also be mental and emotional changes, Jace. It is hard for me to put those into words exactly. For instance, you'll likely soon experience more peer pressure from your friends, and you might even care more about your friends' opinions than mine for a while. And because all the other kids are going to be going through this and trying to find their way through it too, you'll likely also face embarrassments and hurts as you go through puberty. I just want to prepare you for it, Son, so you aren't caught off-guard."

I paused, waiting for the dreaded sigh and the roll of his eyes. Instead came the shocker.

"Dad, I really think it's good that we're going to read this book together, especially right now," he said.

Dumbfounded, I could only stare at him. I couldn't believe my ears. Unable to muster a cohesive thought in that moment, I eventually blurted, "Why?"

"Well, I've been kind of scared lately."

Scared? My son? "Scared about what, Son?" I asked, perplexed.

"It's just that it's been harder and harder for me to say no to my friends lately. I've been kind of scared—it's been harder for me to stand up to them."

A humbled quiet covered me and misted my eyes. Jasen was hurting and needing to hear from me. That made me even more determined to get him the ball—to make a clean hand-off.

the first half is still the first half

I thought I knew Jasen inside out. Yet here he was, confused and searching, and I didn't even know it. What about your son or daughter? What are you missing? If you are like me, it is probably more than you think.

A short time later as we were reading together, we arrived at a discussion of inferiority and how junior-high teens mock each other at school as if it were a blood sport. "Has anyone made fun of you on the bus?" I casually asked him.

Jasen is so perfect to me—handsome, bright, and funny. I couldn't comprehend anyone teasing him, so I fully expected him to say no. Instead, he responded, "Almost every day. The kids call me hickey face."

Immediately angry, I remembered the birthmark on his right cheek. I had seen it from the day he was born, so I didn't even notice it anymore. Of course, my first impulse was to climb on the bus the next day to straighten out some crooked thinking.

My second impulse was much better. That night, I shared some of my own experiences from junior high with Jasen. "When I was your age, kids made fun of my bowlegs, and that really hurt me."

But Jasen's own words were the highlight of the evening. "I don't really mind, Dad," he said. "We all have things that could be made fun of. I know I'm okay."

I marveled at him. How young to be this wise! As I drifted off to sleep later that evening, I found I was marveling at something else. *Here it goes again,* I thought. *Jasen has been enduring this ridicule every day, and I didn't even know it. How many other things have I been missing?* I was so fortunate I asked! When else was he going to tell me about the bus? When else was he going to tell me that he was finding it hard to say no to his friends?

The answer is that he wouldn't have volunteered that information. Neither will your children, most likely. It wasn't that Jasen had suddenly become sullen or had suddenly withdrawn from me. Jasen was simply starting the second half of the game. In terms of his developmental growth into adulthood, he'd been through halftime, and the halftime adjustments God delivered were merely swinging into play. Simply put, the game had changed.

We've seen it before. There are two halves to any football game, and what a difference halftime can make! In the fall of 2002, the University of Iowa Hawkeyes played the Iowa State Cyclones in their annual intrastate slugfest. Iowa totally dominated the first half, cruising up and down the field to take a formidable 24-7 lead into the locker room. Completely outmatched, Iowa State had no hope of victory. Or so it seemed.

But halftime brings adjustments, and if you saw the third and fourth quarters, you would have thought that Iowa State had suited up an entirely new busload of Cyclones for the second half. When Iowa fumbled here and fumbled there, their once sure victory was suddenly up for grabs. Those who switched off the game at the half received a shock in the Sunday morning paper—Iowa State had won the game!

How many times have you seen that happen? If you are a sports fan, you see it all the time. Things change after halftime. Similarly, there are two distinct halves in your child's life. If you want to win as a parent, you better play well in both halves.

The first half is the prepuberty half of the game. Fathers usually play very well in the first half, because the game plan is quite simple. You set and defend simple boundaries through positive reinforcement and punishment. Many of us find this easy because we are linear thinkers. We know black from white and right from wrong, and we love to paint the sidelines on their field of play. When they run out of bounds, we correct them. They hug us and we hug back, restoring the relationship. Simple game.

Our kids, too, are easy to coach in the first half. They are dependent upon us for their food and clothing and, to a large degree, even for their thoughts. They naturally ask a million questions as they look to us to understand their world. They want and expect boundaries, so they accept them reasonably well.

We usually have time to coach also. For the most part, our careers are in the early stages, so we have a little more time in our schedules. Besides, we look for ways to *make* time because having these young kids is still so fresh and exciting. Our parenting legs are fresh, and our will to win is still strong. We play catch, push swings, float boats, watch tumbling, and curl them up with blankets as we read them stories or watch fun videos with them. We sing them off to sleep and tuck them gently into bed. A strong relationship requires little more than enough time well spent.

Best of all, any mistakes we make have less impact in the first half. My father spent very little time with me when I was a boy. He traveled five days a week, spent all day Saturday in his office to catch up with paperwork, and then devoted each Sunday to watching pro sports from the couch. That was his way to rest up for the next week.

I ached to do things with him. I vividly remember sitting behind his office chair on Saturdays just to be near him. As he typed, I played Tonka trucks. On Sundays I'd sit on the floor between the coffee table and the couch as he watched games and took naps. When my father *was* up and about with me, he was often verbally harsh and very demanding. My emotions were his personal whirlpool, and he could dip in his finger and spin me any way he willed.

And yet he paid little for his actions in the first half. Fathers easily dominate the first half of the game. As kids, we ask for only a little…a little attention, a little fun, a little direction, and a few boundaries. And what happens when Dad makes mistakes? We forgive him early and often. We just want to please Dad. We want him to tousle our hair and wrestle on the floor with us. We want to be the gleam in his eye.

INTERMISSION'S OVER

But halftime brings what I call the Triple-P adjustments—Puberty, Piaget, and the Pride of Life—and these are huge.

The first of these, puberty, hits with a cascade of physical and emotional changes that I needn't outline for you if you can recall what puberty was like for you. I certainly remember every aspect of mine. Puberty brought a million *new* questions, but few that I cared to ask my dad about!

For instance, I remember Marianne who sat beside me in my eighth-grade French class. She wore tight jeans and a jeans jacket to class every day, and she had long straight dishwater blonde hair streaking down her back. She wore a perpetual scowl of rebellion across her lips, and she liked to hang out and smoke with her cool friends after school. I wasn't into the smoking crowd, so why did my heart tremble as my eyes ran up and down her denim-clad body? What were these wild, wet dreams I kept having about her every single night? I could *never* ask Dad such questions!

Jasen was no different, struggling with why he was having trouble saying no to his friends. How do you ask your pure, superman father a question about your sniveling little weaknesses?

This trouble with saying no begins with the second of the Triple-P adjustments, which I call the Piaget effect. It hits with a vengeance too. Jean Piaget, whom I first heard about in Psych 101 at Stanford, discovered that the human brain changes dramatically around halftime.

This Swiss thinker and psychologist, who died more than twenty years ago, said that young men and women in the throes of early adolescence were able to think abstractly for the first time about God, life, rules, and relationships. All new questions arise when a young person is on the cusp of adolescence: *Is God real? Is He my God too? Does Dad really have the right to speak to me like that? I can't ask Dad these questions!*

This is serious business, but the ability to reflect on their own thoughts, combined with all the physical changes, brings forth some comedy, too. As they imagine that others are thinking about them as much as they are thinking about themselves, a pair of comical distortions can appear in their lives.

The first is called the *imaginary audience.* Young teens regard themselves as always on stage, convinced that they are the focus of everyone else's attention. And since they are so sure that others are thinking about them and observing them, they may develop an inflated opinion about their own importance called a *personal fable,* so sure that they are reaching depths of feeling and experience that their parents and peers can only imagine.

From these changes flows a third adjustment that I call the pride of life. It is the search for identity and popularity. Who could describe this more eloquently than Rebecca, my seventh-grade daughter?

"In fifth grade, everyone was accepted, simply by being a member of the class," she said. "It didn't matter if your clothes were poor or you were homely or you got bad grades. You belonged. Everyone was your friend and you were everyone's friend, and really, no one made fun of each other or tried to be different. Nobody cared about popularity.

"That began to change in sixth grade. People began to break into cliques, and all of a sudden some of my friends who used to talk to me and used to have me over for sleepovers hardly ever talked to me. It's in full swing now that I'm in seventh grade. I see so many kids without friends, and so many people getting cut off from everyone else. Like me." Then, with a tear dripping out of the corner of her eye, she said, "I just wish it could go back to like it was. I just want everyone to like everyone again."

But it won't go back to the way it was, and the jostling for position in the popular groups creates questions and confusion as well as upheaval in your child's world. Rebecca had discovered cliques, which become increasingly common and more exclusive in middle school. Cliques are based on common interests and social status, and they develop dress codes, ways of speaking, and behaviors that separate kids based on how the others view them.

But there's more to this pride of life thing than your teens' dealing with how others see them—they're dealing with how they see themselves too. I caught Rebecca one day staring off dreamily into the distance.

"Whatcha thinkin', girl?" I said.

"Oh, just wondering about stuff—like what I want and what I like. I was thinking about Jasen and Laura—I envy them. They seem to know just where they're going. Most of the time, I'm up in the air about it, if I can even get off the ground in the first place. Did you ever feel that way?"

Introspection like this is a sign that your child is beginning to form a personal identity. This is a natural part of the halftime adjustments as teens begin to formulate who they are—their personal values and the directions they will pursue in life. Let's face it: They will naturally become more independent of the family as they grow, and if you expect to have the kind of impact on their identities that you want, you must revise your parent-child relationships along with these changes.

Clearly the game has changed, and parenting isn't as easy in this second half of your child's life. Remember how one team can make halftime adjustments and look entirely different in the second half of a football game? The Triple-P halftime adjustment—Puberty, Piaget, and the Pride of Life—has a similar effect. Your child will be different. He will be harder to read. He'll stop asking questions.

Why isn't he asking? Let's look at it from his view of the game.

WHY WOULD HE ASK AT ALL?

Your son is seeking to establish his manhood early in the second half. It makes no sense to admit his weaknesses unless pressed by you. Don't real men stand tall, like John Wayne and Arnold Schwarzenegger?

Jasen sees me like I saw my dad.

Quarterback.

Valedictorian.

Athlete of the Year.

To him, I'm the strong, handsome guy who has been setting all the boundaries for years and the guy who never seems to have trouble living with the rules himself. He has seen little weakness in me.

How easy would it have been for him to walk up to me and say, "Dad, it's been hard lately to stand up to my friends. Can you help me?" Asking that wouldn't seem very manly. Why would he ask? *How could my strong dad possibly understand, and how could he do anything but be embarrassed by my weakness? I'm embarrassed myself!*

WHEN WOULD HE ASK?

As fathers, we are too often playing as if we're still in the first half, assuming that roughhousing on the living-room floor or watching him run a radio-controlled race car in the streets is enough for a close relationship. So we take him to a minor-league hockey game or a big-league baseball game or fishing in a mountain creek.

But it isn't enough. He's got real issues tearing at his heart and preying on his mind. When can he ask you? While the Zamboni is clearing off the ice between periods? During the seventh-inning stretch? He needs a quieter, safer place to really get at it with you.

But that's the rub. Even if simply spending time were enough, we have less time to give to our kids in the second half. We're usually in our late thirties or early forties—decade of horrors! Frankly, we are too busy to parent.

Unlike in the first half, our careers are demanding more time of us than ever before. Our parents are getting sick and sometimes dying. There are the endless soccer games and choir rehearsals and dance recitals and Little League games that seem to go on forever. You don't even have time for sex with your wife. Who has time for questions from kids?

Your *son* doesn't even have time for questions, and they're his questions! He, too, is busy with middle school and core classes and homework and sports. When do you see him?

The simplicity of parenting is gone, along with the thrill. Your son has Triple-P adjustments spilling out all over the place. He's seeing things like never before, feeling things like never before, and questioning your decisions like never before, all while you are desperately trying to keep all of your balls of responsibility in the air.

Your will to win as a father fades. Right now, you would settle for just a little peace. So you redouble your efforts and demand obedience to your ways and decrees. Yet the tighter you squeeze, the more it all slips through your fingers. Frustrated, you withdraw a little more, and you seem less open to talk about anything.

When would he ask these questions at all?

How Would He Ask?

The male brain is more oriented to facts and logic than to emotions and intuitions. Why? Because of brain differentiation during fetal development. The female brain has more lateral transmission points between the two hemispheres of the brain. A recent study by the Indiana University School of Medicine revealed that women use both hemispheres of the brain when listening, but men use only one. We're communicating with half our brains tied behind our backs! This spells double trouble when trying to build communication with a son.

In our book *Every Woman's Desire,* we described the Ten Love Chillers—natural traits in men that actually impede our success in marriage without our even trying. These same traits will impede the communication links we need with our sons in the second half. Let's look at a few:

- Men tend to be less sensitive to the needs of others, so they won't naturally sense their son's need to talk.
- Men have large but fragile egos, so they'll naturally resist sharing their own weaknesses from their pasts—experiences that might help their sons.
- Men are less willing to express emotions and feelings verbally, so talking about feelings can feel weird.
- Men tend to desire peace from their relationships more than anything else, so they'll be quick to settle for mediocrity rather than work for a successful one with their son.

Your son has the same type of brain. He, too, will find it hard to access his feelings and verbalize them. How will he verbalize these questions?

WHY WOULD HE ASK YOU OF ALL PEOPLE?

You sense you don't even know him anymore. He *knows* you don't. Why would he ask *you* his questions then?

It's early in the second half, and you are confused about how to parent. You resist the "listen to him" mode in favor of the "talk at him" mode.

On top of that, those first-half mistakes you made that cost you nothing at the time are suddenly coming home to roost. Back then you could handle him harshly or clumsily, and he would still adore you. Now he's turning into a little abstract thinker! *What does this mean about Dad's love for me? Does he even know me? Does he even care?*

It's Time for Second-Half Adjustments

Is the light starting to come on? The game has changed. Now you can see why a young guy won't naturally come to you—especially if you don't have much of a relationship. Like many, you may be feeling a bit uneasy about what you are seeing in your relationship with your son.

Given the obstacles, it is easy to get discouraged in this parenting game. Statistics show that two-thirds of us believe we weren't adequately trained to be parents. Lack of training is demoralizing in itself, and our will to win can flag.

And yet this Scripture still stands:

> Fix these words of mine in your hearts and minds; tie them as symbols on
> your hands and bind them on your foreheads. Teach them to your children,
> talking about them when you sit at home and when you walk along the
> road, when you lie down and when you get up. (Deuteronomy 11:18-19)

If you accomplish this hand-off, you and your son will both be winners. Passing down a godly character is one of the things that determine your success as a father. If you pass down character, you'll win. If you don't, you'll lose.

Sure, there are obstacles. So what are you going to do in the face of overwhelming odds?

Change.

Make your own halftime adjustments.

Figure out a way to get him the ball.

Signs of the Times

If your son won't naturally come to you with his questions, how will you know when to start? What blips will show up on your radar screen?

One thing is for certain: The game will be well into the second half if you wait until you see signs of sexual awareness in your son. In today's culture, once you see those sexual signs, you've waited too long. It's kind of like running the marathon but waiting until you're thirsty to start drinking water. You need to start drinking water long before thirst grabs your throat.

As for your son, his friends already flood their talk with jokes about sex well before the onset of their own sexual awareness. Like weeds in a garden, these sexy thoughts spread everywhere and defy control or understanding in his young mind.

Second, students begin experiencing the social pressures of their halftime adjustments well before they are fully sexually aware. Remember Jasen's comment about finding it hard to stand up to his friends? At the time he wouldn't have known a hot babe from a bale of hay, but if I had waited until he did, I would have left him at serious risk. Why? Because too often, in their inexperience, our sons will grab hold of anything that gives them a sense of being part of the in-crowd. If sex is held up as their boarding pass, they may walk through the Jetway and try to get on board, even though their plane hasn't yet reached the gate.

Third, and most important, pornography's treacherous, choking tentacles reach early for our sons' throats. The average boy views his first pornography at age eleven, well before he is sexually aware. That's why it's important to watch for the onset of the Triple-P halftime adjustments rather than full sexual awareness. The Piaget effect will be the first *P* to arrive, around age eleven. This serves as your early wake-up call, heralding the approach of puberty's sexual awareness that is sure to follow in just a year or two.

You want to look for signs of abstract thinking. Is he harder to read? Is he introspective or suddenly questioning—even defying—your authority in ways you haven't seen before? Have you gone from telling the world, "What a great son I have" to the baffling "Where has my good little boy gone?"

If you listen and look closely, you may see signs that your son is living his own grandiose personal fable before a huge imaginary audience when he proclaims his passionate insights on every topic. Is he making these pronouncements like he was the first person to ever come up with these thoughts?

Later, signs that he is becoming sexually aware will present themselves in subtle and obvious ways. Where once he didn't care if his hair stuck up like a rooster's tail, now he makes sure it's plastered down. Where once his breath smelled like a toilet, now he's sipping your bottle of Listerine. Where once he was happy running around in old army surplus clothes on weekends, now he has to wear Old Navy when he goes to the mall. Where once he rushed to josh around with the guys after church, now he casually leans against the walls with a friend or two, trying to act cool as he banters with the cute girls flitting about.

It's amazing what you hear just by listening to the conversations he has with his friends. Rich told me, "Whenever I'd drive my son and a bunch of his friends to some event or whatever, I'd keep quiet. I didn't try to dominate anything, nor did I interject with my opinion. I simply drove…and listened. For years, their conversation turned on snow forts and ball games and who could pound whom. Soon enough, however, the conversations turned to girls and who was hot and who was going out with whom. That's when I noticed that the times were changing."

The times are going to change—and rapidly. It's time to get with it, Dad. The fifteen-minute halftime intermission will soon be over. You've got an entire second half to play. Not only that, but you're *the* man—the one with the most experience. You're not in this game by chance, but by God's choosing. He has allowed you to be here as quarterback at this time in history to fulfill His special purpose—raising that son of yours.

Are you fired up and ready to make the hand-off?

Great, because you can do it!

diving deep

You can't make a good hand-off to your son unless you have a good relationship with him. It's like the old saying: Rules without relationship equal rebellion. Dads may be good at laying down a laundry list of rules, but we're pretty poor when it comes to building a foundation for two-way communication. That's too bad because many of us start out with a winning relationship with our son in the early years. As he grows, however, we keep on emphasizing rules when we should be emphasizing the relationship more.

Blam! Puberty hits, and he's got questions and you've got answers, but he's not asking yet. He doesn't feel confident enough to ask you why he can't keep his eyes off Lisa's well-developed breasts in science class—which he can't help but notice when she wears those fluorescent-colored, low-cut tube tops she likes. He thinks he knows why he gets erections sitting behind her in class, but he hasn't the foggiest idea why he gets erections on Sunday mornings in church.

And then there are all those kids at school—especially the older ones who make fun of him when he takes a shower in PE class. They've got hair and all he has is a couple of eyelashes poking out down there. And the way those jocks swagger about, snapping towels at the twerps and picking on everybody. They lose a game by thirty and act all week like they won by fifty points! It irks him to have to keep his head low and not get on their bad side.

Lately, he's been noticing Kara in his junior-high group at church. Everyone else thinks she's a goody two shoes, but he likes her. What would happen if he showed some interest in her? Social suicide, he reckons. His buddies would tease him about Kara, that's for sure. "Why do you like that prude?" they'd laugh. "You're as weird as she is." Still, he wonders what it would be like to approach her and talk with her.

Arghh! Why can't I make sense of all this? Will someone at least tell me I'm not weird?

He's got questions to ask, Dad. Are you going to be the one to hear them, or will his friends get the call? Your young running back is looking for the ball. He's starting to strike out on his own. Are you, God's first-team quarterback, up to the task? To do it, you'll need a relationship, and you'll have to work to get something going. Things won't fall into place naturally.

You'll have to chart a new course. Now, for most of us, changing course means one of three things: taking a left, hanging a right, or slamming on the brakes and doing a 180-degree turn.

But if you were a submarine commander, there would be a fourth option: Dive down! As fathers, we must think like sub commanders. We must dive deep with them.

But I live in the same house with my kids, for heaven's sake! How much deeper do I have to go?

That's a natural question for any guy. After all, in the past, sharing space and hanging out with your friends was about all it took to go deep with them. I can remember at the end of seventh grade when Mom moved my sisters and me from Linn-Mar Junior High to Roosevelt Junior High at the opposite end of the Cedar Rapids metro area. Brian became my new best friend at Roosevelt. He was the humorous little kid with funky black glasses and curly hair that wouldn't lie down. I was the intense, fragile kid who couldn't throw a baseball like a real man. Sound like a match made in heaven? It was.

If you read *Every Man's Battle,* then you probably remember all those stories I told about my sexual sins. Brian knows the names of nearly every girl in every story. Then again, I know how the term "Mack Truck" applies to a girl he once knew. He knows which girl of mine we affectionately dubbed Woodhead. If I was making out in the front seat at the drive-in, he was in the backseat doing the same.

My life was football…and his life was basketball, but that didn't keep us from cross-training together throughout high school. On hot summer days, he ran pass patterns while I flung passes. On other days, we played one-on-one basketball on blazing concrete, and he endured more than his fair share of hacks. We traded our dreams about becoming state champions. I'll never forget sitting stunned in Marshalltown High's Roundhouse Gym as his dreams went up in smoke at the playoffs, and he's never forgotten the bone-chilling cold in foggy Brady Street Stadium when my hopes evaporated beneath the fourth-quarter heroics of quarterback Terry Rubley and Davenport West High. Whether we were in celebration or in tears, we'd head to Leonardo's Pizza after home games for a large Canadian bacon.

Brian was the only guy who ever saw me wearing my acne medicine. Then again, he had the same dermatologist and the same treatment, so it went both ways.

We were so close that we went on to the same college together—Stanford University in the San Francisco Bay area. We organized an intramural basketball team, and our team, the Woosies, won the championship. Off the court, we worked security together at countless Bay Area concerts. Once a drunk took Brian down and grabbed him by the throat. In an adrenalin rush, I grabbed the drunk's collar in one hand and his belt in the other, and I tossed him out the front door and into the bushes like a sack of potatoes.

Brian and I were tight. We went deep with each other, and it happened as naturally and effortlessly as breathing. We practically lived together…his room was mine, and mine was his.

Is it realistic to think we can go deep like this with our sons? We can, but I am the first to admit that it's not so effortless anymore. Merely living under the same roof won't cut it.

We're adults with responsibilities everywhere. Because of that, relationships are never effortless anymore, and if left to nature, our relationships will bob on the surface forever. Think about your relationship with your wife. It's important to go deep with her because a lot is riding on it—including sex. But even that relationship doesn't go deep naturally and effortlessly. I know that I must be proactive by scheduling regular dates with my wife, Brenda, every other Thursday night. I've found if they don't get written down on the calendar, we let those date nights slide by.

Spending time with Brenda is a priority to me, and I know that I need to talk with her every day if I expect to go deep with her. With four kids, Brenda and I don't get much time together during normal waking hours. Yet I've learned over the years that she needs time just to sit and talk with me. She draws interpersonal intimacy from sharing conversation. Trouble is, I'm a morning person, and I'm practically on life support when 10:00 P.M. rolls around. If I lie down on the bed, I'm fast asleep for the next eight hours.

So I had to figure out a solution. If Brenda needs to stay up and talk, I do everything I can to engage her and not fall asleep. I made a hard-and-fast rule for myself that, when I retire to the master bedroom at night, I can't lie down immediately. Instead, I must sit down in what I call my talking chair, the La-Z-Boy rocker in the corner of our room. This way my rear end never hits the bed until it first hits the chair. You've got to actively, intentionally decide to do things like this if you expect to go deep with your wife.

Why would it be any different with our sons? Left to nature, a deep dive is unlikely. What's more apt to happen? Surface drift. After all, when left to nature, the average father only talks to his children thirty seconds a night, remember? That's some serious bobbing and drifting.

For a submarine at war, surface drift means almost certain death. If the enemy stumbles across you, *poof*, it's over. In this spiritual war for our families, surface drift risks spiritual death for our sons.

Death? Look, my Dad never went deep with me, and I turned out all right.

Maybe so. But we can do better than this! We were created in the image of God, the greatest Father ever. Most of us can do so much better than our fathers.

Sure, my dad did okay and certainly made some good choices. He didn't have to stay around Cedar Rapids after the divorce to help raise me. He didn't have to be so generous in paying for Stanford. He stayed and he paid because he loved me and wanted to be a part of my life.

And though he often crushed me, I stand by what I said at his funeral: I wouldn't trade him for any other father I've ever known. He was a superman, bigger than life itself. He captured every room he ever entered, and as for pure toughness, he had no peer. From wrestling to poker to sales, he'd beat you up one side and down the other. Most kids brag, "My dad can beat up your dad!" My father really could.

But he never went deep with me when I needed him most. We must do better than this, because if we don't, our sons will pay the same price that maybe we paid in the sexual arena. Patrick Middleton, a good friend and a gifted addictions counselor, recently told me, "I deal with a lot of men, and it never fails that the men with the deeper sexual issues also have uninvolved or missing fathers. Their sexual issues are directly and severely impacted by their dad's failure as a father."

That's to be expected because there's a point in the development of a boy into a man—say from eleven to thirteen—when the boy needs to move into a deeper relationship with his dad. "I know this sounds a bit weird," said Patrick, "but I've never found a better way to say it: Dad has to be close enough to his son to be able to call the 'heart of the man' out of the boy. If this does not happen, the next window of opportunity for a young man to try to feel like a man is through his emerging sexuality. So, if Dad isn't there early in adolescence to help answer questions, the boy will use his sexuality as an arena to answer his questions about being a man."

Men become men in the company of men, through the connection of acceptance and understanding. Your son often thinks about sex and his own sexual identity and security. This is of utmost importance to every young man, and if you do not choose to connect with him on this issue, you may lose the opportunity to connect with him in many other important areas as well. Besides, your connection here may be his key to his connecting with other men and even to a wife someday.

Since I had no one to talk to, I was forced to climb through that second window of opportunity and sort out my manhood in a swirl of pornography, masturbation, and premarital groping of girls.

How about you? Sure, we can slough through fatherhood. We don't have to go any deeper with our sons than our own dads did with us, and we can be satisfied to merely raise another productive member of society. But that is stopping way short of our call, and it certainly stops far short of what we ought to be doing. That's a mediocre middle ground if I've ever seen one. My sons won't need that other window, and sexual exploration won't be their teacher. Not without a fight, anyway, because I'm going deep.

My dad stopped short. He never grabbed the helm to take us deep. I paid a heavy price, drifting aimlessly on the surface, tossed by the waves of my sexuality, randomly clunking hard against the flotsam and jetsam until I was covered in bruises and wounds.

My wife also paid the price of my father's lack of parenting, but my daughters-in-law are not going to pay that same price, and neither are my sons. I'm grabbing the helm. You should too, because our sons have questions: *What's up with these wet dreams, anyway? What's this masturbation thing all the guys are laughing about all of a sudden?* We've certainly got to go deep with them there.

Their questions are boundless. *In life, what works and what doesn't? What is success? What should I be concerned with? What is worth pouring my life into?*

They've got more than sex problems. They've got vision problems. They need a clear vision of purpose, something to pour their lives into so they can look back and say, "That was worth living for. I made a difference."

They need a clear vision of manhood...God's vision, which is straightforward and simple: He who hears My Word and does it is a man. When God looks around, He's not looking for what everyone else calls a man's man. He's looking for God's man.

As fathers, we have a simple command:

Fathers, do not exasperate your children; instead, bring them up in the training and instruction of the Lord. (Ephesians 6:4)

We're commanded to not frustrate and annoy our kids by withholding from them the instruction of the Lord they so desperately need. When we do, they become embittered, and so we break a second command:

Fathers, do not embitter your children, or they will become discouraged. (Colossians 3:21)

What have we seen in such cases as the Columbine High shootings? Annoyed and frustrated young men. What are they taking revenge upon? Fatherlessness? Likely so.

Of course, few of us go to this extreme type of revenge. Most of us still become productive men, but that isn't the point. The point is that if we don't take this issue seriously, all of our sons, no matter how successful, will have holes in them that haunt them for years.

I'll never forget the first time I saw Bo Jackson run the football for the Oakland Raiders. My mouth fell open in awe. His acceleration on the football field was unmatched, and I don't care who you stack him against. You can have your Walter Paytons and your Barry Sanders and your Marshall Faulks. For my money, Bo Jackson was the most unforgettable running back I've ever seen.

Sadly, his painful words remain just as unforgettable. During one poignant interview with *Sports Illustrated*, he said, "My father has never seen me play professional baseball or football. I tried to have a relationship with him. I gave him my number and said, 'Dad, call me. I'll fly you in to any game.' Can you imagine? I'm Bo Jackson, one of the so-called premier athletes in the country, and I'm sitting in the locker room and envying every one of my teammates whose dad would come in and talk with him after the game. I never experienced that."

Granted, few of us fathers are *that* bad. Most of us have regular contact with our kids. But this sense of drift can even happen in homes where dad is present and involved. We're often giving our kids the good things but not the best things—a biblical vision for manhood, a biblical vision of treating women with honor, and a challenging vision to give their lives a purpose that is something greater than themselves.

We can do nothing now about our own father's leadership, but *we* have the helm these days. It's high time we give the command: "Dive, dive, all dive!"

the swapping place

To go deep with our sons, we need to do two things:

- Spend time talking with them.
- Be open and transparently share our lives and our walk with God.

Those two directives sound simple enough, don't they? Sure, but life's hectic nature works against them. Obstacles keep popping up like gopher heads in those arcade games. But though the obstacles and our natural traits as men work against us in this game of relationships, we need to flail away and keep on swatting.

More often than not, we'll beat those gopher heads down in the areas where it really counts. After all, we can go deep with our wives. I've got the talking chair with Brenda; perhaps you have a favorite coffeehouse that you frequent once a week. I've studied her essence and found her heart. Can we build such a place for our sons in spite of the obstacles and time pressures?

It's clear enough that it really counts. I think we can if we really want it. There may be gopher heads everywhere and we may have our weaknesses, but we're still men. We've got what it takes.

God's description of Christ's role as the high priest is very instructive for us in this effort:

For we do not have a high priest who is unable to sympathize with our weaknesses, but we have one who has been tempted in every way, just as we are—yet was without sin. Let us then approach the throne of grace with confidence, so that we may receive mercy and find grace to help us in our time of need. (Hebrews 4:15-16).

In a sense, you play this same role in your home, as the Father's chosen representative of Christ for your sons and daughters. And you have at least part of the role down pat already. For instance, you are certainly able to sympathize with your son's weaknesses, because of your own. And you've surely been tempted in every way your son has been.

But you probably still lack one thing. Have you built a place for him to approach with confidence, a place where he can find mercy and grace and truth to help him in his time of need...in this rugged second half of play?

You must build such a place. How? Like the talking chair, you must construct a place and set times to talk with your son, or you can't complete that role God gave you.

Talk? I thought you said we aren't good at talking?

For the most part, we're lousy at it. We can all relate to the letter one young man wrote to his absent father in his diary, saying, "I don't know how to talk about these things, and I know you don't either, but maybe we can help each other."

Fortunately we have a secret weapon, a special category of male communication that connects us every time it's tried—we can swap stories, tell tales, and regale listeners. Storytelling is right up our alley, and nobody does it better.

Years ago, I heard an accomplished linguist describe on the radio the differences between the brain structures of men and women and why men have difficulty accessing their emotions and expressing them verbally. His explanation, which I found fascinating, described how the mother's androgens naturally break down many of the communication links between the two hemispheres of the male brain during fetal development. The two halves of the male brain cannot talk to each other very well, but the two halves of the female brain communicate with each other just fine. He told how men are less able to express emotions and feelings verbally than women are because of this.

Now don't get me wrong. These differences don't make us inferior—the differences in the male brain bring some clear upsides along with the downsides. But when it comes to communication, they're a reminder that there is a reason that guys have a hard time keeping up with gals when it comes to *saying* how we feel. Still, we aren't hopeless communicators. In fact, we're far from it.

The linguist added that there was one little area of communication at which men excelled and that would help men access their emotions. I hunched forward in my car to catch this pearl of wisdom.

"The brain differences between men and women have shown one thing clearly, and it's this," he said. "A man's emotions can best be reached through a story."

He then followed with a statement that will forever remain indelible in my mind, and it was this: "A good pastor will recognize this and use stories in his sermons to reach the hearts of men."

I nodded my head in revelation. That's our secret weapon! That's why storytelling connects us every time…we're built that way.

And if a pastor is urged to use stories to reach the men sitting in the pews, then what about fathers who want to relate to their sons? A good father must deploy this same weapon and use stories to reach the hearts of his sons.

When I heard all this, I was so excited. *For once I'm fully equipped by nature for a task at hand. Bring it on!*

I was reminded again about this concept recently when a Canadian Christian band named downhere stayed in our home. The band was deeply touched by *Every Man's Battle,* and we came into contact shortly after that when we asked them to provide some music for the *Every Young Man's Battle* video. I enjoyed getting to know these guys. When I heard they were traveling through Des Moines on their way to a show, I invited them to flop at our house for the night.

Like all guys, we began to swap stories, hanging out and laughing in the family room well into the night. I kicked it off with this one. It seems that one Christmas break, my friend Dave joined Brian and me to visit our favorite high-school teacher, Rick Baylor.

Mr. Baylor had been bragging about his trip to Jamaica and the prized box of Jamaican cigars he'd carried home. When we arrived that night, he hadn't made it home yet, but he'd left the back door unlocked and open for us. Entering the house, we soon spotted the cigars displayed prominently in the den. Instantly, we hatched a plan.

Hustling to the nearest 7-Eleven, we bought a bunch of cheap cigars approximating the size of his prized Jamaicans. Hiding the Jamaicans, we set the empty box on the coffee table between us. Lighting about four cigars each, we puffed them down to the nubs as quickly as possible without burning our lips. (We didn't smoke 'em, of course. We just didn't inhale—like Bill Clinton.)

We squashed a dozen butts into three ashtrays and, for good measure, emptied three-quarters of his bottle of Jack Daniels into a bowl and hid that, too. Through the smoky haze, it looked for the world as if we'd smoked all of Rick's prized Jamaicans in a drunken bash of glory.

Rick finally arrived with his wife, Melissa, who opened the door only to be assaulted by the fragrant aroma of cigar smoke and booze. Slurring our words, we called out tipsy greetings to our dear friends. Spotting the cigar butts piled high and a drained whiskey bottle crowning the ashy mess, Melissa marched straight up to her room, livid. With great effort, Rick maintained an even keel, but his lips pursed tightly as he struggled to contain his temper. Meanwhile, we laughed and carried on, complimenting him on what a fine host and friend he was to provide us with stogies and drink.

We originally wanted to keep up the charade and hold his feet to the fire well into the night, but the clouds were beginning to rumble ominously over Rick's head. When we thought he couldn't stand the indignation one more minute, we blurted out the truth—while laughing quite hysterically at him. Rick managed a tight smile, but the shock was still too real for him.

When the boys in the band heard me retell this story, the floodgates were opened. As the night wore on, the stories got a little deeper and a little more serious.

We shared stories of family.

Stories of pain.

Stories of amazing coincidences.

That's how men are. The longer we swapped stories in the family room, the deeper we went. We connected in the way guys connect…through storytelling.

I'm sure from the kitchen, where Brenda was tidying up, it all looked like much ado about nothing. I'm sure my wife was thinking, *Why does Fred love to tell that story about Rick Baylor and the cigars? That doesn't have anything to do with anything, and it doesn't exactly put him in a good light. Guys are so weird.*

A few nights later we were driving late in the darkness on the way to Quad

Cities. Talking to Brenda and my eleven-year-old Michael, I offered, "You know, I really feel that my dad's pressure hurt my football career."

Absently, Brenda replied, "How so?"

"I was always so afraid of making mistakes that I was even afraid to call the best plays. I was as good as any running back on the team, but I avoided calling my own number because I didn't want Dad to call me a ball hog. My coach really chewed me out at the halftime of our homecoming game because I hadn't called a single running play for myself in the whole first half. We lost that game, and I really think that is why," I said.

"The week before, my running had won the game," I blathered on. "It was drizzly, and my plays were the only ones working. Of course, Washington's guys were really big, but in the mud, my running style worked out great. I was picking up the third-and-shorts to the right all night, even though Darrell Hobbs was on that side. He was six feet four inches tall and a human bull. Still, I couldn't break anything long because Craig Roalson, their all-state defensive back, kept blasting me down short of the secondary. This one time, though, I looked up and he wasn't there—nothing but grass to the goal. I took it sixteen yards for the score."

Dumbfounded, Brenda exclaimed, "Men are so weird! You can remember every detail of every game from almost thirty years ago! I just can't believe you."

IT'S A MATTER OF CALLING THE RIGHT PLAYS

Stories root deeply in our emotions. You want to know what I think? I actually think men are as sensitive and emotional as women, but we just have trouble accessing it all, except through story.

While Brenda was amazed, Michael was all ears, as you might expect. *That coach chewed out my dad? This I gotta hear!* He learned a valuable lesson about confidence and calling your number regardless of what others might think.

Brenda thought I'd simply shared a dusty old football story. But Michael and I had connected that evening. What if I'd simply declared, "Michael, you should always call the right plays no matter what others think"? Do you think he would have remembered? Maybe, but how much would it stick? I'm not sure.

But I *am* sure of one thing…my younger son is a guy. That story will stick somewhere and have an impact down the line.

Just like a story Dad once told me as we traveled down Highway 30 on a forgettable business trip one forgettable afternoon about a year before I married Brenda. I can't remember where we were going, but I sure remember the story. Dad asked, "Whatever happened to Polly, that girl with the big brown eyes that you used to date?"

Embarrassed, I looked out the window and mumbled that, while we had broken up about three years ago that spring, I had never really gotten over her. Though she was married, I was hoping for a divorce so I'd have another chance with her. Why I told him that, I'll never know. The moment those words left my mouth, I expected a big fat lecture. What I got instead was priceless…a story from him.

A far-off look settled over his eyes. "I had a girlfriend like that once," he began. "I usually didn't get caught like that by girls. In all the little towns around Benton County, I was known as the Casanova of Keystone. The nickname alone tells you I didn't get smitten very often. But one little princess really nailed me."

"So who was the girl, Dad?" I was really interested.

"Janie Monroe!" he answered. "I'll never forget that name! What a girl she was, Son! Even after I'd left home and had all the girls at Iowa State Teachers College to sort through, she always kept a huge piece of my heart. Even after I married your mother, I thought back longingly to those days with her, wondering what had ever become of her. I always thought that we'd get back together someday."

"Boy, I sure understand *that* feeling, Dad."

"Well, after your mom and I divorced, I was playing cards one night with some of my old buddies from Keystone, and one of them told me where she had ended up out west. I risked sending her a letter, and was I ever surprised. She, too, was divorced, and she was thrilled with the thought of seeing me again. My heart hadn't fluttered like this in years, and my memories of her danced and danced endlessly in my mind as I waited for the day to fly out and see her."

"You got the chance to see her again?"

"I sure did, and when I arrived, it was great to see her. She seemed as lovely as ever to me. But as the evening wore on, wow, what a disappointment! She'd changed so much over the years—or maybe I had. Life had dealt her many blows, and that light, airy, lovely spirit I'd known years earlier had flown. She got a bit tipsy that night and began crying, saying, 'Freddie, I've never stopped loving you all these years. Can't we try again?'"

"What did you do, Dad?"

"I turned her down. It wasn't the same. I spent the whole flight home musing over all the wasted years loving a memory that didn't even exist anymore. My Janie was no more."

I sat amazed, gazing at the cornfields slipping by. *My dad has feelings like me!* I had no idea. Not that his story changed my feelings for Polly on the spot. If you remember from *Every Man's Battle,* it would be two years and one wedding later before God dealt with those simmering feelings I had for Polly. But that story Dad shared rooted deeply in me, and it was a great encouragement to me as I struggled to crucify my memories of Polly a few years later. Somehow, I was never alone in the battle with Dad's story in my heart.

Do you swap stories with your son? How many of your stories could help your son if you took a chance and shared them? You shouldn't wait for such moments to arise, so what can you do to trigger the process? Maybe you can't put a talking chair in his bedroom, but you can build a swapping place.

As I mentioned in chapter 1, I built my first swapping place with my firstborn, Jasen, years ago by going through a book on adolescence with him. This book served as a trigger to launch hundreds of stories and precious moments between us. I've gone on to build such places with Laura and Rebecca and will soon build another with my younger son, Michael. By now we've gone through a number of different books together, and the connections we've made are priceless.

We call this "doing book." (The phrase *doing book* did not grow from the Left-Coast slang "doing lunch" or "doing Hawaii," and I know full well it is a grammatically incorrect Stoekerism that won't pass muster with you English teachers out there. "Want to do book?" is simply short for "Want to do some book reading?" Granted, it's not the most creative name in the world, but humor the Stoekers on this one!)

Why books? Years ago I tried the approach of simply spending the last ten to fifteen minutes of my kids' day with them, talking with them in their bedrooms before they went off to sleep. While we all enjoyed it, we never really went anywhere, rarely venturing beyond discussion of the events of the day. We shared what *we did,* rather than what *we are,* falling far short of my call in their lives. With books I find that the author's stories trigger memories of my own stories, providing a push to dive into deeper waters.

It's too late for my son and me. We can't talk at all, and I don't see any hope! You are wrong. Your son still longs for it, regardless of how things look now. We *all* need that connection with our fathers and will seek it to the very end if given half a chance.

At the age of seventy-one, my dad's life was winding down. With a congestive heart and two diseased kidneys, life had become a big shell game—which organ would go first? My once-powerful father could no longer walk fifteen feet without stopping to rest, and his once strong arms had atrophied to pencil thin.

You think your relationship with your son is bad? My dad had never accepted my wife, Brenda, and after an argument thirteen years earlier, he had literally kicked me out of his house, bellowing, "And don't you ever come back!" During those thirteen years, I never saw my dad except at required business conventions. But one fine day, I found Dad's letter nestled in my box. He asked me to come back.

It was during those last two years of his life that my father built me a swapping place. I entered that place without hesitation. It is never too late.

Whenever my day called for me to be in the Quad Cities for business, I'd arise at 4:30 A.M. at my home in the Des Moines suburbs and drive the 180 miles to the Quad Cities so that I could work a full morning of appointments. Then I'd pick up Dad for lunch, after which we would return to his home, where I put Dad on stage and prompted him to tell me stories from his life. I had a million questions, and he had a pile of time. Sometimes this went on for three or four hours, but that didn't matter: I just loved to hear him talk.

I must confess that little of what I heard was earth-shattering revelation. Most of what he talked about was slice-of-life stuff, like the time when my father was fourteen and hanging around the Turner Hall one night in downtown Keystone, Iowa. It wasn't long before three guys his age began picking on him. Breaking free, he rushed inside to tell his seventeen-year-old sister, Dorothy, that he needed help. Instantly leaving her date speechless on the dance floor, she flew outside and waded in with fists flying, sending those boys packing! Way to go, Aunt Dorothy!

When Dad was stationed out west at a naval base in the state of Washington, he befriended a girl and her family, with whom he corresponded by letter until the day he died. "Yeah," he said, "they used to take me skiing practically every weekend!"

"You liked skiing?" I exclaimed.

"I dearly loved it!" he said.

He was seventy-two, and I was forty-three. I'd never heard of these people that he corresponded with his whole life, and I never knew he liked to ski. How can this be? All I know is that this happens way too easily.

On one level, so what? After all, the stories themselves were often no big deal.

Still, with each story my dad seemed a little more human and our relationship a little deeper. Little details of someone's rich life history are unearthed when a father and son connect through stories, and Dad and I connected more in the last two years than we had in the previous forty-one combined. How? He had the time, and I *made* the time.

We schedule date nights with our wives and talking time with our dying fathers. We swap stories into the night with rock bands breezing through town. Are you scheduling times to swap stories with your son? Or are you sitting back and waiting for something to happen?

You don't have time to wait. You need to build a swapping place where he can find mercy and grace and truth from *you*. He needs you at his side as he leaves the locker room after halftime. He's got a rugged second half coming up, and he doesn't want to battle adolescence all alone. That's why he needs a swapping place today.

In the next two chapters, we'll show how to build one by doing book.

"you go first, dad"

To build a swapping place, what's the key?

You must go first.

Your son is becoming a young man, and he aches for you to count him as one. But, as we said earlier, there are natural obstacles, and it's unlikely he'll bring up the questions himself. We must make it easy for our sons to share, and there is only one way to ensure that. We must go first. We must be the ones to initiate the conversation.

When I'm interviewed on radio about sexual purity, a very interesting thing happens. Early in the show, women flood the switchboard because they seek to understand their husbands better. It's an easy call to make because it involves little personal risk.

But the men often hold back when it comes to talking about their sexual integrity on talk shows. They don't feel safe enough to admit their need. In that sense, I have to go first, and I try to do it early in the show. Once I share my own painful, choking story of life stuck in the dark depths of sexual prison, men *do* light up the switchboard, and we can really get rolling.

Can we expect our young men to be any different? Of course not. That's why they need you to go first. Besides, what did we learn from Bart Starr about the art of the hand-off? A clean hand-off is not the running back's responsibility. His eyes are looking upfield at the chaos around the line of scrimmage, and that's where his focus should be.

But you are the quarterback. You must call his number. Take the snap and set the ball firmly in place. Go first.

Swapping stories is right up our alley, and it shouldn't be scary in the least. In light of this, our call to teach our children isn't really something to fear anymore, either:

> Fix these words of mine in your hearts and minds; tie them as sym-
> bols on your hands and bind them on your foreheads. Teach them
> to your children, talking about them when you sit at home and when
> you walk along the road, when you lie down and when you get up.
> (Deuteronomy 11:18-19)

I used to wonder how I could accomplish all this. Like most families, my kids and I lead busy lives, and we don't sit around home, nor do we walk or work together very much, unless you count shopping in the malls as a walk. Our culture is vastly different from that of the Hebrews.

And that's perfectly fine. God understands the fast-paced society we live in, but He still wants us to teach our kids how we apply Scripture to our day-to-day lives. Since our kids aren't with us much during the day to see *how* we apply Scripture, fulfilling this call won't look the same today as it did back then.

We need to do the next best thing...we need to *tell* them what happened during our day and our weeks and our years. I think the swapping place serves that role well, and that's how we can fix these words in their hearts today.

So you're saying that this swapping place will be all about me and my life and my stories. If so, how is this going to fix God's words into my child's life?

Exactly like the verse says: by telling them how you live Scripture in day-to-day life. That will fix that scripture in their heart. They will see how it works. They will get it.

Of course, showing them still makes the most impact, and though you are all busy and aren't with each other all day, your life itself will always still serve as the foundation of your swapping place, a foundation that rests on the very Rock upon which the church itself is built...God's Word:

I will show you what he is like who comes to me and hears my words and puts them into practice. He is like a man building a house, who dug down deep and laid the foundation on rock. When a flood came, the torrent struck that house but could not shake it, because it was well built. But the one who hears my words and does not put them into practice is like a man who built a house on the ground without a foundation. The moment the torrent struck that house, it collapsed and its destruction was complete. (Luke 6:47-49)

REJECT HYPOCRISY

So your first step in building a swapping place is to walk rightly before God. Hypocrisy is like an unstable fault line running through a solid rock foundation. If you ever expect to build a useful swapping place, please consider how you've lived your life up to this point. You must do so for the sake of your son.

Pastor Alan McAllister, a dear friend whose face brings a smile to me every time I see him, grew up as a huge James Bond fan, especially those early films featuring Sean Connery as 007. Recently, his local station had a James Bond week, broadcasting a different Bond film each night. Alan was pumped!

Monday evening, he settled into bed next to his wife with great anticipation. While she read, Alan hit the remote, bringing the British secret agent bursting to life. Of course, when suave 007 isn't busy saving the world, he's either in bed with, about to bed, or maneuvering into bed the latest "Bond girl." It's almost a cinematic cliché: James Bond wearing a bathrobe while holding a martini—shaken, not stirred—as he charms the pants off some supermodel with a preposterous name like Pussy Galore or Holly Goodhead. The womanizing is part of every slickly produced Bond film.

Alan always thought that was part of the Bond mystique—the sophisticated and inventive secret agent with a license to kill who scores in and outside the boudoir. That first evening, when he was engrossed with the latest Bond adventure, he never noticed that his ten-year-old son, Daniel, had slipped into his bedroom to watch his first Bond movie.

About an hour into the show—after another Bond sexual conquest—young Daniel popped up and asked, "Daddy, why are you watching that?"

Startled, Alan struggled to think. He knew that his son had never watched such a sexually charged film. "Because I love James Bond movies, Daniel. If you'd sit down with me, I think you'll like them too."

Putting his hands on his hips and shaking his head back and forth firmly, Daniel simply declared, "Girls, girls, girls, girls, girls!" Then he vanished down the hall as quickly as he came.

A few days later, Alan and Daniel were watching television when they saw the Bond week promo. "Look, Dad. There's a James Bond movie coming on tonight."

"Yeah, but I've decided not to watch those movies anymore," replied his father.

His son shrugged his shoulders. "Can I go out and play?" he asked.

"Sure, Son," Alan replied.

When Alan related that story to me, I said, "Wow! Do you suppose he was testing you, checking you out?"

"I don't know," Alan smiled. "He's only ten…maybe, maybe not. But either way, my message was delivered. That's the main thing."

Make no mistake, when we open our lives up to our kids, they'll find out what we're all about. If they notice hypocrisy's fault line, they might just point it out in their innocent way of saying things. If they happen to say something, no matter how innocuous, use that opportunity to go deep with them and repair the fault line by submitting yourself to Scripture, the way Alan did. After all, your son needs answers from you, not more confusion.

You must reject hypocrisy, and you must also be humble and open to receiving further instruction, whether it comes from your son, your wife, or the Lord.

The righteous man leads a blameless life;
blessed are his children after him. (Proverbs 20:7)

Your son will learn from you without your having to say a word. Let's not forget that your very life, lived before him, is a sort of swapped story in its own right.

If you've read *Every Man's Battle,* you know the history of my family tree. I came from a family in which the men ditched their wives or were caught up in sexual affairs and pornography. This has happened for *generations*.

When it was my turn, I jumped in feet first. I can still remember the pictures I viewed in *Playboy* and *Gallery* magazines more than twenty years ago. I can also remember the many girlfriends and intimate times together. But in the end, the Lord and I won this battle, and the generational sin in my family tree was broken. I didn't have to say much to my sons. My life spoke a story that fixed God's truth in their hearts.

When my older son, Jasen, was eleven, I simply told him, "Jace, pornography is like taking drugs. When we look at women without clothes on, there is a chemical reaction that happens in our brains that is much like the reaction the brain has to taking cocaine. There were studies showing this way back when I was in college. I'll never forget watching some of my rich Stanford friends blow thousands and thousands of dollars on cocaine in just a few days over spring break…they just couldn't get enough.

"Son, I've never done cocaine, but I *have* viewed pornography, and once I did, I was hooked and wanted to see more and more, just like those guys with their drugs. It was a brutal habit to break, Son, and I just don't want you to make the same mistake that I did."

Two weeks later Jasen's friends brought some pornography to school—a *Hustler* magazine. They called him over to have a look.

I was impressed—and grateful—that Jasen told me about this incident. "What did you do?" I asked.

"I walked away, just like you said I should."

"That's great, Jasen. I'm really proud of you for doing that."

Jasen turned his back on looking at a magazine of beautiful naked women, but the only conversation we ever had about looking at porn happened just weeks earlier. On the surface, one direct conversation may seem like puny firepower against a formidable fortress of generational sin. But let's face it: Jasen had also seen me live a life consistent with God's principles for years. That spoke volumes to him as well, and so that one conversation turned out to be what God needed to break a generational stranglehold that had bound the men of my family for decades.

These days Jasen may be a step purer than I am. He recently took some birthday money and bought a videotape of a *Star Trek: Next Generation* film. With excited anticipation, we all sat down to watch it. Midway through the show, First Officer Will Ryker and Counselor Deanna Troi suddenly appeared on opposite sides in a deep hot tub with soap bubbles covering everything up to their necks. There was nothing directly sensual or sexual about the scene. Before I could even think, however, Jasen was up and out of the room in a shot. He reacted merely to that whiff of sensuality.

If you want to go deep with your sons in the swapping place, you've got to crush hypocrisy early; otherwise it will shut their ears to you. One time, when I was seventeen, Dad decided that it was high time that he said something to me about the facts of life, although it was a little late since I had already heard so much in the locker room. We went away on a fishing trip to Canada, and when we were alone in a fishing boat out in the middle of that Canadian lake, he said, "I really think it's time for me to talk to you about the birds and the bees."

But Dad divorced my mom for a mistress, and he still had multiple girlfriends and sex toys lying about, so I shut him out. "I don't want to discuss it," I said.

He kept insisting. "Now, Freddie, it really is time, Son."

As he kept pressing, I got annoyed. Before long, my anger bubbled completely over. Gritting my teeth, I snarled, "If you open your mouth, I am going to jump into this lake and swim to shore. Don't even think I won't, either."

My jaw was set, and he knew I meant it. His life of sexual hypocrisy had shut my ears to him.

SWAPPING PLACES

So our own lives will speak stories and serve as the foundation for our swapping place, but we will need to build a place in which to share our words regularly as well. And we still must go first. Going through books will make that easy. What does this look like in practice?

doing book

Now that it's time to build that swapping place, it's also time to get down to business and "do book." This may sound intimidating, but it's no big deal: You and your son read some material and talk about it. No need for this to make your blood pressure soar like a kite!

But going through books! Isn't that a lot of work? Most fathers wonder if they have to prepare before each evening's reading session. The answer is no. Although it doesn't hurt to glance at the section titles and mentally calculate how much ground you want to cover that night, you can just open the book and start reading until you've reached your fifteen-to-twenty-minute goal.

TOUCH FOOTBALL

The mechanics of doing book are simple. Two or three nights a week, Jasen and I would read six to eight pages in silence separately as we sat in his bedroom. Of course, the book is not the end game here; while you're reading, you're also looking for opportunities to talk later on, ask leading questions, and regale your son with stories. So as I read, I'd underline thoughts that I'd like to come back to, especially those words or phrases that triggered a memory of something that happened to me in junior high or high school.

Jasen and I always sat casually facing each other. I thought it was important that we could look directly into each other's eyes as we read. That way, when I stopped reading and looked up, his eyes met mine, and I could see by his eyes where his mind was going. Sitting across from each other also helped me to be honest about my past, because I felt more secure if I could be reading his eyes and gauging his reaction to my story.

Once we finished the reading, we'd drop back to the beginning of the section and go over the points I'd marked as I read. I'd like to give you more of the how-tos, but you'll understand quicker if I just show you how it played out. In the next chapter, I'll share more of the rules of the game for building an effective swapping place for the long haul. For now, let's just roll through a little highlight reel from doing book with Jasen as we paged through *Preparing for Adolescence* together.

One of the earliest passages spoke of how common it is to be mocked at school. I remember the time I asked him, "Has anyone made fun of you on the bus?"

As I mentioned earlier, I fully expected him to say no since he was so perfect to me.

"Almost every day, Dad," said Jasen, confiding that his classmates called him hickey face because of the birthmark on his right cheek.

I attempted to explain how common that is by recalling something similar when I told him how kids teased me about my bowlegs. "Jasen, I used to walk to school every day with my toes turned in, trying to get my legs to straighten somehow. It didn't work."

"I know it didn't," he grinned, and his little joke got us laughing, and you and your son are going to laugh too when you share similar stories. Just as storytelling makes for great books, storytelling also makes for memorable and fruitful father-and-son interactions. Stories will humanize you to your son and remind him that you know *exactly* what he's going through because you've been there before.

And notice how easy this all is with the help of a book. The book never dominates the swapping place. It just gets you started in a useful direction. From there, you both get to talking, and things begin flowing naturally in the direction you feel they should go. One story flows to the next story. For instance, after hearing my bowed legs story, I reminded Jasen that guys should never say mean things about other people, especially about stuff they have no control over—like birthmarks. "That's not to say teasing has no place. Teasing keeps us all from getting too far out of line with everyone else. Hey, my philosophy is this: If someone paints their hair purple, maybe they need a little teasing. That's to be expected."

Jason nodded.

"Which reminds me of a great Millis story," I continued, referring to Dave Millis, the starting center of my high-school football team. "Ever heard of Broadway Joe Namath?"

Jasen shook his head no, but I expected that.

"When I was your age, Broadway Joe was the hottest quarterback in pro football, both on and off the field. Before he came along, everyone wore black cleats. Some even wore black high tops, like Johnny Unitas. Not Joe Willie. He wore the coolest white cleats and had a Fu Manchu when he played for the New York Jets. I couldn't grow a moustache, but I sure wanted to wear white cleats, so some of my teammates and I made sure we were decked out in white shoes. I'll never forget the time, though, when Millis lumbered onto the field in his black high tops. Now, centers weren't supposed to be cool enough to wear white shoes, but that didn't stop us from giving him the business.

"We teased him about his 'nice shoes,' but he didn't care. 'Hey, I like them, you kumquats!' he said. 'Besides, it's not the shoes, but the man who fills them that counts. I feel sorry for those of you wearing those sissy little white shoes.' We all laughed, and there's nothing wrong with dishing it out, as long as it is all in good fun. But the lesson here is that we never made fun of anyone for something they couldn't help or couldn't change. I don't have to tell you how that feels."

"I know how it feels," said Jasen, "but I really don't mind about that hickey-face stuff, Dad. I look at those guys making fun of me, and I can find a lot of things I can make fun of, but I just don't want to play that game. I know I'm okay."

His growing wisdom felt great to me, which is no surprise because:

A wise son brings joy to his father. (Proverbs 10:1)

Our times doing book forced a natural change in the way I viewed Jasen. He was no longer simply my son—he was my brother in Christ, albeit younger, wise in his own right and capable of teaching me a thing or two. You, too, will be pleasantly surprised to find how mature your youngster is becoming, and your relationship will change as he continues to grow and mature. And like the talking chair I did with Brenda, doing book was taking my relationship with Jasen deeper and changing my view of him along the way, effortlessly.

Soon we came to the section in the book regarding conformity. Jasen declared that both he and I were nonconformists—people who weren't afraid to be different from everyone else.

"Yeah, you've got us both pegged pretty good," I said. "But I wasn't always a nonconformist, at least not in everything."

"That's not true, Dad. You were never afraid to be different."

"Oh, I don't know, Jace. I went along with the crowd a lot more than you might think."

I could tell that he didn't believe me, so I decided to prove how much of a conformist I could be. The next night we skipped the reading and headed for the storage room to go through old photo albums. It didn't take long to find the photo I was looking for—a fading color photograph of me standing before the camera wearing blue-suede shoes. Blue-suede shoes may have been hip sometime during the seventies, but I must confide that I'm now mystified why. Those blue boats in size thirteen had to be the goofiest shoes ever made. That didn't matter back in the seventies. I obviously wore them because I wanted to be part of the in-crowd.

"Those shoes—look…" Jasen wasn't quite sure how to describe what he saw in the photograph, but I could tell what he was thinking: *Man, those shoes are stupid and ugly!*

We spent the next hour laughing at dozens of old pictures of me trying to look hip, and it was certainly instructional. Jasen never dreamed that I dressed exactly like everyone else back in junior high and high school—but I had visual proof.

Remember, the key to doing book is being flexible. If it makes sense to skip the book one night so that you can blow the dust off some old photo albums or high-school annuals, why not? Point out the old prom pictures and other candids taken of you and your old buddies. They don't say that a picture is worth a thousand words for nothing. Pictures of your youth are visual evidence that you grappled with the same struggles your son does, twenty, twenty-five years ago. This knowledge will help you and your son tie your hearts together, and he'll be much more receptive to your advice.

Your son may not believe that you ever had acne or any pimples. If so, show him a photo of you with a blotchy face and describe how inferior you felt each time an ugly blackhead announced its presence. Watch out, though. Some photos are *beyond* explanation. I'm talking about those canary yellow tuxedos, frilly Edwardian shirts, and platform shoes that were so big in the seventies and eighties!

A SURPRISE TWIST

Two important moments occurred when we were reading through the conformity section. I told Jasen one evening, "If someone I know had conformed one Friday night long ago, neither you nor I would exist today."

Jasen's eyes got big with wonder.

"Yep, it's true," I continued. "When my dad was a teen, four friends pulled into his driveway on the farm to pick him up. Getting into the car, he noticed some beer in the backseat, so he told his friends that he was going to take a pass, and he got out of the car. His friends roared away, spitting gravel and jeering that they didn't want to be friends with a sissy anyway. A few hours later all four teens were killed in a fiery car wreck."

"Wow…that really happened?"

"It sure did, but Dad's strength not to conform saved his life…and mine…and yours."

I let that thought sink in for a while.

I told Jasen that sometimes he wouldn't know beforehand what harm he might save himself from by not conforming. He must simply do the right thing.

I used that as a springboard to talk to Jasen about pornography. I said, "You know, sometimes you must simply trust another person's experience, even when you don't fully understand the dangers yourself. One of those things would be avoiding pornography."

Porn, like sexual intercourse, is tough to talk about. Your son may squirm or feel embarrassed because his friends have been showing him pictures of naked women and it didn't feel right for him. Maybe he has come across porn sites on the Internet, which is so, so easy to do.

We must build a deep enough relationship with our sons that they will simply trust our word and avoid the trap, even if they don't fully understand the dangers themselves.

As I mentioned in the last chapter, I continued by telling Jasen that looking at pornography has the same effect on our brains as drugs and is also addictive.

Jasen nodded his assent that evening. He had heard those DARE cops talk about drugs in his classroom, and so he understood the comparison.

Still, Jasen didn't have much to say after this conversation, so I wasn't sure how much he understood. Would he trust my words and avoid the trap? I got my answer a couple weeks later when his friends brought those *Hustler* magazines to school and Jasen walked away.

Over the next few days, I was just sky high in my emotions. *Jasen walked away!* You can only dream what that means to me. Both my grandfathers left their wives for other women, and at least one of them was hooked on porn. My dad was hooked on porn. In college I memorized the dates of the month when the new issues of my favorite porn magazines would hit the campus drugstore.

Yet here was my son walking away. *Could this be the first crack in that wall of generational sin?* As the years passed, time confirmed that it was just that… Jasen hasn't dabbled in porn yet.

As we said earlier, a wise son brings joy to his father. But Proverbs also teaches:

A wise son heeds his father's instruction. (Proverbs 13:1)

Sure, our sons will stumble upon some wisdom themselves, as my son did when classmates teased him for being a hickey face. But the greatest joy comes when they heed our instruction, although the key to this joy does not lie in the obedient hearts of our sons. We are the key, as fathers, because they can never heed our instruction if we never take the time to instruct them. It's that simple.

Rules just don't make it, at least not by themselves. Sure, I could put in some software to block Internet porn and lay down some sensible rules for computer use, but my son is studying to be a computer engineer. He could skirt any defenses my puny brain could devise. Likely, your son could too.

We have to go beyond rules. In the *Star Trek* series, a Class M planet is one whose environment is like Earth's. It isn't hostile to human life, and men can move about such planets without spacesuits. As parents, we often spend all our time creating Class M environments in our homes…employing filters and defenses and bubbles to create a nonhostile environment. But what happens when they leave the friendly confines of "Earth"?

My son has launched and splashed down at Iowa State University, and we knew this going in: ISU is no Class M planet! Some have questioned our wisdom in not sending our son to a Class M Christian college. But let's face it: Eventually all of our sons will explore hostile planets as they travel through their own college and career galaxies. They'll need spacesuits built with internal filters and beliefs to protect them in these hostile environments. Jasen has his own spacesuit.

Rules don't provide these filters. Only instruction can. While our home defense perimeters are fine, we must also prepare our sons to stand on their own on any planet.

Doing book dropped seeds that grew into Jasen's own *internal* rules and boundaries that kept him clean through high school and now defend him on the foreign planet we call ISU.

GIRL TALK

A few days later Jasen and I moved into the section on girls.

"You probably still think girls are dumb. Right?" I asked.

"Well, I don't really think they're *dumb*," Jasen replied. "I mean, I've noticed in school that they get the same kinds of grades we do, so I know they're smart. I just think girls are *weird*," Jasen replied.

"You've got that right. They are different!" I responded. *Little do you know how different they can be, but I'm going to let you find that out for yourself. Besides, you wouldn't believe that you'll one day love that weirdness and even cherish those differences, even if I told you so tonight. We'll have other nights.*

I then pointed out that if God hadn't given us the appetites for girls that puberty brings, none of us would ever choose to live with someone as weird as a girl. "How many marriages would happen if us guys felt like you feel toward Jennifer or Megan?" I watched Jasen nod his head, and I knew he understood completely.

"Jasen, did you know that God created our emotions—our anger, fear, attractions—in a kind of chemical base? Our desire for girls, in many ways, is a product of our hormones. This was God's answer to the 'weirdness' of girls.

"It's like this. God created a chemical soup that makes us attractive to them and makes us attracted to them as we grow up."

His eyes twinkled after hearing this. "I'm going to drink acid and blow His soup up!"

"I don't think you'll get out of it that easy, my boy!" As the days passed, we went deeper into this girl thing, and came to this passage:

Now let me describe for you the feeling that sex will bring in the next few years. Boys will become very interested in the bodies of girls—in the way they're built, in their curves and softness, and their pretty hair and eyes. Even their feminine feet may have appeal to boys during this time.[1]

With this statement, things had finally gone far enough for Jasen. He emphatically declared, "Even if this *does* happen to me [which he was clearly not conceding], I'm *not* going to find their feet attractive!"

We'll just see what kind of soup God whips up for you, I thought.

But I didn't say it. *I'll save him the worry for now,* I mused, *but the soup's on the stove.*

Which led us right into the dreaded page 78 a few nights later—the one describing sexual intercourse.

Now I was skating on thin ice, and I could feel the cracks forming. I was totally freaked out and wanted counsel badly. I asked Brenda to read the section beforehand and to let me know if we should skip the section for now. She read it, emitting laughter interspersed with ominous mutterings. She was nearly finished when our son Michael, then a toddler, began stirring in his crib. I went up to settle him, and when I returned, Brenda was at the kitchen table, shoveling cereal into

---

1. James Dobson, *Preparing for Adolescence* (Ventura, Calif.: Regal, 1989), 77.

her mouth as fast as she could chew and swallow. "I'm eating to get away from *that* book!" she said.

Now I was really nervous, so I suggested getting a second opinion. We shared the section with some of our female friends, and they all had similar reactions (minus the cereal, I presume).

"It's too direct, with no romance at all," they unanimously declared.

That's just great, I thought.

In the end, regardless of how unsettling the description was to my wife and her friends, I decided to proceed. I headed for Jasen's room with these final instructions ringing in my ears: "Honey, just save us some self-respect."

I thought about turning around and schlepping back downstairs—just like I did when I was pumping up my courage to enter Jasen's bedroom to talk about puberty the first time. Instead, I decided to storm the ramparts. I knocked and entered his room, where I strapped myself in and hung on. As Jasen and I read each sentence, it got…very quiet. Somehow we got through to the part where the author describes how a man and wife slide back and forth together until they both get this tingling feeling all over them.

"You and Mom do *this?*" Jasen interrupted.

For the first time in my life, I felt shame about making love to my wife. "Well…yes, Son. I do—I mean, yes, we do."

"Oh, *yuck!*" he cried out as he rocked and fell to the floor laughing.

As we moved through the text, he learned that some couples actually do this intercourse thing two to three times a week.

"*What?*" he squawked with amazement. "How often do you and Mom…do this?"

Now it was my time to be surprised. I certainly didn't expect this question.

Remembering Brenda's last words, I deftly deflected his query like the finest goalie. "Listen, Son, I knew a couple that did this two to three times a *day.*"

"A day!" he gasped, and then he burst into the sort of belly laugh you get on a really good night of *America's Funniest Home Videos.*

We did not wrap this section in one quick evening because the topic of sexual intercourse tripped all sorts of topics: how babies grow in the womb and how they come out, the importance of purity prior to marriage, and why it was God's plan that we wait until marriage before having sex with our wives. I told him only a little bit about my sex-soaked past, but I promised full disclosure when he got older.

Jasen and I formed a bond when we went through the section on sex. We really could talk about anything after this. Your son needs more than a sex talk from you—he needs an ongoing sex *discussion* as well as discussions on all varieties of relationship issues. How do you keep your swapping place strong for the long haul? We'll take a look at this in the next chapter, followed by a few chapters showing what you'll gain in your relationships by doing book.

Oh, and by the way, from here on out, I'll be sharing a few stories about doing book with my daughters as well as my sons.

But I thought this was a father-son book! It is, but many of my experiences with my daughters demonstrate the full value of doing book. I think they are too important to leave out, because my experiences with my girls have helped me in doing book with my younger son, Michael, and they will help you with *your* sons too. Besides, we fathers need as much help with our relationships with our daughters as we do with our boys.

rules of the game

When I started doing book with Jasen, he responded as if the cavalry had arrived to save the day. That wasn't the case for my two daughters, however. Let's just say that Laura's and Rebecca's responses were underwhelming.

I remember the first time Laura headed down to the basement, book in hand, to begin reading with me in Grandma's Room (the guest room where Grandma stays when she visits). Her wariness told me that she wasn't very dialed into the program. "This isn't going to be a 'let's talk about everything that's wrong with Laura night,' is it?" she grumbled, assuming the book was just a cover for my real intentions. Not a promising opening attitude, right?

Rebecca was worse—her attitude stunk throughout the whole first session. She'd had a hard day at school, worked all afternoon on her homework, and was ready to bury herself in a favorite old movie. And then I came along, asking her if she would like to do book with me.

"When?"

"I was thinking that now would be a good time," I said cheerily. "Let's head into Grandma's Room and have some fun!"

Fun? Reading a book on puberty with Dad? That didn't sound like fun to Rebecca on *this* night. With a resigned "you're putting me out" pout, she fell in behind me as we walked down to the basement, where she promptly sprawled across Grandma's bed with a deep sigh. She hadn't said a word, but her body language screamed, *Let's just get this over with, okay?*

As we got into it, our first session didn't seem to improve her attitude much. She seemed bored out of her gourd, but I resolutely stuck to the schedule. I noticed her interest picking up a bit at the end, giving me a glimmer of hope for the next time. As for this night, I was getting pretty anxious for the finish line myself. After twenty minutes, I declared that we were done. As we got up to leave, I commented, "I think you're really going to enjoy this. You want to try it again tomorrow night?"

"I suppose," she responded. "I guess it wasn't too bad."

"See, I told you it wouldn't be too bad. But you know that it would be better for both of us if you got into it a little more."

Rebecca's face flushed as if she had been caught red-handed raiding the refrigerator twenty minutes before dinner. Tossing her head back, she said with a light air, "Oh, you noticed? I didn't know you knew I was feeling that way."

"Oh yeah, it was pretty obvious. Besides, I'm pretty old. I know these things."

Giggling, she pranced up the stairs to her bedroom. "Okay, Daddy. Next time I'll put some heart into it," she smiled.

And she did. Two weeks later, she was washing dishes with her mother when she said, "You know, going through this book with Dad is my favorite thing right now. I just love it."

When you start doing book, your children have no clue where you're going, so how they react is often a by-product of their personality types. Jasen, my firstborn, has a temperament that makes him want to get things done right. He saw doing book as something fun and challenging, and he couldn't wait for the next installment. Laura, on the other hand, is skeptical by nature. If something is new or different to her, her default position is one of suspicion, so her reaction was not too surprising. Rebecca is a happy bubble floating merrily over life's currents, and she loves doing things the easy way. Her reaction to Dad's latest plan was predictable too.

Which goes to show you, you just never know how your children will react when asked to do book. Give them a break. If you don't get a great reaction at first, be a man and take the early heat with grace. Don't chew and rant and rave. Carry on as if you don't notice.

They'll get it soon enough. Maybe you'll even get a card of thanks. Laura recently wrote, "Dad, thanks for all the times we go through books together. It is so great to get to know you so well, and I'm learning a lot."

Not a bad sentiment from my suspicious one, huh?

SWAPPING-PLACE SPECS

Where should you do book? Any room that has a door and some privacy will work. You need to be totally alone together. Make the spot you pick *your* spot. Do you both feel comfortable there? For instance, you might not want to meet in your home office, since that has Dad's Territory written all over it. Ditto for the master bedroom, which could be embarrassing for both of you since that is where you make love with your wife. The child's bedroom will almost always work, as would a basement bedroom, a sewing room, or a cordoned-off nook in the back of the house. Finally, since this area will probably have lifelong implications in your relationships, you might want to pray and ask God to bless this space.

Whatever you do, make the swapping place special. When Jasen and I first started, it was on the floor in his room. Soon thereafter Grandma's Room became our place. Whenever one of my kids and I enter Grandma's Room, he or she always knows something unusual is going to happen. When they come with anticipation, they listen well and open up, often in the mood to talk instantly. It is our place to connect, just like the talking chair is my place to connect with Brenda every night.

I always give my child the most honored spot in the room. As your kids' father, you are the Big Kahuna in their lives, the one who is always in charge. Show them that the normal roles don't apply in the swapping place, that you are like any special friend who would sit around the campfire and talk to them one-on-one, friend-to-friend. I like to sit in the corner on the floor by the chest of drawers, and lean against a throw pillow. My kids get to sprawl on the bed in comfort, looking down and over at me. It seems right.

LOGISTICS

Essentially, you mark the book as you read so you can come back with questions later on to jump-start the all-important discussion. What kinds of questions should you ask? Personal ones. Ones that ask about feelings, what they're thinking, and what they think something means. Your questions need to be as direct and personal as possible. General questions will result in generalized answers.

Let me give you some examples. Let's say you're reading a section on conformity. You might ask, "Have you ever noticed the effects of conformity before?" But that would be pretty general.

The following questions, however, would really get the fires cooking and get the spotlight on you and your son:

"Son, are you a nonconformist or a conformist?"

If he answers, "Nonconformist," and you agree, follow up. "Why do you think you're a nonconformist?"

But don't be all over his case. Keep the tone light—even neutral. Ask: "How do you know you are a nonconformist? Can you give me an example? Do you remember a time that you did something that no one else in your class would do?"

If he gets stuck, flip the spotlight back on yourself, and ask: "Son, would you say I'm a conformist or nonconformist?"

I guarantee that will get the conversation going. Whatever his answer, tell him what you think you are and give him examples of why you think that. He'll start coming up with his own examples, and you'll be rolling from there.

As another example, let's say you've read the section on friends and friendship. You could ask, "What do you think about this section on friendship?"

While it is a decent open-ended question, it's not very personal. Again, remember that you want the spotlight on you and your son, so you can swap stories. How about this: "Jasen, who would you say are my best friends?"

Once he answers, you can ask him why he thinks that or ask something like this: "Jasen, what do you see in these guys that you think made me choose them as friends?"

Man, you can talk an hour on that one. When you're finished, you do it all over again by discussing your son's friends.

Of course, sometimes you don't need questions to get a discussion going. You can tell a story. One time, when Rebecca and I came across that section about people making fun of each other, I skipped the questions entirely and went straight to my story.

"Rebecca, when I was in sixth grade, my best friend was Dan. He and I were in the same class at Linn-Mar Middle School. His dad was a Boy Scout leader, and Dan asked me to join up so we could go camping together. I did so, unaware that Dan already had a close friend in that group named John, and John was jealous of my friendship with Dan. Well, I happened to be in a kind of 'big-head stage' back then," I said. We both laughed at my inside joke. In our house, we've noticed that at various stages of growth, sometimes your head grows a bit before the rest of your body catches up. We call that a big-head stage.

"Anyway," I continued, "John started calling me 'Fathead' all the time. That really, really hurt. Every night after Mom tucked me in bed, I'd sneak out to the bathroom and look in the mirror at my big head. Putting a hand on each side of my head and lacing my fingers together on top, I'd squeeze my head as hard as I could, hoping to make it smaller over time. Sometimes I'd cry when I squeezed my head, not because it hurt, but because I was so desperate to get rid of that horrible nickname."

Rebecca gasped. "That is so sad! What happened?" she asked.

"Well, one night when I was squeezing, I pulled a big muscle right in the center of my back. It felt like a stabbing knife, and my back hurt for days. That made me so mad! I suddenly realized how silly I'd been to allow John's ridiculous nickname to bother me. I just decided I wouldn't let anyone do that to me anymore."

"Hey, that happened to me too!" Rebecca exclaimed. "Remember that orange-and-white outfit that was my favorite? I wore it to school one day, and some girls laughed at it. I didn't have the courage to wear that outfit for a long time, and when I finally did work up the courage, I couldn't. I had outgrown it. That made *me* so mad! I decided that day I would never let anyone decide what I wore ever again."

"Yes, that's exactly the same thing," I said. We had a great time talking about this for the next half-hour. I brought up other stories, Scripture—whatever came to mind.

You know, we can tell our kids for years to get tough in the face of mockery. But sometimes a single story like this can cement these truths in ways that a "you just gotta get tough" lecture never could.

RULES OF THE ROAD

There are two major rules you must follow to avoid destroying your swapping place. First, your book room should never be used as a place for finger-pointing or scolding. You have the rest of the house for that. If you do it even once in your swapping place, every time your son walks the stairs to the swapping place, he'll be wondering, *Just great. What am I getting into trouble for this time?*

You can't build a good relationship under that cloud. Randy and Celia are dear friends of ours. We married in the same year, and we've spent countless hours together at softball diamonds, restaurants, and church nurseries. We've grown up together as couples and as parents, learning as we go.

During their first few years of marriage, Randy had a very bad temper, not unlike mine. "Trouble is," Randy admitted, "Celia knew just how to light my fuse. I used to yell at her so menacingly that she'd cower. Once I even grabbed her and pushed her. Just one time, Fred. Of course, I promised never to do it again, and I haven't. But for years, any time I'd get angry at her and move toward her, she'd flinch. It used to tear my soul every single time that my precious wife flinched when I moved toward her. In my pain, sometimes I'd lash out and say, 'Why can't you get over that! I made one mistake! You are so unforgiving, Celia!' But every time, tears would just well up in her sad eyes, and she'd simply say, 'You so terrified me that day. I don't want to flinch, Randy. I just can't help it.'"

He paused, still hurting at the memory of those words. Then, quietly, he continued, "But you know, she didn't have to say it. I knew the truth—it was my fault she flinched, not hers. Though I was so, so sorry, some things don't get erased quickly. It took years for Celia and me to get back to square one."

The same thing is true of your swapping place. This is a place to swap stories, to connect, to grow. To bring a reprimand into the swapping place would be the same as my bringing a *Playboy* magazine into a Sunday morning church service.

And I assure you, it takes forever to wash these polluting memories out of the relationship and out of the swapping place.

The second rule is to never, ever say no when your child asks to do book. That's not easy to do, especially if you, like our family, don't have set times. For the younger kids, I might do it two to three nights a week. Once they are juniors and seniors in high school, they are in AP classes or mock trial or a play or basketball—any number of things. With them, I might only do book once a week…sometimes even less when their school lives get crazy. Remember, doing book shouldn't be a legalistic, schedule-busting chore. It should be a couple of friends getting together.

Normally, I'm the one who invites them downstairs to Grandma's Room, since I know all the schedules. But when one of my children asks me to come down, the invitation has little to do with schedules. They've got something on their mind. Grandma's Room is the place to get answers, and they need to go there *now*.

Michael, my youngest, was ten years old when he came urgently to me one night and said, "Daddy, I'd really like to go down to Grandma's Room with you." Now Michael had never done book with me in Grandma's Room or any other room—he was about a year away at that time, since I usually start all this at age eleven, around puberty. But he'd seen his brother and sisters enter that room for years, and he knew what went on in there.

In fact, it all sounded so good to him that for some time he'd been pressing me, "Daddy, when will it be my turn to go through the books with you?"

My answer was always simple. "When the grass sprouts under your arms, you're there."

But the urgency of this night could not wait for the grass to grow. Something was eating at his little heart. I couldn't imagine what it was.

That particular evening was so busy that it took me an hour to clear the decks and head down to Grandma's Room. Once there and settled in, I simply looked up into his little face and said, "Well, what did you need to talk about?"

He instantly burst into tears, sobbing. "Daddy, I'm just so scared about 'Uncle' Bill and Carrie. Why are they getting a divorce? It seems so sad, and Ryan seems so sad."

Over the weekend, we'd spent New Year's Eve at Bill and Carrie's house here in

Des Moines, as we've done so many times before. We've vacationed with their family, fished with them, canoed with them, and so on. But this time Carrie wasn't present.

As the old year wound down that evening, we gathered for a time of family prayer. Bill and his son, Ryan, Michael's treasured friend, joined our prayer time, and we began to cry out to God for Bill's marriage. Bill was just crushed, as his wife had left him for another man. After the prayer, Ryan remained slumped in his chair for nearly forty-five minutes. Michael walked up to him to pat him every few minutes for encouragement. The memory of that prayer time had Michael by the heart now. He needed me.

Once you have a swapping place, you can't say no to such a request. Sometimes you can't drop everything and meet right away, but don't delay for long.

We can't. We just have to find the time.

PROACTIVE SWAPPING

How do I choose which books to go through? Whatever makes sense at the time! Choosing the right book is part of being proactive and intentional in the swapping place.

I always begin with a broad-based book on puberty and adolescence, such as *Preparing Your Son for Every Man's Battle,* the book you're holding in your hands. Such books are foundational to everything that comes later in building your swapping place with your kids. Believe me, after you've given them a taste for what the teen years will be like and shared your experiences from the past, you and your children will be tighter than you have ever been.

After laying the foundation with a broad-based book or two, I then choose age-appropriate books based on where I think my child is currently. Sometimes I've picked books that have stretched my kids, but again, that was based on some parental instinct. For instance, I'm going through some of Tim LaHaye's old temperament books with my kids right now. Everyone knows Tim LaHaye for the best-selling Left Behind fiction series, but fewer are aware that Tim was known back in the late sixties for a book called *The Spirit-Controlled Temperament,* which did a great job of explaining the four basic personality types that we are born with.

My two daughters share a bedroom, but they are as different as night and day. Laura is a driven, focused girl who never rests and lives life to the hilt. Rebecca is a laid-back, carefree feather on a breeze.

My daughters are living quite peacefully with their differences, but I want more than that for them. Over time, I want them to marvel at their differences, to grow a love and passion for the essence of the other. With LaHaye's books, we're working toward that end.

Of course, some books are chosen for more urgent needs. One of our house rules states, "No dating until age sixteen." When Laura turned fifteen, she fixed one eye on the clock and the other on the starting gate, champing anxiously at the bit. As the months ticked by, I became very concerned. Not so much because of her, but because of the other horses circling the Stoeker homestead.

The names of two young stallions in her class were rearing up in her conversations far too often. I didn't mind it so much until they started hanging around the house more. Instantly, my heart cried, "All hands, red alert! Shields up!"

A single lovely thought emanated from my consciousness: *Where's my baseball bat? Because if those studs so much as make a hoof mark in Laura's corral, it's time for some batting practice.*

Miraculously, a better thought pushed through. Why not make this a lesson? Why not do book with a book about dating? I'd seen Joshua Harris's *I Kissed Dating Goodbye* swamping the bestseller shelves, and I loved the title's sentiment right about then. So I bought two copies, along with two copies of a book making the counterargument called *I Gave Dating a Chance* by Jeramy Clark. I figured I'd give both sides equal time.

Hold it. Why didn't you read both books and then pick the one closest to your own thoughts? Don't you want her to think like you?

Yes, but I don't have to force it. The truth speaks for itself.

I'll admit it. I don't like one-on-one dating in high school. But I can't make that decision for Laura. That's got to be a personal decision, especially with a child as strong-willed as she is. I really can't coerce her or convince her. But gratefully, I don't have to, and that doesn't scare me nor bother me in the least.

If the truth *is* the truth, I'm confident that Laura will come to the same truth herself as she continues to read Scripture and continues to gather life experiences.

At sixteen, she knows and understands God's Word better than most adults. Her handicap? She's inexperienced when it comes to things like dating. That's where I come in. I'm in my midforties. I've seen plenty.

When doing book, we explore how the author brings God's truth to the topic at hand, which, in this case, was dating. Remember, our call as parents is to *share* our lives, not clone our lives in our kids. I simply need to tell Laura about some of the things I did right and some of the things I did wrong when I was dating. Those life experiences will help her understand how to apply His Word. She can sort things out without having to experience the crushing times herself.

As fathers, we have to be humble enough to admit that our way may not be exactly the right way down to the last turn of every path. Sure, there *is* a single right way and a single right answer. But at least for now, we still see through the glass darkly. We may not always be right.

Granted, the odds are with us as fathers. If Laura and I disagree, I am more likely right. After all, I'm older and have a wealth of life experiences. But she still must have a voice and a place on the path to search out that truth as we walk together.

BOTH POINTS OF VIEW

So what happened to the young stallions? Well, Laura and I began doing book. This time, we couldn't get through the books quickly enough for her—she was too hungry—so we did it a little differently this time. I gave her both books to read on her own and told her we'd go through them together once she was done. Besides, I wanted her to receive both points of view to get her juices running before we got together again.

Again, be flexible. Doing book is not a legalistic chore. It is just a couple of good friends getting together to talk about something they read recently.

When Laura was finished with both books, we started discussing *I Kissed Dating Goodbye* together. Early on, the author said that serial dating could bring a lot of pain as you open your emotions freely to people who are not the least bit committed to you in the long run.

I told Laura about my first real girlfriend, Calley, whom I dated during my sophomore year. "Laura, she really stole my heart," I began. "She had long blonde hair and a cute silvery smile because she wore braces. I tell you, she had my number. Calley had this certain way of standing next to me and patting my chest with the flat of her hand. I felt so strong and so happy when I was with her. I was kind of shy, while she was outgoing and the center of the popular gang. I got to go with her to all the best parties, where we'd quickly find a make-out corner for some fun. I was so in love."

"You really did this, Daddy?"

"Yes, I did, but I didn't really know anything about love or relationships at all—only what I'd seen in movies. I wanted to express it so deeply, something romantic, something in writing. I wrote her a note telling her how much I loved her, and I even naively dropped the word *marriage* into the mix to show that my passion was no average passion."

"Gee, Dad, you must have really liked her," Laura said.

"That's for sure, but let me tell what happened after I wrote that note. A buddy of mine took her the note between classes. For fun, he watched her open it by her locker. When she read the word *marriage,* it was all over. She laughed out loud, and then she told my friend to go tell me I was a nut. She spread the news about what a big dork I was to all her popular friends and never really spoke to me again, though I tried to call her several times."

As I finished the story, Laura saw the pain in my eyes. She knew I still felt it twenty-five years later. "Laura, Josh Harris is right. When you let your emotions out freely in situations where there is no real commitment, you can be crushed."

But she didn't really need my words. My eyes revealed the truth.

I spent many nights sharing my early dating days with Laura, and I'll share some of the rest of our discussions later on in the book. But as I opened my heart to her, she saw a side of dating that she hadn't considered before.

PRIORITIES IN LIFE

How did our trip through the dating books end?

As quickly as it began.

One night we sat down to do book and before we began, Laura simply said,

"You know Dad? I've been thinking, and I've decided that dating needs to take a much smaller priority in my life at this time. I can really see now that dating could take me away from my dream of being a veterinarian, and I just can't have that. I've decided that group dating is okay, or if I do go out with a guy, we'll go out as friends and not for romance. I think this romance thing needs to wait because I don't really see what it gains me and, given what I've learned about guys and what they're looking for in dating, I don't think it makes sense to risk my emotions or my dreams on dating, at least for now."

I sat stunned. We hadn't finished going through the dating books and never did. She found enough truth and I'd shared enough of my life experiences for her to make her decision…so neither one of us really cared to go on.

But what effect do you think that decision had on my blood pressure as she approached her sixteenth birthday? I put my baseball bats away, as she had gone from being hot to trot to being satisfied remaining in the barn, pursuing God's dreams for her life.

How grateful I am for God and His truth! I never had to tell her what to do. She found the proper application of the truth for herself. All she needed was some perspective from an overexperienced father.

And remember, doing book is not about finishing all fifteen chapters by next month. It isn't about finishing the book at all. If you do, fine. If not, so what?

Doing book is like a day dawning over the rises and rolls of your favorite golf course on the morning of an impossibly busy day. It's not about the failure to get in the full eighteen holes. It's about the nine or fourteen you *do* get in, and about the dew that glistens on your shoes and about the meadowlark's call and the peace that opens your soul. It's like tubing down a lazy river on a hot, hazy summer day. Don't worry—you'll eventually get to where you need to go. It's about the journey. The journey *is* the goal.

Doing book is about you and your son and your daughter. It's about fun and relationship. Laura never quite kissed dating good-bye. That was fine with me. Would she give dating a chance? At some point, I suppose. But her attitude was awesome in my sight. The moment I heard my daughter's voice wisely and decisively put dating in its place was one of my greatest, most indelible, breathtaking moments as a father. I'll cherish it to the edge of my grave. Such grace she had!

It was pure silk, like a Michael Jordan jumper with the seconds waning. It doesn't get any better than that.

THE RICH REWARD

As we respect our children and invite them to confide in us, they will slowly but surely open their hearts more deeply. Where your son had once stopped asking you his questions as he entered puberty, he will now start coming to you more and more often with his questions without prompting and without books. There will be a place to go, a place he can be alone with only you, where any question is safe and there are no accusations. This may sound familiar to those who feel like they have a secret place with the Lord, a place where you can tell Him everything.

Graced by the fruit of the Spirit, you can be your children's go-to guy for hope and help. You've provided the place and the quiet moment to listen to their most painful questions. And the Comforter—God's Holy Spirit—is there with you, even when you go so deep together that you feel like you're in over your head.

> But when they arrest you, do not worry about what to say or how to say it.
> At that time you will be given what to say, for it will not be you speaking,
> but the Spirit of your Father speaking through you. (Matthew 10:19-20)

THREE SIT IN THE SWAPPING PLACE

Remember when Michael came to me about Bill and Carrie's divorce? He burst out crying because he was tortured and broken by the news, so desperate for answers.

Those moments are etched deeply in my mind, even now. I wondered what I should say. Where should I start? Then I remembered that the Holy Spirit promised to lead me. I sensed the Spirit's tap when He said to me, *Fred, can I go first here?*

Relieved, I replied in my spirit, *By all means, Lord.* Then He gave me what to say to Michael about the devastating divorce.

"Michael, I know you want to know what Daddy thinks about all this, and I'm going to tell you, but let me first show you what the Lord thinks about it."

As I opened the Bible, I continued, "Now, I'm about to read you what God thinks about divorce. Sometimes it is hard to understand what God is saying in the Bible, and sometimes it isn't. I want you to listen closely, and I want you to tell me whether God is making Himself clear in this passage, okay?"

Putting on his most studious face as he wiped his tears, Michael said, "Okay, Daddy, I'll try."

So I read Malachi 2:15–16: "Guard yourself in your spirit, and do not break faith with the wife of your youth. 'I hate divorce,' says the LORD God of Israel." I looked up and said, "Okay, what do you say? Has God made Himself clear enough for even a ten-year-old to understand?"

Now grinning, Michael chuckled, "Yeah, He's pretty clear, all right."

"He wanted to be clear on this one so we'd never miss it," I continued. "God hates divorce, and we need to do everything we can to avoid it. And I want you to know that your mom and I are never going to get a divorce, because of what God says here. Besides, my parents got divorced, and it was awful. I won't do that to you."

Palpable relief washed over his face as he breathed a deep sigh.

"As much as we all love Carrie, and as much as we all wish she'd come back home, she seems to have no plans to do that. And while we don't like to think badly of Carrie, I want you to look closely at how this sin is affecting everyone she loves."

"I think I've been seeing some of that already," Michael said.

"You're right, you have. Remember Daddy's favorite saying? 'There is no such thing as fair...there is only righteousness.' I think you'll understand this saying a lot better now after our talk tonight. You see, we don't have to fight for things to be fair. Jesus never concerned himself with whether things were fair. He talked mostly of righteousness. Do you know why?"

Michael shook his head. "When a person is living right," I continued, "all the people who love him will automatically feel like things are fair in their relationship with him. But when a person isn't righteous and chooses to sin, suddenly nothing seems fair to anyone. That's one of the reasons God hates divorce so much."

"You saw Uncle Bill during the prayer time we had, right?" I said with all seriousness. "He was so sad and in such pain. He had invested more than twenty years building a home and a life with Carrie, the only woman he ever loved. He never had eyes for anyone else. He worked to buy a house and to give her everything she desired, and he looked forward to growing old and taking great vacations with Carrie when Ryan got into college.

"Carrie took that all away without warning. Is anything about this fair in the least?"

"No," said Michael.

"And what about your buddy Ryan? I haven't talked to him, but at some point he may wonder if his mom really loves him. At least that's how I felt after my mom and dad divorced. I've lived through that pain myself, and the pain of betrayal never really went away. Is that fair to Ryan?"

"No," Michael replied.

"Look at your mom and me. We've been crying and praying for weeks over this, and it's going to hurt for a long time. And Michael, look at yourself! Look how scared you are over all this! When we are unrighteous, nothing around us seems fair to anyone."

When Michael and I talk about difficult issues like a family breakup, I know the Holy Spirit is right there with me to help with my answers. Do you believe that the Spirit is interested in what you are passing on? He is right there on the edge of His own seat in your swapping place.

As our Comforter, He's as concerned with providing us wisdom as we are in receiving it. He wants us to answer well. He wants our sons to have confidence in this safe, secret place that we're building for them. So as you build, relax. Know that God Himself will be there with you always, just as He promised.

outside the swapping place

If you're champing at the bit to start doing book, that doesn't surprise me because as I've spoken before audiences on this topic, the response has been as overwhelming as when I've taught about sexual purity out of the *Every Man's Battle* playbook. Men who catch the vision see doing book as an avenue to being a good, effective father in this crazy-busy, light-speed culture we live in. They are just as desperate for help in how to reach their sons and daughters with the sexual purity message as they are for help in staying sexually pure themselves.

I'll never forget the group of fathers who approached me after one of my presentations. One sharp-looking guy, athletic and dashing with his dark hair and mustache and bright polo shirt, approached me with tears streaming down his face. "Fred, I'm losing my sixteen-year-old daughter, and I'm so desperate to get her back!" he whispered in an aching voice. "We just can't talk anymore. Can you tell me anything more? I'll take any handouts you've got. I've just *got* to do this right."

My eyes get moist today when I think back to that incident. What that man said is every father's heart cry. We desperately want to connect with the most special people in the world to us—our children.

GOING THE OTHER WAY

At the same time, not every father immediately sees the value of doing book. One father told me, "This might work with my oldest son, but my youngest just isn't wired to sit down and read with me—he's all sports and running and action."

He could be right, but he'll never know unless he gives doing book a solid try-out. If there's anything I know about men, it's how we are quick to make snap judgments on these sorts of things.

Listen, my son will never sit still for this. I know my son!

I don't doubt you know your son, but let me remind you of the power and the draw of the swapping place. You don't have to have kids who love reading to do book. If that were true, then doing book would have never worked in my family. The fact is, when I started doing book with Rebecca, I learned how deeply she hated to read.

Jasen and Laura liked to read; we would quietly page through our sections together and finish at about the same time. As for Rebecca, I would read four or five pages for every two of hers, and I waited long periods each night for her to finish before we could get on with the discussion. I began to understand why she hated to read: She read too slowly to really pick up the pace of the story. (I eventually took her to a tutor, and she reads much faster today.)

It would have been easy for me to throw up my hands and say, "Rebecca just isn't wired for this book thing." But I didn't. I exercised patience and waited. Once she was ready, we started our discussions. It turns out that she loves those times with me in Grandma's Room just as much as her older brother and sister.

Why? Because doing book isn't really about reading, and it's not some glorified study hall with Dad as the proctor. Doing book is simply a gateway to swapping stories, that's all. Being wired to read or sit still has less to do with it than you might think.

Rebecca and I often did a lot more talking than reading anyway. Doing book became, for us, a time for Rebecca to laugh. It became a priceless one-on-one time between a father and a daughter. And though she didn't like to read, the price of reading a few pages was well worth the conversations that followed.

Do not be too quick to judge whether your son is wired to do book. For heaven's sake, we're only talking about reading six or eight pages…that shouldn't be a big deal, even for a high-strung jock. If it turns out that it *is* a big deal, then take turns reading out loud together. That'll keep you turning pages before you go to the discussion time and start swapping stories.

MORE THAN ONE WAY

That being said, doing book is not the only way to swap stories. In fact, the goal of doing book is to make every place a swapping place as you grow closer to your kids. My brother-in-law Brent owns a concrete-cutting business in Illinois, and my nephew Nick, a high-school student, regularly works jobs with him on weekends and during the summer. They do most of their swapping as they crisscross the freeways of Chicagoland between jobs.

Gary Rosberg, cofounder of *American's Family Coaches* radio program, used to spend the last fifteen minutes of his girls' days flopped down on their beds as they prepared to nod off to sleep. Gary shared much of himself throughout the years on those countless nights. He recently told me that even now his youngest still tells others, "My dad is my very best friend."

My friend Gil told me, "Our swapping place varied throughout the years, but nothing worked better than our hot tub. Maybe seeing me with my shirt off showed my son that he had nothing to worry about when talking man to man with me! Seriously, the feeling that 'Dad's not so perfect' opened up personal matters between us."

I asked Gil what tips he could share. "When the kids were real young," he said, "I worked hard at asking questions that didn't allow yes or no answers. They had to learn to answer in short sentences. That got them talking, and that was key later on, because by the later grade-school years, we'd settled on the fact that Dad wasn't afraid to talk about anything. I could talk to my sons about pornography and masturbation when they reached the midteen years. Of course, my goal wasn't to make every single talk something heavy. Maybe one in five of our hot-tub discussions carried something of real significance."

As you can see, you can make your whole life a swapping place if you show a willingness to be a transparent friend. My friend Patrick Middleton is like that. "In terms of sexual issues, my son and I talk all the time," he told me. "I watch for situations on TV shows so we can discuss them. All it really takes is asking an intriguing question like, 'Do you really think it would work out the way they say on the show?'

"I also listen for comments about pregnant girls at school or gossip about who is easy. We talk about that girl's side of things in terms of her motivation. We talk about the nonphysical consequences of being sexual, like the lost chances at *real* intimacy and the hurt and the loneliness. I'll ask, 'What do you suppose goes on inside of people that makes them think they are only good for sex? How hurting must they be?'"

"You must get some interesting responses," I casually observed.

"I sure do. But I try to see things through their eyes. I remember one time when I dropped my boys off at school. I said, 'I don't know how you guys make it through the day with all this skin in your face.'

"My oldest son replied, 'You just get used to it.' To which I replied, 'How sad. I never want you to get used to it. When your wife comes out in some sexy outfit on your wedding night, I want you to fall out of bed. I want sex with your wife to blow your mind.'"

I laughed, but Patrick wasn't finished. "I go as deep with my boys as I can at any moment," he said. "Once, on another occasion when I was waiting in line to drop them off at school, I commented, 'I have no idea what I would do if I had two fleshy globes on my chest that gave me so much power over half the human race. I'd probably show them off too.' My sons chuckled, but I could tell it got their wheels turning. I let them ponder that a moment, and then I asked, 'So what do you think motivates them to show off their breasts?' For the next few minutes, we had a great discussion about the effect that this part of the female anatomy has on men. And you know what, Fred? Just being willing to comment on the reality of it seems to have drained away some of its secret power."

Can you imagine having that conversation with your dad? I can't. But my life would have been different if I'd had a few talks like that!

The key for you, as the father, is to understand just how valuable your wisdom and the stories of your life are to your kids. Your stories teach as well as warn. But they can also warm them and make them laugh, connecting souls and bringing the Scriptures alive to young hearts.

GETTING INTENTIONAL

Lots of times you'll hear the experts say that parents need to be "intentional" with their kids. Intentional can mean a lot of things, of course. Willie told me, "My dad avoided the talk by giving me a Christian book on sex back in high school. Granted, I know that's intentional in a technical sense, but that was awful! I had *so* many questions and wanted badly to ask him about them, but I had no way to do it."

Willie's dad didn't go first, and he didn't go deep. Like Willie, maybe you had a father who handed you a book on the birds and the bees, so you have no role model on how to do this with your son. Maybe you've even decided to check out on the job.

Let me make one thing perfectly clear: You have no right to avoid this issue with your kids. You're a father, whether you like it or not, and you've been given a job to do by God. You must press ahead no matter how scared or how far it pushes you out of your comfort zone. This is not the time to take yourself out of the game.

When my son Michael was ten, he picked up a ball and glove and played his first year of Little League. All the other kids had been playing organized baseball for five years. Needless to say, the live pitching overmatched him at times.

Being a ballplayer from way back, my heart was with him in spades. I tried to give him some extra batting practice when we didn't have practice or a game. I schooled him on how to hold the bat up and take a level cut at the ball. After one particularly good week of practice, Michael was looking forward to his Saturday game in the worst way. "Daddy, this time I'm going to hit that ball and not strike out!"

In his first plate appearance, however, Michael promptly struck out swinging. He was crushed. Struggling bravely to hold his head up on the way to the dugout, he collapsed into my arms in quiet tears. "I'm not good enough to be here," he said.

I just held him and rubbed my hand gently over his hair. The third out was called, and now the other team was up to bat. "Michael, you've got to get out there," I said. "Grab your glove."

Instantly, his emotions crumbled further. "I can't, Daddy. Not after striking out again. I just can't."

"Son, you've got to go."

"Daddy, I can't go out there. I'm just not good enough."

"You have to," I gently urged.

His emotions were now nearing a quiet but frantic panic. "No, I can't. I can't go out there."

"Son, your manager is depending on you. He put you in center field. You've got to go."

An amazing thing happened. Michael looked at the ground intently for a moment and thought about his manager. Suddenly, I watched him set his jaw resolutely. Grabbing his glove, he wiped his tears on his sleeve and ran bravely out to center field, knowing full well that he could embarrass himself yet again.

Dad, you've got to run out into the field and take your position too. It doesn't matter if you don't know what you're doing. Your Manager has filled out His lineup card, and you're playing father. You've got to go. There's a game being played.

Look, I'm a guy like you, so I understand how we often react to something new. Either (1) we're afraid that we'll look ridiculous and fail or (2) we feel that new thing won't work for us.

C'mon. You read my story. You remember how I waited outside Jasen's room with books in my hand, too chicken to step inside his room. But when I pushed ahead, I found my fears to be unfounded. Not only that, I began enjoying myself because swapping stories is right up my alley. Most guys like to do this sort of thing. Let's get intentional and get at it.

And as for you single moms out there, you may feel handicapped, but you really aren't. Who knows more about relationships than women? You've got an edge in this game too, and your son could benefit from your insight. Besides, there's no other parent on duty.

I know what you're thinking. *I'm not a guy. Why would my son want to talk to me about girls?* Granted, he won't likely come to you on his own with his questions, but that would be true if there were a father in the house too. You can still do it. You just have to go first.

running all the way

If we master the art of the hand-off and get them the ball, they'll run normally—just as Coach diagrammed the play. They'll be regular, normal Christian sons and daughters.

Rich, a youth pastor, once expressed to me his vision for his youth group. "We want to raise up a generation of young people with uncommon character!" he said.

That is a great sentiment, and I understand fully what he is saying. A Christian teen *should* look different from the average non-Christian teen. Too often our adolescent Christians are indistinguishable from their non-Christian peers, watching the same movies, listening to the same music, catching the same shows on television—and even having the same attitudes about premarital sex. Kristin, a teenager, told me, "Our youth group is filled with kids faking their Christian walk. They are actually taking drugs, drinking, partying, and having sex. If you want to walk purely, it's easier to hang around with the non-Christians at school than to hang around with the Christians at church. I say that because school friends know where I stand, and they say, 'That's cool—I can accept that.' The Christian kids mock me, laughing and asking, 'Why be so straight? Get a life!' They pressure my values at every turn." She described how Brad, a lay leader's son, told her, "I know intercourse is wrong before marriage, but anything short of that is fine. I love to get up under a bra."

Obviously, if this sort of behavior is common, we want to push the uncommon. But why measure ourselves from the mark set by what's common in the world around us?

God doesn't use terms like *common* and *uncommon,* and He doesn't measure character in relation to the *world.* He measures character in relation to the *Word,* and He uses words like *sin,* which means "missing the mark." What mark?

The one set by Jesus. Jesus was the Word in flesh, so Jesus is our mark. When God speaks of character, He speaks along these lines: *Jesus is My beloved Son in whom I am very well pleased. He is the most normal person ever to walk Planet Earth. You are a Christian, My child. Are you walking normally like My Son, Jesus?*

As Christians, we should measure from this mark. As parents, our vision and our challenge must be to rear a generation of youth with *normal* Christian character. That is what the hand-off is all about. And what of that "uncommon character" spoken of by Rich? We should call it what God calls it: normal. And that all-too-common behavior seen in youth groups today? That should be called abnormal. Otherwise, we get confused.

CONFUSING OURSELVES AS PARENTS

On a recent Friday, I was speaking at a denominational regional singles conference in Cedar Rapids. A pleasant woman approached me and said, "My son really liked your book *Every Young Man's Battle.* He's in school today, but I'm going to have him pulled out of class so he can come over here and hear what you have to say."

"Thank you," I said. "That's nice to hear."

She smiled wearily. "I need *someone* to talk to him. He doesn't listen to *me* anymore. He's sixteen—you know how they are!"

I nodded and smiled, but honestly? I don't really *know* that's how sixteen-year-old boys really are. I understand the current literature on adolescence. I know what is *common* in teenland. But I'm not at all certain that's how they *are!*

At Stanford I focused on the disciplines of sociology and psychology. With teens, as with all groups, we could study and survey and measure endlessly and finally label the most common behavior normative. Calling the common thing normal would be considered scientific truth. Even Christian parents accept this "normative" behavior as just part of raising teens. But it isn't.

For me, Christianity turns secular sociology and psychology on their ears. That is why the rise of Christian psychology has had such a profound impact on our world. A sociologist, if devoid of God's absolute truth, is really little more than a news anchor reporting what he sees in the world every day. What he reports is no more the truth than the repeated horrors on our daily newscasts prove that we all live in a perpetual state of catastrophe and violence. Yet we are told to expect that same behavior from our own teens, and when our children turn twelve, we start to cower before the adolescent years while gripping our Bibles with white knuckles.

But sociologists and psychologists are only reporting what they commonly see *today.* They aren't reporting the *truth.* For instance, sociologists say that teens don't want to be seen with their parents. This is normal behavior, we are told, and it's repeated so often that we believe it. But it isn't normal. God's Word defines what is normal. Normal behavior for a Christian teen is Christian behavior, not the common behavior we see everywhere else.

CONFUSING OUR TEENS

As Christian parents, we can't afford to define normal by what the rest of the world considers common behavior. If we do, our teens can get pretty confused too.

One time while we were doing book, Rebecca and I came across a passage noting an "emotional problem that usually arises during adolescence; we call it 'the conflict between generations.' This phrase refers to the irritation and harsh feelings that are likely to occur between you and your parents during the teenage years."

As my first question of the night, I asked, "Rebecca, what do you think about that passage?" A boring question, to be sure, but I couldn't help it. To me, the so-called generation gap was accepted old news, and to my brainwashed mind there was no way to put a new or interesting spin on it.

But Rebecca found one easily. Without warning, her face crumpled a bit and tears pooled up. "I guess pretty soon I'm not going to be talking to you for a while," she said. She was torn to think she'd have to endure this conflict with her father and mother, but it was clear to her from the passage that there really wasn't any choice. This was a natural part of adolescence, and she'd be treating us roughly whether she liked it or not.

I was dumbfounded. We can confuse our kids when we mix present-day sociology with our Christianity. I now wonder how much of this "natural," unpleasant teen behavior is simply a self-fulfilling prophecy?

Quickly stepping in, I dried Rebecca's tears by saying, "Hey, wait a minute. Let's stop and think about something. Jasen is eighteen. Do you ever remember his going through something like this?"

Pausing to think, she replied, "No, he didn't, did he?"

"What about Laura? She's sixteen, and you *know* how strong-willed she is. Do you ever remember Laura's going through a stage like this?"

"No, neither one of them has."

"And neither will you, sweetheart. Sure, it's natural for you to become more independent. But normal Christian kids don't have to drive everyone crazy in the process, and normal kids don't have to withdraw into some grouchy stew. Remember the fifth commandment? What does it say?"

"Honor your father and your mother," she answered.

"See, there it is," I said.

"See what?" Rebecca asked, puzzled.

"God says that it's normal for Christian teens to have a great relationship with their parents and to keep talking with them. They shouldn't be embarrassed to be seen with them, and they shouldn't be storming around slamming doors and lying about where they've been. Jasen and Laura are normal. Rebecca, you will be normal too."

Relief swept over her face. She could avoid this awful stage. *And all I have to do is be normal?* She was happy! She didn't have to become some witch just because some psychologist told parents all teens are this way. She simply had to relax and be normal.

No Incentive to Change

But there is another reason it is important to allow God's Word to define normal. I'll let Rebecca express this one to you. It began when I asked her, "Beck, do you see why it is important to define normal correctly? What happens if we call 'the conflict of generations' normal?"

Without hesitation, she responded, "If we call that normal, I don't have any reason to change if I slip into being nasty and treating you rotten. After all, I'm being normal, right? No problem. Why change and be nice?"

This thirteen-year-old girl gets the picture better than a conference room of sociologists.

We shouldn't expect common behavior from our teens, nor should we *accept* the common from them. You see, while many sociologists and psychologists call these generational conflicts and grumpy teen attitudes "natural," God calls them red flags marking areas in the relationships that are out of line with Scripture.

If these conflicts and attitudes aren't normal and are merely red flags, then why are they so common? Simple—our culture is sick to no end, hopelessly out of line with Scripture. Low commitment to Christ is pandemic in the Christian church today, so teens haven't a clue as to what's normal. On top of that, the pain of life may have knocked them off-line early. For instance, multiple generations of 50 percent divorce rates have left millions of teens wounded.

Parents are also out of line. Never in our history have so many parents been raised without a Christian heritage. They had poor parental role models, and the resulting baggage they bring with them into their young families can easily drive their kids to wrath.

These conflicts are red flags that point to the places where we can better apply God's truth in our families. Look, I'm not saying there are no developmental reasons behind the generation gap. When the idealism of teens bumps up against their parents' more realistic outlooks on life, tension can pop up.

What I *am* saying is that we can expect more from our teens, and we can do far more to ensure great relationships with them. They weren't born to drive us crazy. They were *reborn* to bring God glory...you know, by being normal, like Jesus. Because of His truth, we can know what's normal. Because of His victory, we can walk normally.

I stand on this statement from God:

He who dwells in the shelter of the Most High
     will rest in the shadow of the Almighty.
I will say of the LORD, "He is my refuge and my fortress,
     my God, in whom I trust....

A thousand may fall at your side,
> ten thousand at your right hand,
> but it will not come near you....
Then no harm will befall you,
> no disaster will come near your tent. (Psalm 91:1-2,7,10)

What does this mean? A thousand teens may stand at my side "acting that way," and ten thousand parents may stand at my right hand proclaiming, "My son won't listen to me anymore—you know how they are." But this won't touch my teens nor come anywhere near my tent. They will listen to me and will be open to me. My teens will be kind and respectful to all adults. We can expect greatness from our teens.

Sure, sullen, withdrawn, and rebellious teens may be common elsewhere. But we are Christians. We aren't common. We are called out and set apart. We aren't conformed to this world. We are transformed.

It is not normal for a Christian teen to be embarrassed to be seen with his mom or dad, regardless of how common it is elsewhere. It is not normal for a Christian teenager to ignore me when I greet him in the church foyer, though it is quite common.

Quite the opposite should be true. Our teens ought to be our finest witnesses for Christ. Not long ago Dale attended his daughter Holly's parent-teacher conference. Her biology teacher, a non-Christian, said, "Your daughter is one of the most hardworking, diligent students I've ever met. She is also a great leader and very kind to the other students. I've heard that her brother Tanner was the same way. I know you have a great relationship with your kids. What is your secret? I have two young children, and I'm trying to learn."

God says Holly is normal, and He says we should expect our sons and daughters to shine:

Do everything...so that you may become blameless and pure, children
of God without fault in a crooked and depraved generation, in which
you shine like stars in the universe as you hold out the word of life.
(Philippians 2:14-16)

But because we've mixed the common with the normal, our kids are confused and so are we.

IT'S ALL ABOUT PARENTAL GUIDANCE

Calling normal behavior "uncommon" and calling abnormal Christian behavior "natural" has not only warped our expectations, but it's devastated our leadership. Our parental guidance suffers greatly in this fog.

Consider raunchy movies, for example. Parents will often say, "Oh, they will watch those movies anyway. Everyone goes to see those things. It's natural! What's the big deal? We can watch the shows with them and point out what's right and wrong."

In her book *Kissed the Girls and Made Them Cry*, Lisa Bevere expresses horror at such thinking:

> [After speaking], those who wanted to stay for prayer or just to talk and ask more questions were invited to remain.... What I heard for the next two hours broke my heart. I was told stories of an abuse—so subtle you may mistake it as harmless: parents who watched movies filled with sexual promiscuity, innuendoes, and often, partial nudity with their children in the shelter of their homes or beside them in the dark theatre. Young girls shared how uncomfortable they'd been watching this with their parents, especially with the *fathers*. They'd feel shame and fidget, then look at their parents and notice they weren't flinching.
>
> After a few such movies or TV shows, they pushed the uncomfortable feelings away, but couldn't see their parents in quite the same light. It was as though by watching their father view the naked breasts of another woman presented in a sexually suggestive manner, their own virgin breasts had been uncovered. They left the experience feeling vulnerable and violated and not even knowing why.[2]

---

2. Lisa Bevere, *Kissed the Girls and Made Them Cry* (Nashville: Thomas Nelson, 2002), 8-9.

The whole world screams that watching this kind of show is normal and natural. We need to sound a clear, opposing voice, but Christians remain silent, unwilling or unable to distinguish the common from the normal. The chances of making a clean hand-off are slim in this confusion. How will our sons ever run normally if we're fumbling the ball this way?

We need to straighten up. Take voyeurism, for instance. What's a voyeur? A fancy French name for a Peeping Tom. A voyeur gets his jollies watching other people have sex. Do you approve of the practice? Few of us would—or should.

And yet most Christians engage in voyeurism all the time. But because we've sanitized it and put up ticket booths and popcorn stands, and because we do it together in the dark, cozy comfort of our theaters, we think it is okay. We're blind enough to call voyeurism normal for us.

Wait a minute! I'm not sneaking around in the bushes peeping through windows!

That may be a distinction in America's legal system, but not in the realm of God's kingdom. God says it is never normal for Christians to watch others having sex.

Feature films pollute as surely as pornographic Web pages, but we ignore the truth because everyone else is watching them too. These films damage our oneness with Christ as surely as cyberporn, but we've watched them so long that we don't even notice.

And so our leadership becomes bizarre. We demand that our sons avoid viewing the nude women found on the Web—but we rent PG-13 and R-rated movies for ourselves. And honestly? There is no difference between you, in the padded comfort of your home, watching others have sex and your son having sex with the deacon's daughter in the padded comfort of the backseat of his car. Not by God's way of thinking anyway. Both are sin and one is as abnormal as the other.

Let's get serious—how can we get them the ball when we're falling down? How can we give them internal standards when we've compromised our own? When we compromise, the enemy attacks. He drops a veil over our eyes so we can no longer see to lead.

The veil's effect? We're perplexed. Some guys think, *Why can't I get my masturbation under control, though I've prayed a billion times? Why can't I pray five minutes without sexual thoughts racing across my mind?* It's because we aren't living normally. We aren't fleeing sexual immorality. The truth would set us free if we'd walk in it.

We're perplexed when our daughters leave for school dressed modestly, then change into something sexy in the rest room before the opening bell. *How can this be?* We're perplexed to see our sons consumed with girls and struggling with their sexuality. *Isn't he awful young to be struggling so?*

But why be perplexed? What do you expect? You haven't taught them to flee sexual immorality. In fact, you've done the opposite, sitting with them in sexual training sessions at the theater and in your family room. You've opened a door that was supposed to remain closed. You've *sexualized* (see additional information on pages 103-107) them early.

I was out to dinner with a dear friend from church. Wrenchingly, he told me of his son's wild, promiscuous ways. But then he followed it with the most amazing statement: "I don't know why he is so promiscuous! We don't teach him this at home!"

I was blown away. I'd seen the videos stacked up in his home entertainment center. He most certainly *does* teach it at home, just as surely as rain falls downward. But because he isn't living normally, there's that veil and he can't make the connection.

It is abnormal to set sin before our kids as a form of training. God says it is abnormal for a teen to set any unclean thing before his own eyes (see Psalm 101:3). How can it be normal for you to set it there?

God says it is normal for a young man to keep his way pure (Psalm 119:9) and to flee sexual immorality (1 Corinthians 6:18). How can it be normal for you to encourage further practice?

We've called God's ways too hard and tight. Call them what they really are—normal.

No Confusion Here

Mixture is so subtle in our culture. I stumbled again recently, once more confusing the common with the normal. At the time, Jasen was eighteen and a senior in high school, and yet he had never dated. One night I casually asked, "Hey, Jasen, I noticed you haven't really dated anyone yet, and here you are getting ready to head off to college. That's kind of uncommon. Any particular reason?"

He looked me in the eye and replied, "There just isn't anyone out there, Dad."

Hmmm. That makes him only five thousand times more mature than I was at his age. He's got his standards, and he will keep them. No rush, no hurry. Is that odd? Should that be rare? Still, I densely pressed on a bit more, asking, "Well, some of your friends have had steady girlfriends and all that. Have any of your friends ever asked you why you don't date?"

"Some. Jan asked me about it just the other day. But I'm glad it doesn't come up so much. The whole topic is very annoying."

"How so?"

"People are so strange about it, Dad. They are all so convinced that you have to use high school as some practice ground. Remember Mr. Peterson?"

"Sure. Everyone's favorite teacher."

"That's him. He is one of my favorites too, and I really loved his class," Jasen continued. "But I'd often hear him talking to kids about opening up and getting on with dating. I didn't want to talk to him about it, but one day he and a couple of the guys cornered me. I knew they were only concerned for me, but they piled on about my need to start dating before I went off to college. They also said it would be good practice for picking out a wife.

"I stood there patiently listening, while chuckling to myself inside," Jasen continued. "I thought, *If all this practice is so helpful in learning how to pick wives, why are our divorce rates so high?* But I didn't say it, because I didn't want to offend him. Still when they kept going on and on, I finally got so annoyed that I told them, 'But *I* don't want to be practiced on!'

"You should have been there, Dad! It was really funny! They all just fell quiet and stared. None of them had ever considered that while *you* are practicing on the girls, *they* are practicing on you, using you as their own little practice field."

I, too, fell quiet and stared at Jasen. In all my "sophisticated" years of dating, I'd never thought of that, either. Then I burst out laughing. The joke was clearly on me. Some might say that Jasen has uncommon insight. But he doesn't. He has normal insight, so normal that many of us don't recognize it.

But we should. Our chief commandment is to love our neighbors as ourselves, and it is quite normal to do so. Practicing with a girl's body and emotions isn't loving, and it seems quite odd to God, to say the least.

You want to know what I think is the greatest thing about this story? All along, I worried about getting the ball into Jasen's hands. I was so worried that I never noticed that I had *already* made the hand-off much sooner than I had realized. He was off and running, blazing his own trail. As ESPN's Chris Berman would say, Jasen…COULD…GO…ALL… THE…WAY!

the spiritual inheritance

It's amazing and yet strange. An entire decade has passed since *Every Man's Battle* first hit the streets, but as I write this chapter in honor of the tenth anniversary of the Every Man series, it seems like only yesterday I was clumsily punching out the original rough draft of that manuscript. But it seems as if God's done three decades of work in that short time. After all, its message has been translated into some thirty languages and has spread throughout the world, and eleven more books have followed in this popular series, along with eight in the best-selling Every Woman series.

Readers often ask, "Which is your favorite book in the series?" That's like asking me which of my children is my favorite. A far more intriguing question is, "Which is *God's* favorite?" I believe it's this one, *Preparing Your Son for Every Man's Battle*. As I pressed into the Lord one morning while praying over the first draft of this manuscript years ago, the Lord whispered into my heart, *This is the most important book you will ever write. It won't have the most readers, but it will have the most impact, as this book will turn the hearts of many fathers toward their sons, so that many young men who would have otherwise been entangled in sexual sin will instead run hard with Me their entire lives, from their youth.*

As those years passed, the evidence of that impact has become stronger and stronger, starting in my own home. Consider again these sentences from the end of the previous chapter:

All along, I worried about getting the ball into Jasen's hands. I was so worried that I never noticed that I had *already* made the hand-off much sooner than I had realized. He was off and running, blazing his own trail.

To be sure, Jasen *was* off and running, and quite free of the encumbering burdens I'd carried as a young man. At the age of twenty-three, I had four girlfriends. I was sleeping regularly with three of them and was essentially engaged to be married to two of them. Though I was born again later that same year, the years of sexual sin had strapped heavy, crippling weights about my ankles. I could barely step onto the course laid out for me by the Lord, let alone race freely with Him to the finish (Hebrews 12:1). God had to push me through many years of strenuous biblical training at home before I could run with Him.

Not so for Jasen. At that same age of twenty-three, I watched him step up to his wedding altar and share his very first kiss with his bride, Rose. Talk about blazing your own trail! Jasen had avoided the sexual sin that entangles so many young men and was already running hard with God. By the age of twenty-five, Jasen had already discussed celibacy and sexual purity on national television in England and coauthored his first book, *Hero,* which tells the story of how he managed to stay sexually pure from those early chaotic days of puberty to that wonderful day at the altar.

Jasen had been given a head start. In other words, he'd received a huge spiritual inheritance from my wife and me. Spiritually speaking, my ceiling had become Jasen's floor. Because of that, he was able to set out from a higher spiritual plane than I did, embarking from a place of purity that took me most of my lifetime to reach.

As Proverbs 13:22 says, an inheritance is a commendable thing: "A good man leaves an inheritance for his children's children." Like most of us, I want my kids to have it better than I did, and of course that's what a financial inheritance is all about. But most of all, I want my kids to have it better than I did *spiritually*. I don't want my kids spending their first ten or fifteen years as adults *preparing* to run, like I did. I want them racing freely from the start.

A SPIRITUAL INHERITANCE

If I bequeath the fruit of an entire lifetime of economic effort to my children and grandchildren, they'll get a head start in their financial lives. But if I manage to bequeath an entire lifetime of spiritual effort, it's even more valuable. I can plant that inheritance earlier in their lives, and I needn't even split it up between them. Once I make that hand-off, they can start from where I left off, and our family line will be far more effective for God over the years.

Leaving a spiritual inheritance takes special work, of course. Unlike a financial inheritance, it requires a deep connection with your kids, and that connection doesn't just happen. There is a practical side to providing this spiritual inheritance. Since it takes intentional, timely effort and a lot of talking and sharing, it's our first responsibility before God to make that connection happen.

Perhaps you came from a broken home like I did, and you're not even really sure how to connect with your wife effectively, let alone your children. If you've never seen it, you'll have fewer practical ideas on how to get it done.

You're not alone. But you're not excused, either. That hand-off is still yours to make, and your entire call as a father will depend upon your ability to connect with your children:

> Love the LORD your God with all your heart and with all your soul and with
> all your strength. These commandments that I give you today are to be upon
> your hearts. Impress them on your children. Talk about them when you sit at
> home and when you walk along the road, when you lie down and when you
> get up. (Deuteronomy 6:5–7)

I've never experienced anything more practical or effective at building this family connection than doing book. Where would my kids be without it? Even as I wrote this chapter, I received this e-mail from my daughter Rebecca, who is experiencing a very difficult and teary time in college:

> Hey, Dad! Thanks for talking with me last night. It was all very encouraging, and I'm feeling better about a lot of things this morning ☺. I love our times in Grandma's room. They are always so fun and helpful, and I want to thank you for setting that up years ago, so that we can all have a place to go and talk freely with you and to learn. It really does mean a lot to me. I love you very much!

It means a lot to me too. She needs her spiritual inheritance, and I promise that my ceiling *will* be her floor. It's just a matter of time.

It's just a matter of time for you and your children too, if you get started now. *Preparing Your Son for Every Man's Battle* has already taught many parents how to make that connection with their kids in a simple, practical way. So turn your heart toward your sons and daughters. Take what you've learned and build your swapping place, and make your ceiling their floor. From that higher plane, they'll launch onto trajectories you've only dimly imagined in your wildest dreams.

To support your efforts in building that connection, let me answer a few of the most common questions from readers over the years as they began to build their swapping places.

How do you choose the books you use with your kids? You started with Preparing for Adolescence *by James Dobson and* Preparing Your Son for Every Man's Battle *or* Preparing Your Daughter for Every Woman's Battle, *and now we've done that too. What books should we use next?*

This is easily the most common question I'm asked about doing book, so I will answer this one in some detail. I'll share some of the books we used along the way, but I'll also share why I chose them so you'll be better equipped to choose the right books for your children.

In short, I choose the books based up both my kids' *developmental* and *personal* needs at the time. To follow are the four categories I used to help me pick these books.

1. Universal Developmental Issues for Teens. Certain developmental issues exist for every teenager. For instance, everyone moving through puberty will develop an interest in the opposite sex—usually sooner than later. I figured that was a good place to start, so certain books on dating and courtship became required reading in the Stoeker household. Understanding dating is critical for my children's protection, both emotionally and sexually: *I Kissed Dating Goodbye* and *Boy Meets Girl: Say Hello to Courtship* by Joshua Harris and *I Gave Dating a Chance* by Jeramy Clark.

Once dating begins, of course, sexual pressure naturally develops. Since every teen also goes through this process, we stretched beyond dating books and into those focused on *staying pure* while dating. *Every Young Woman's Battle* by Shannon Ethridge is great for girls, and *Hero,* the book I wrote with my son Jasen, is perfect for guys.

Because of the sensitive female issues involved, my wife covered *Every Young Woman's Battle* with my daughters, while I did *Hero* with both my sons and daughters. *Hero* teaches young men the proper mind-set and strategies needed to handle dating purely, and it also teaches what kind of leadership women should expect and receive from those pursuing their hearts.

2. Personal Book Selections. You'll find other developmental topics to cover by looking over your own life for the topics that impacted you most along the way. As I mentioned earlier, no topic has had a bigger impact on my marriage than the study of temperaments and understanding the difference between personalities. I wouldn't dream of sending my children out into the world without that basic understanding, nor would I attempt to raise them together in close quarters without it either. Comprehending and honoring their differing temperaments helped my children understand one another better and treat one another with deeper care and respect.

There are many books about temperaments out there, but I prefer those written by Tim and Beverly LaHaye because of their excellent coverage of the "temperament blends" in individuals. You might start with the *Spirit-Controlled Temperament,* written by Tim LaHaye.

What do you find when you look back over your life? Perhaps temperaments weren't it for you. Perhaps your relationships were revolutionized by learning and understanding the various love languages. If so, you might instead choose to do book with the best-selling classic by Gary Chapman, *The Five Love Languages: How to Express Heartfelt Commitment to Your Mate.* By choosing a topic that has transformed you personally, you'll be sure to have plenty of enlightening stories to swap with your children as you do book together.

3. Today's Generational Issues. You might also look for widespread developmental issues among the teens in your son's generation. As a group, how are they stumbling? Choosing the right book will provide your kids the weaponry necessary to fight off common failures being experienced by others their age. For instance, so little is expected of teens today that many aren't living up to their capabilities. To counteract that in your kids, I'd recommend *Do Hard Things: A Teenage Rebellion Against Low Expectations,* written by Alex Harris and Brett Harris.

4. Your Child's Own Personal Issues. Consider the lives of your own children to find where they need help. Perhaps there's something in your son's life that you've talked about until you were blue in the face, but little has changed. Why not do book on the topic? For example, being suave and minding manners hasn't always been at the top of the priority list for my son Michael. While he hasn't always been a six-foot-five, 291-pound offensive tackle, he has always had a rugged, scruffier mind-set.

As a result, Brenda chose a very special book for Michael to do with me: *How to Be a Gentleman: A Contemporary Guide to Common Courtesy* by John Bridges. This book was good for him, and frankly, it was good for me as well. Did you know, for instance, that a gentleman always wears a T-shirt under a dress shirt to catch his perspiration? My dad never taught me that, but it's good to know. I've never gone without a T-shirt since I learned this.

In the end, there may be no better way to pick a book than to listen in on your children as they're growing through life. We were sitting around the kitchen table at suppertime recently when Rebecca snorted, "A bunch of the guys in my dorm are going on a survival trek next month. They'll march dozens of miles with the barest of provisions, living off the land and sleeping under the stars. That's all they can talk about. Ugh! Why do they like that stuff? It just seems so childish and weird to me."

Alarms started clanging from every corner of my masculinity. Maleness has been under a blistering and withering attack in the media for decades, belittling men and "civilizing" our boys into oblivion. I wondered if all this propaganda had seeped into my daughter's brain. After all, Rebecca's a young woman. She should adore maleness, not bristle at it. It should intrigue her, not annoy her. Clearly, times were desperate. I had to come to her rescue.

Mounting up quickly, I rode in upon the John Eldredge classic, *Wild at Heart: Discovering the Secret of a Man's Soul.* Rebecca needed to understand the male heart. Though slightly dangerous in its intrinsic strength, a guy's heart is a stem of God's victorious stock, created after God's own image. Genuine manhood has great value and ought to be treasured.

The rescue went flawlessly. After only the second chapter, Rebecca giggled over the phone one evening, "Dad, I used to be bugged by the guys with all that bravado stuff, but after starting *Wild at Heart,* it's really kind of exciting to hear them talk now…and very attractive!"

Mission accomplished. Keep your ears open, Dad. You'll know just the book to ride in on.

I travel a lot. Can we do book over the telephone?

At one time I would've answered with an emphatic no to that question, but not since my other daughter Laura recently moved to North Carolina to begin her graduate studies in biomedical research. She soon discovered what many who have gone before her learned: without the dorms to help build friendships, graduate school can be downright desolate. The hours are just too long and the homework too stifling. It wasn't long before Laura was desperate for a little more human connection in her life.

As part of the solution, Brenda suggested we schedule an hour each Sunday night to do book together by phone. I didn't think it would work, but I agreed to give it a shot, as it had to be better than nothing.

And it has been. In fact, I've been blown away! I purchased a headset to keep the neck kinks at bay, but beyond that, little has changed. I still sit in my corner of Grandma's room to talk, and I still spend half the time laughing my head off with her. I recently gushed, "I just love doing book over the phone with you, Laura. I really didn't think it would work without being able to see you, but this is just as much fun as it ever was."

"I think so too, Daddy," she said. "All I miss is the hug at the end!"

Hmm. Come to think of it, so do I.

At what age do you stop doing book with your kids?

While I haven't given this question too much thought, perhaps marriage would be the finish line:

> For this reason a man will leave his father and mother and be united to his wife, and they will become one flesh. (Genesis 2:24)

Once my kids are married, they need to be doing book with their spouses. Jasen began the process early—during his engagement to Rose—by working through some of Dave Ramsey's budgeting and finance books and DVDs.

But until your children's wedding day, I see no reason to stop. After all, whatever their age, my children are still my children, still under my spiritual protection and guidance. My call from God to impress His truths upon them still stands. The same is true for you.

If you've done little to build your relationships with your twentysomething children over the years, you certainly can't force doing book with them now. They are adults, and they're on their own. But if you do have that relationship, the odds are good they'll still be receptive.

My two oldest are now adults, but they're still young, which means they still have questions about life. That's to my advantage because I've got thirty years on them, which means I still have some answers. Granted, by now they're making most of their decisions on their own, and I know they're plenty smart already. My twenty-four-year-old daughter, Laura, for instance, is a brilliant young scientist who recently traveled to Paris to present her biomedical research to an international symposium. I can assure you, it's been years since she's asked me for help on her science homework. But consider what happened when we recently read the following passage together from the eighth chapter of *Wild at Heart*:

What the Scriptures call the flesh, the old man, or the sinful nature, is that part of fallen Adam in every man that always wants the easiest way out. It's much easier to masturbate than to make love to your wife, especially if things are not well between you and initiating sex with her feels risky. (page 143)

While Laura is well read and a rising young star in the scientific community, that passage still tossed her for a complete loop. "Daddy, why would any husband ever choose masturbation over his wife? That makes no sense! And why would it ever feel risky to initiate sex with your own wife, who loves you dearly?"

She may be an adult, but she still has some difficult, insightful questions. I want to be the one answering those questions as long as she'll have me. Sure, it takes effort. It took me forty-five minutes to answer those two questions to my satisfaction because I first had to explain some basics of male sexuality and the male ego before I could cover the challenges of marriage, intimacy, and the likelihood of differing expectations. But that's the job, and I'm fine with that. Now she has a new understanding, and God's truths about sex and relationships are a little more deeply impressed into her heart.

Do you ever go through the same book at the same time with your kids?
I never go through a book with the kids grouped in the same room together, as each of them needs one-on-one time. But I often go through the same book with more than one child simultaneously. In fact, I recently set a family record by going through *Wild at Heart* with three of my kids at once!

But I think it's important for you to understand that even when you're going through the same book with multiple kids, it's rarely for the same reasons. In this case, all three—Laura, Rebecca, and Michael—had different circumstances to address. It just so happened that this one book could address all of them.

We've already discussed what Rebecca learned in the book, but Laura's situation was quite different. If you'll recall, at age sixteen Laura had been chomping at the bit to get out of the corral and start dating, but then a few visits to Grandma's room convinced her that high school wasn't the right time for romance in her life. But now she was twenty-four, and with her friends marrying one by one and the loneliness of grad school piling higher over her heart, the time seemed "righter" for romance with every passing day. Once again, I sensed a potential for danger in her eagerness to date if it was motivated by fear and loneliness. I hoped to lead her into an even deeper intimacy with the Lord, which would soften some of that urgency. This passage from *Wild at Heart* tripped a trigger in her:

> God wants to be loved.... From beginning to end, the cry of God's heart is, "Why won't you choose Me?"... "You will...find me," says the Lord, "when you seek me with all your heart" (Jeremiah 29:13). In other words, "Look for Me, pursue Me—I want you to pursue Me." Amazing. As Tozer says, "God waits to be wanted." (page 36)

Laura's response provided one more indelible moment in our lives together: "Daddy, I've never seen God's desire for me in such a personal, intimate way. I've never understood His hunger and passion for me quite like this." Over the next few months, she dug toward His heart through many hours of personal worship time, prayer, and revelation. Soon her relationship with the Lord had settled into a much deeper level of intimacy, and that overeagerness to date faded once more into the mists of time.

Separately, my son Michael was struggling to reconcile the raw masculinity of football with the softer "turn the other cheek" tenderness of the Gospel. "Where does manhood start and stop for a Christian guy? Just how hard can I hit someone on the football field before it becomes sin? We're told to turn the other cheek when confronted in life. Is it really okay to pancake the guy who's been talking smack to me all game and relish it with a smile? When my coach tells me to 'get mean out there,' what exactly does 'mean' mean? What would Jesus do in a set of shoulder pads? Would He get mean out there?"

I doubt if I had the right answer to every one of his questions, but I did know one thing—the confusion had to stop for Michael. Male strength is not a bad thing. Societies need maleness to survive, and families need maleness to excel. I had to introduce Michael to the man Jesus. He had to finally know, once and for all, that it's okay to be a male and to express it like a man. Gratefully, author John Eldredge introduces Jesus like no other:

Be honest now—what is your image of Jesus as a man? "Isn't He sort of meek and mild?" a friend remarked. "I mean, the pictures I have of Him show a gentle guy with children all around. Kind of like Mother Teresa."

Yes, those are the pictures I've seen myself in many churches. In fact, those are the only pictures I've seen of Jesus.... They leave me with the impression that He was the world's nicest guy. Mister Rogers with a beard. Telling me to be like Him feels like telling me to go limp and passive. (page 22)

You see, that's the kind of image that was confusing my son. But Eldredge didn't stop there, and quickly shared the glorious side of Christ's maleness. Mr. Rogers with a beard? Hardly:

Christ draws the Enemy out, exposes him for what he is, and shames him in front of everyone. The Lord is a gentleman? Not if you're in the service of his Enemy....

Jesus is no pale-faced altar boy...speaking softly, avoiding confrontation.... He is the Lord of hosts, the captain of angel armies. And when Christ returns, He is at the head of a dreadful company...with a double-edged sword, his robe dipped in blood (Revelation 19).... No question about it—there is something fierce in the heart of God. (pages 25, 29)

Needless to say, Michael was soon seeing Jesus—and himself—in a new light.

How can one book speak so eloquently to three different issues at once? Well, it's partly because John Eldredge has his finger so tightly on the pulse of the masculine heart. But frankly, it's also because doing book isn't really about the book at all. It's about your opportunity to swap your own stories with your kids, and your opportunity to swap God's stories in a way that is relevant to their lives at that moment.

Isn't that what God meant when He told us to impress His truth and commands upon our children when we sit at home and when we walk along the road and when we lie down and when we get up? He was asking us to make His truths relevant in the moments at hand, as our children grew. We may not work side-by-side with our children in our trades like they did in the Old Testament, and we may not be with them as often during the day as the patriarchs were, but we can still get the job done as men and as fathers.

You can still give your children that rich spiritual inheritance, and your ceiling can still be their floor. Make sure your kids have it better than you did spiritually. Connect with them, and then watch them run!

Watch for Early Sexualization

What does it mean to be sexualized early? I believe it happens quite simply through early exposure to content and situations that convey inappropriate sexual messages and images. These stir up passions of desire and lust long before they should be stirred up and long before children can understand and manage them responsibly. I was sexualized early when my grandfather threw an ice pick like a dart at pictures of nude women he'd pinned on the wall of his office.

Fred was sexualized early by exposure to pornographic magazines and his dad's nude velvet painting. Today's young generation sees nothing but sex—on television, at the movies, and on the Internet—which forces kids to grow up too fast and experience too much too soon.

With our society saturated with sexual imagery and content, your job is to protect your children from as much of it as possible. Here are some suggestions for protecting your children from early sexualization:

Do Not Allow Them to See Movies with Explicit Sexual Content

Younger children should be prevented from seeing sexually provocative movies, even when they are not explicit. You cannot depend upon Hollywood's standards to do this. For instance, the PG-rated *Runaway Bride* has no nudity, but the film has plenty of sensual joking that is out of place for Christians in light of Ephesians 5:4. How many sexual fires has Julia Roberts kindled by playfully teasing that she'd already "charmed the one-eyed snake" long before marriage?

No, you will have to set your own boundaries and limits. You will have to model appropriate viewing yourself. Fred and I are appalled at the number of parents who allow their kids to see PG-13 movies that would have been R-rated just ten years ago. Watching such films and videos reinforces the idea in boys that women are objects for men to use. Taken to its extreme, such

(continued)

behavior can also plant the idea that the boys themselves are also objects for men to abuse. The leap from one to the other is not far.

Society's standard might change, but God's standard will not. Kids who see this stuff when they are too young want to experience it too early. They come to believe that sex is all right because they see the adults on screen doing it and they see their parents watching the movies with them. The problem is, they are too young to understand that some adults can and will allow things in their own lives that are simply wrong or unhealthy, and that the behavior of the actors and parents does not necessarily make watching or having sex right.

Help Them Choose Their Music Wisely

Another adult allowed my daughter to hear a song about "taking your clothes off because it is just too hot." I could not believe that this mother allowed her children to hear this stuff. "They listen to it all the time," she said with a shrug.

We need to teach our kids the power of words—especially words that are set to music and played over and over again in their heads. These musical messages can undo much of the good teaching you have put into your children. Listen to their music. Make a point to let them know what you do and do not approve of. You are entitled to decide which music is inappropriate under your roof.

How can you set these boundaries? I (Fred) have had little rebellion against my boundaries because they've become "our" boundaries. Simply setting the standards and demanding obedience can work, but by building relationships through sharing my own stories, I have helped my children understand that I know where they are living and that I understand the dangers of crossing those boundaries. They don't chafe under the rules the way that they might otherwise.

Explain where your personal convictions come from, including the words that the Holy Spirit has spoken to you in the quiet places of your heart. After one discussion where I shared with tears the Holy Spirit's instructions to me, my kids actually said, "Dad, how can we ask you to let us break your convictions on movies after hearing what the Holy Spirit has said? We will follow you."

Train Their Eyes

If you are always pointing out certain body parts of attractive women ("Get a load of those ———!"), you will be stirring up things inside them. You will be feeding their budding interest in sex rather than helping them understand it and manage it. Instead of indicating that women are a collection of attractive body parts, help them to look at what a young woman or girl is like on the inside. What does she stand for? What does she mean when she says something? What hurts her? Help them see her as a young person worthy of honor and someone to be cherished for who she is inside. Do this, and you will be downplaying the sexual side and playing up the emotional and spiritual sides of her personality. When young men react to women as complete, honorable creations of God, the chance for early sexualization diminishes.

Protect Your Son from Early Romantic Relationships

We often think of adult-child relationships as nonsexual, but that is not always the case. When I was quite young, I had a crush on a high-school senior. This must have been quite flattering to her because she reciprocated with trips to Dairy Queen and long good-bye hugs and kisses. Her attention made me feel like a million dollars, but it also sexualized me and turned me on to the drug of romantic euphoria long before I was ready to manage it. Watch who your son spends time with, and be sure it is an appropriate relationship.

Don't Encourage Boy-Girl Relationships Too Early

Some fathers are so worried about their sons' becoming gay that they are thrilled when they start dating or meeting girls at the movies long before it is appropriate. As the father of a twelve-year-old girl, I have had to be the strict parent compared to the parents who wanted their sons to pair off with my

(continued)

daughter. I have had to talk directly to those parents and let them know it was just too early to be encouraging romantic opposite-sex relationships. It's better to encourage opposite-sex friendships in groups with other young kids.

Stand Guard Against Molestation

I never dreamed that this one would have to be one of my major goals as a parent, but it is. I would not recommend allowing your children to spend a night at a friend's house unless you know the parents and family well. You must not assume that every member of the church staff and leadership is safe either. Some are not, as we have learned from reading the headlines over the past few years, so please wake up.

You must talk to your children about this, but you must also help them avoid situations where molestation could occur. The impact of this level of sexualization is lifelong, and your vigilance is worth the trouble, especially considering that research reveals that a good percentage of homosexual behavior begins with early male-to-male sexual abuse. (If you suspect your son is gay or confused about sexual identity, you might consider reading the book *Desires in Conflict* and going through it with your son.)

Set the Example of Sexual Integrity

Your son needs to see that you are a sexual being and know that you have sexual urges and desires. He needs to know that you have boundaries and limits that you adhere to as well. He needs to know that while part of who you are is sexual, not all of who you are is sexual. He needs to see the spiritual and emotional parts of you integrated with your sexual side. If all he hears is sexual innuendo and your single-minded focus on sexuality and women, then his sexualization will be unbalanced. When you present a whole, healthy, and integrated sexuality, you are demonstrating sexual integrity.

To be a man of sexual integrity as a Christian, you need to ask yourself questions like these in everything you do:

1. Could this movie be shown in heaven? (Or could this song be played, or could this joke be told?)
2. If this movie (or song or joke) is not appropriate for my teenage son, what makes it appropriate for me?

These questions keep your double standards at bay. As a parent, if you are seeing rebellion to your standards in your home, your first instinct is to look for the flaws and weaknesses in your child. Ignore that first instinct and look instead for the flaws and weaknesses in your own example and your own sexual integrity. Are there double standards? Do you place sensual and violent films off-limits for your son, only to watch them yourself?

If you don't live a life in line with that second question above, you'll have rebellion to your standards at home. Hypocrisy breeds rebellion every time.

Book 2

for son and dad

introduction

Reading for discussion: As you both read, mark those phrases that remind you of a story or event from your own life or anything that you simply want to come back to for discussion.

You're about to read an unusual book because we'll be talking about some things that you have probably never heard before. But you don't have anything to worry about because you're in good hands. Why is that? Because you're reading this book (we hope) with your dad. If you're reading this book with your mom or a close family friend, that's okay too. The important thing is that someone you love is reading this book with you and will be available to answer any questions you have.

Now, we know what you're thinking: *How come I'm starting to read a book in the middle?*

That's a great question, and we're glad you asked it. The reason you're starting in the middle of the book is because the first part was for your dad to read. You see, we're going to be talking about things that dads and sons usually never get around to talking about—adolescence and girls and all these crazy feelings inside. Steve Arterburn, my coauthor, and I (Fred Stoeker) feel that this book, *Preparing Your Son for Every Man's Battle,* is so important that we had to give your dad some homework before he could read this with you. Your father probably hasn't done homework for years, but it was good for him to study the first half of the book before proceeding to start *Preparing Your Son* with you.

Now he's ready to "do book" with you. We recommend that you and your father read this book together for fifteen to twenty minutes and then talk about what you just read. This would be the time to ask questions or talk about whatever's on your mind. Don't worry if you're embarrassed. Once you ask an embarrassing question, you'll find it much easier to ask the second and the third. And Dad will find it easier to talk with you as well.

You definitely want Dad to be the go-to guy with your questions, and the fact that he's willing to do this with you is pretty cool. But take it easy on him. He's probably just as nervous as you are. I know that I was a big, fat yellow-bellied chicken when I wanted to read a book similar to this with my older son, Jasen, who was eleven years old at the time. Every night after dinner I would tiptoe up to his room while he did his homework or played with his Game Boy, carrying two copies of a book with me. And every time I would chicken out. I felt like a sissy.

One evening, however, I told myself that I wouldn't turn around and slink back to the living room with my tail between my legs. Instead, I marched right into Jasen's room. My son looked up from his Game Boy, and I could tell that I had startled him.

"Hey, Jasen," I said with a hopeful smile. "I have a copy of this book called *Preparing for Adolescence,* and I thought we could read it together." Settling down onto his bed, I opened my copy and said, "Jasen, I know this might feel a little uncomfortable, but you will soon be entering a very interesting period of development."

"Oh yeah?" he responded. "I've heard of that. It's called perverty, right?"

"Well, it's actually called *puberty,* Son." I chuckled but pushed ahead. "Anyway, puberty will be bringing a lot of physical changes in you. You know how Uncle Brent is always tickling you and checking for 'grass' under your arms?"

"Yeah. He did that again at Thanksgiving. I love it when he does that."

"Well, the grass is about to start sprouting. And you'll also be getting a beard, and you'll have to start shaving like me, if you can believe it."

His eyes lit up at that one.

"But there will also be mental and emotional changes, Jace. It is hard for me to put those into words exactly. For instance, you'll soon experience more peer pressure from your friends, and you might even care more about your friends' opinions than mine for a while. And because other kids will be going through this and trying to find their way through it too, you'll likely also face embarrassments and hurts as you go through puberty. I just want to prepare you for it, Son, so you aren't caught off-guard."

I paused, waiting for the dreaded sigh and the roll of his eyes in reaction to my plan. Instead, Jasen shocked me.

"Dad, I really think it's good that we're going to read this book together, especially right now," he said.

I was very surprised and couldn't believe my ears. "Why?" I asked.

"Well, I've been kind of scared lately."

Scared? "Scared about what, Son?" I asked, perplexed.

"It's just that it's been harder and harder for me to say no to my friends lately. I've been kind of scared—it's been harder for me to stand up to them."

As a father, this really touched my heart deeply, and tears came to my eyes. My son had been noticing the changes in himself that adolescence brings. He was worried about these changes, and he really wanted help...but he must have not known how to ask me.

You know, dads are great people to ask questions of. I know another father named Greg, and he told me recently that he was shaving in his bathroom when his little Timmy came in and dropped his pants to go to the bathroom. But his penis was standing straight up, making it difficult to go. Putting his hands on his hips, an exasperated Timmy said, "Dad, what makes this wood get in here sometimes so I can't go?"

That's a great question! And Timmy was asking his father, which is usually a great place to start. The trouble is that, as we grow older, we have other questions that we would *love* to ask our dads, but they seem too embarrassing.

Questions like:

• Why do girls look so nice all of a sudden?
• What are these tingly feelings I get when my leg brushes up against hers?
• Why do strange things happen to my body when I lie in bed at night and think about certain girls?
• Do these strange things happen to everyone else, or am I just weird?

But it's tough to ask Dad those questions because...well, he's Dad and those are questions about sex. You don't ask questions about sex because you just don't.

That's how guys have thought since Cain and Abel were kids. In fact, it's part of the time-honored Sexual Code of Silence, which states that it's okay to joke, wisecrack, cut up, or even lie about sex, but other than that, it's your solemn duty—as a male—to keep silent whenever a *serious* discussion about sex takes place.

Since everyone is determined not to talk about sex, or maybe is too embarrassed to do so, you may even wonder what healthy sexuality is all about. That's one of the reasons we wanted to write this book for you. We want you to have accurate information about a wonderful subject that's prone to misinformation and ignorance. You deserve to know what's going to happen to your body (we're assuming that you haven't gone through puberty yet). In a very short time, your body's sexuality will be awakened by the natural work of chemical hormones in your body. If you and your dad can talk about puberty, then you will have the greatest chance to navigate your teen years without making mistakes that can hurt you and others.

We're not saying this is going to be easy. If it makes you feel better, it probably isn't any easier for your dad. Maybe he's never done this before, and it's unlikely that his father ever went through a book like this with him. Like you, he may not know quite where to start. He may also be worried how you'll respond to going through this book with him, like I was with Jasen.

From your side, you may feel odd talking to your dad about these changes you'll be going through, and it may just seem easier to talk to your friends about these issues. But for your own sake, you need to get used to talking to your dad about these things, no matter how you feel right now.

Sure, Dad is much older than you, and when he was a boy, dinosaurs roamed around in his backyard. But he's not *that* old. He hasn't forgotten what it was like to go paddling down the Adolescence River. Take it from me. The world hasn't changed so much that your dad doesn't understand and remember. He knows a lot.

In fact, I'm betting that he can't wait to tell you what he remembers about growing up and how difficult and weird and exhilarating that was. Better yet, he probably has a ton of stories to share with you—stories that will amaze you and probably make you laugh. So give him a shot, won't you?

I never really gave my dad a shot. My dad left my mom for another woman, and he left me to grow up in a home without a father. Though my dad lived in the same town, the divorce blew a gap in our relationship that was hard to bridge. I could never quite trust him again to talk about important things. I'll never forget the time we were fishing on a lake in Canada, and he cleared his throat and announced that he wanted to talk to me about girls and sex. I blew him off. I really thought I was showing him, but in the long run, I really wasn't. I needed his advice.

If your father is living outside your home, I hope you have a good relationship with him. If you don't, and he still comes and asks you to go through the book with him, cut him some slack. Go ahead and read *Preparing Your Son* with him. I believe this book will help you bridge the gap.

Maybe you don't have a dad nearby, and your mom has offered to go through this book with you. If so, you have an even greater responsibility to step up and help out Mom. She's doing this for you, so make it work with her. It's really, really hard for single moms to talk to their sons about sexuality, so be extra nice to her.

We all love our moms. I know that I thought my mom was the bravest woman in the world. After my parents finalized their divorce, life became an emotional and financial horror for Mom, my two sisters, and me. The pressures of single parenting nearly flattened her, but Mom tenaciously fought through it. She'd come home from her receptionist job, touch base and grab a bite to eat with us, then head out to her second job—selling grave plots at night.

As she battled on to make enough money to support us, I'd sometimes catch her crying over the pressure of it all. She was tormented in other ways, too, sometimes wailing, "I'm so sorry that I don't know how to be a father to you. I'm so sorry I can't make up for what you've lost." My young heart ached for her, and I vowed I'd never do anything to make Mom cry. I became a man as best I could to help lighten her load.

Your mom has likely shed the same tears in the quiet of her bedroom. She can't be everything a dad can be for you, but she *can* go through this book with you, and she's willing. And though she's no guy, she'll surprise you with how much she understands your struggles. As a son, you need to be a real man and help her to help you. Put your whole heart into this process. We guarantee God will bless you for it.

In fact, God will bless you for going through *Preparing Your Son for Every Man's Battle* with either one of your parents. You're going to learn about yourself, you're going to learn about your dad or your mom, and you're going to learn what God has to say about sex and being with girls.

This is important because, as you change and become sexually mature, you may feel pressure to experiment sexually with girls. You may feel pressure to look at pictures of naked women in glossy magazines like *Playboy* and on the Internet. Actually, pictures of unclothed women are found nearly everywhere these days, from *Newsweek* magazine to *Sports Illustrated*'s swimsuit issue to billboards alongside the freeway. And if your parents let you watch PG-13 and R-rated movies, you're taking in scenes of naked women. That's often why those films get those ratings.

One of the goals of *Preparing Your Son* is to encourage you to not get into looking at pictures or films of naked women. Steve Arterburn and I did when we were your age, and it really messed us up. That's why we're going to be talking a lot about sexual purity in this book.

To be sexually pure means to live God's way as you deal with the changes in your sexuality. If you can remain sexually pure during your teenage years, you won't get into pornography, won't get into trying to get girls to take off their clothes, and won't get into other sexual activity.

So let's get ready to roll. We're going to be blunt with you, but you're a young man now. We think you're ready for some blunt talk. Don't forget: If you have any questions, ask Dad what he thinks.

He'll be glad you asked.

> Discussion: Go back to the beginning and read through your highlighted phrases. Discuss them together.

Optional Discussion Questions

1. Share your feelings with each other about starting the book. Do you feel a bit like Fred did? Or like Jasen?

2. Dad, tell your son about the discussions you had with your father about your sexuality.

3. What kind of a role model of sexual purity was your dad? What did you learn from watching him? What did he read?

4. Tell your son how much you want to be the one to answer his questions, even though it may seem hard at first.

Closing Scripture

He will turn the hearts of the fathers to their children, and the hearts of the children to their fathers. (Malachi 4:6)

Closing Prayer

As that verse indicates, God wants fathers and sons to be close. Commit to talking through this book together. And commit to God that you are willing to allow Him to turn your hearts toward each other in deeper love and respect. In fact, why don't you stop and pray about it together right now?

Dad, kneel next to your son and pray out loud to God, committing your heart to finish this book with him and to be as open and transparent with your answers as you can be. Ask Him for His presence, guidance, and wisdom in your book times together.

Son, promise God that you will make this book a priority and that you will be open and honest with your questions and answers. Ask Him to help you learn His ways quickly as you go through this book with your dad.

PART 1

Changes

This section of the book is for eleven- and twelve-year-old sons who are approaching the outer boundaries of puberty but are still largely sexually unaware. This does not preclude sons who are thirteen to fifteen years old from starting here as well; please note that some of the information will be elementary. Fathers with older sons may want to consider skipping ahead and reading chapters 6–11 before embarking on part 2 on page 195.

the planet "pupiter"

Don't forget. As you both read, mark those phrases that remind you of a story or event from your own life or anything that you simply want to come back to for discussion.

Girls. Now there's a loaded word for you. Does the word *girls* stir something in you it never stirred before?

When my son Michael was nine years old, he came home from church one time and whispered, "Dad, there's a girl I like in my Sunday school class."

"Well, well!" I said. "Just what is it about this girl that you like so much?"

He got a little grin on his face and simply said, "She's nice!"

That's it? I thought. *She's nice?*

I thought back quickly to when I was nine years old. Ah! Her name was Susie Barnes. She had a round face and a cute smile and always made me laugh. She was great to goof off with at recess, and she could run like the wind. She was nice...and that was all that mattered.

But girls were about to get a lot more complicated for me, and they will for Michael, too. He got his first hint a year later at age ten when he viewed his first film on sex education. I was home early that day when he rushed in from school, clearly in a panic.

"They showed a film today about pupiter!" he exclaimed, rhyming *pupiter* with the planet Jupiter. "Dad, I have a bunch of questions. Can we go downstairs and talk?" he asked.

I had a good chuckle. "It isn't pupiter, Son. It's puberty." Pausing a moment, I said, "Although, come to think of it, puberty *is* kind of like landing on a bizarre planet. Maybe we *should* call it Pupiter." Ever since that day, Michael and I have called this growing-up thing Pupiter. It seems like a natural fit.

Michael is now eleven years old, and his growing body has entered the outer reaches of Pupiter's gravitational pull. Soon he'll splash down on this unusual planet, and girls won't quite look the same to him. Girls will be looking nicer and nicer to him, as they will for you.

Michael told me that he's not sure if he's looking forward to life on Planet Pupiter. Oh, he likes the thought of having big muscles and a chest full of hair and playing high-school football. But he turns his nose up a bit at the rest of the trip. I know he's wondering why he has to go through all this at all.

I'm sure you are too. What *is* the point of all these changes you are going through? Well, here's the quick answer: to make a man out of you. Adolescence is the dividing line between childhood and adulthood, kind of like halftime at a football game. You've got a great second half coming up, and it's going to be fun. You'll be learning how to drive, going out on dates, and going off to college. You have a lot to look forward to, but God needs to get you ready.

Why? He wants you to play well in the second half. With a lot of fun comes a lot of responsibility. You'll need to be able to think wisely on your own and to develop more independence from your parents if you expect to play well and not get hurt along the way.

How does God get you ready for the second half of play? Like any good coach—by making halftime adjustments.

THE THREE Ps

If a football coach were standing before a blackboard during this halftime, he just might write "Triple Ps" on the board.

What are the Triple Ps? They are Puberty, Piaget, and the Pride of Life, and all three taken together add up to God's halftime adjustments in your life. The first one you understand because you've heard about puberty at school already. The other two you're not sure of. That's okay. We'll get to those in later chapters, but for now let's review what we mean by puberty.

PUBERTY

When you plant your feet squarely on the surface of this vaguely weird planet called Pupiter, you'll notice that your body is changing. Maybe a few pimples will pop out. Maybe you'll shake a dandruff flake or two off your shoulders. Maybe you'll grow so much that you'll stumble a bit when you're shooting hoops with the guys. You'll certainly notice that your body is changing in new and exciting ways.

Of course, that's all off in the future, but right now, you haven't yet reached Planet Pupiter, and you're probably wondering what all the excitement is about. If you are like most boys your age, you have questions—questions similar to ones that Michael asked me after seeing the film on puberty. I'm going to replay a little highlight reel from that evening, and I hope our exchange will start a Q&A session of your own with Dad.

LET IT ROLL

As Michael and I headed downstairs that night, I was relaxed. "Okay, Son, you said you had some questions. Fire away."

Michael wasn't a bit relaxed. Taking a long breath, he blew it out loudly. Then, with deep intensity, his desperate eyes locked on mine and he asked, "Daddy, what's sperm?"

Whoa! *Strap in, Captain, the storm's beginning to blow!* Michael really rocked my boat with that question. I was used to questions like "What's a trap block?" or "How do you snowboard?" He had never hit me with a direct sex question like that, and I was rattled. I was happy he asked it, though. I wanted to be the one to answer his questions, just like your dad wants to answer *your* questions.

I found my sea legs and set my face into the wind. "Hmm. Did you say *sperm?* Well, let's start with their appearance, since they are so goofy looking.

They look kind of like a helium balloon with a long string floating out back. That string is really their tail, which they whip back and forth like a flipper so they can get where they want to go."

"Okay, yeah!" said Michael, processing. "I saw those on the film. They look dorky, all right."

"Dorky but still really cool in what they do, and especially how your body makes them. You've learned that your body is made up of cells, right?"

"Right."

"Every one of our cells has these things called chromosomes and genes. These are the design instructions for your body, kind of like a blueprint of a house. A blueprint tells a carpenter exactly what to do when he builds a house—how long to cut each board, where to put the windows, that sort of thing. Chromosomes and genes tell your body how to build *you*—what color to make your hair, what color to make your eyes, how tall to build you, and all the rest."

Michael nodded, indicating that he was listening.

"Anyway, all people have forty-six chromosomes. That's what defines us as humans. But your chromosomes are different from mine because we each have different genes on them. So even though we are both human, we each look totally different, too. The interesting thing is how God made sure we would all look different, even when we have the same set of parents."

"I've always wondered why I look so different from Laura and Rebecca."

"The way sperm are made has a lot to do with this. It all starts in the testicles...or 'tentacles,' like you called them one time up at the gym!"

"Very funny, Dad!"

"I always thought so. Anyway, sperm cells are made down in the testicles, but they don't just *look* different from other cells. They are quite different on the inside, too. It's a very intricate process to make them—in fact, it all has to happen at just the right temperature or it won't work. Your body temperature is too hot for sperm production, for instance. That's why God hung the testicles down and away from the body, where it is just enough cooler for everything to work out just right."

"So that is what that sack is for!"

"Pretty much. When sperm are made, the testicles begin splitting sets of chromosomes in two, giving one half of the directions to one sperm and one half to

another. In this way, every sperm you produce has exactly half the instructions necessary to build a human being."

"Why? What good is half?" Michael asked.

"Well, that's the awesome part. This sperm takes his half of the instructions
and swims like crazy to find an egg with another half of the instructions somewhere."

"I remember the film talking about eggs, too. Moms have those, right?"

"Yep, and these eggs do the same thing that sperm do—they carry only half a
set of instructions. But eggs aren't made like sperm. Mom was born with all these
eggs inside her body from the beginning, so her body doesn't actually have to make
new ones along the way like we do with sperm. And eggs don't have tails or any
decent way to get anywhere. But they do have a way to let the sperm know where
they are so the sperm can find them. This is one of the best parts."

"Oh?" Michael said.

"You see, eggs work a lot like Mom's chocolate-chip cookies. You know how
that smell draws you to where Mom is standing with the fresh plate of cookies, no
matter where you are in the house? Eggs put out a chemical smell like that. I saw a
film of this under a microscope once—an egg was surrounded by thousands of
sperm, all fighting like crazy to be the first one in to get the cookies."

"Cool!"

"It really is!" I replied.

"But Dad, if there are thousands fighting to get in, why does only one get in?"

"Easy. Once one sperm climbs aboard, the egg drops a putrid chemical bomb
out the hatch to clear the others away. You know how Grandma's dog Mitzie can
clear all of us out of a room if she gets into the wrong food? When she drops one of
those bombs, we all scatter. It's the same thing."

"That's funny!" Michael said.

"Yeah, it is. But it's also really important, if you think about it. Imagine if two
sperm got in. If that happened, there would be too many instructions. But if you
have just one, when you take the half of the instructions from a mom's egg and put
them with the half from a dad's sperm, you have a single perfect set of instructions—
exactly what you need for a baby to grow."

"I think I'm getting it now," Michael said.

"Good, because mixing those two halves and seeing what you get on the other end is one of the best parts of having kids. The chromosomes can split in countless ways, so you never know which of your genes will go to which of your children. When a baby is born, it's like opening a big surprise package to see what you got."

"What was I like when I was born?"

"Michael, when you were born, your nose looked just like Great-grandpa Frank's. Your ears were mine. Your blue eyes squinted shut when you smiled, just like mine. Your hair, though, was thick and dark like Mom's. Every boy looks a little bit like his mom and a little bit like his dad, with different parts of aunts and uncles and grandfathers and grandmothers thrown into the mix as well. The resemblance comes from these genes that are passed down and carried by the sperm and egg."

I paused a moment so Michael could think about what I said. "You and Jasen look a lot alike," I continued. "You both received a similar set of instructions from Mom and me. But your sisters look nothing like each other and nothing like you. Wouldn't you say that they're a whole different mix?"

"They sure are, Dad. Now I understand why, or at least a lot better now."

> Discussion: Go back to the beginning and read through your highlighted phrases. Discuss them together.

Optional Discussion Questions

1. Tell your son about your favorite girlfriend from fifth or sixth grade.
2. Tell him about that first girl who really grabbed your heart after puberty—in seventh or eighth grade. How were your feelings different this time, compared to that nice girl you knew in fifth or sixth grade?
3. Tell your son what it was like the first time you laid eyes on his mom and how the attraction grew.
4. Tell your son what is was like to look at him for the very first time in the delivery room and in the next few days at the hospital. Who did he look like when he was born? Who does he look like now? Whose nose? Whose ears? Whose eyes?

5. Tell your son how badly you wanted to shave as you approached puberty, and how vigilant you were to watch for hair of any kind.

Closing Scripture

For you created my inmost being;
    you knit me together in my mother's womb.
I praise you because I am fearfully and wonderfully made;
    your works are wonderful,
    I know that full well.
My frame was not hidden from you
    when I was made in the secret place. (Psalm 139:13-15)

Closing Prayer

In your own words, take turns praying as you kneel together for a moment, thanking the Lord for His wonderful creation and how much He means to you. Tell Him how much you appreciate how He made you and how much you appreciate who you are. Thank Him for the plan He has laid out for your life.

what does
making love mean?

Michael was really getting warmed up now. "It's really interesting how sperm and eggs work!" he said. "But Dad, there is something I don't get about all this. If the egg is in the mom and the sperm is in the dad, how can the sperm swim to the egg?"

"Good question. I'll give you more details later, but let me give you a quick answer for now. Do you know how sometimes your penis gets hard and stands straight up?"

He nodded, looking very serious all of a sudden.

"This is called an erection, if you didn't know that yet."

"Oh," he said.

"Well, your wife will have a place where that fits into when it gets hard like that. When you place your penis in there, the sperm come out and go inside your wife. From there, the sperm can swim to find the egg. This is called sexual intercourse. Have you ever heard of it?"

"I'm not sure... I don't think so."

"You'll hear more about it as you get older."

Then, pausing to think, I thought better of that plan. "Michael, I've changed my mind. I guess I really need to say more than I just did, because I made this sexual intercourse thing sound pretty boring, like sticking the nozzle into the gas tank for a fill-up. You want to know the truth, Son? Sexual intercourse is the most wonderful experience there is between a husband and wife in marriage. You know how I love to hug Mom and kiss her?"

"Yeah, I like it when you do that. And I know Mom likes it too."

"You know we're in love," I said, batting my eyes and smiling sweetly.

"That's right! It feels good to see that!"

"Sexual intercourse is even more like that. It is a special gift that God has given a husband and wife to share together. It's so special, in fact, that God says couples should keep doing this as long as they're together. It brings them close to each other, and it strengthens their love for each other. I never feel closer to Mom than when we do this."

"I thought it was just for making babies!" Michael said.

"It certainly *is* for making babies, but that's not the only thing it's for. Remember that place I told you that a wife has where you can put your penis? That place is between her legs, and you do this while lying between her legs and sliding your penis in and out, but that's not all you do. There is hugging and kissing and all sorts of stuff that goes along with it, and it is a lot more fun than it sounds, especially because there are wonderful feelings that go along with it. You know how great it feels to jump into a warm shower after you're really chilled from playing in the snow all day? It's kind of like that, only even better. Isn't it wonderful that God gave us such an awesome way to have kids?"

"Yeah, that makes it nice, I guess," he said a bit blankly.

"But you see, having babies is not the only reason we have sexual intercourse. We do it to show how much we love each other. It is very romantic."

"Dad, I really don't get all this. This part is a lot harder to understand than the rest of what we've talked about tonight," Michael said honestly.

I laughed. "Well, I suppose so! Don't worry about it. It isn't so important that you understand everything right now. I just want to make sure you remember that you heard it here first, straight from your good ol' dad, that sex is a wonderful thing. You should respect it and look forward to it someday."

We paused a moment to catch our breath, and then I began again.

"Well, let me see, where were we? Oh yeah, sperm! After all that, you should have a better idea of what sperm is all about. What other questions do you have?"

"Dad, the film said I'd get tired a lot during puberty, and maybe I'd even get sick with headaches and aches in my knees and stuff. I don't like the sound of that at all, and it kind of scares me. What does that mean?"

"Oh, that's no big deal," I replied. "Mostly you'll feel no different than you feel after playing football all afternoon with the kids in the neighborhood. Your body will get tired from growing so fast, that's all. There's a lot going on, you know. Not only will you grow taller and stronger, but your voice will get deeper, and new hair will be sprouting on your legs and around your genital area and under your arms. You won't feel these things happening directly, but it will still be hard on your body. You'll need extra sleep, that's for sure. Some doctors say that you need even *more* sleep during puberty than you did as a child."

"You don't mean that I'm going to take naps like I did when I was a little kid?" Michael asked.

"No, we're not going to make you take a nap, but sometimes it wouldn't hurt to take a snooze when you get really tired. And you should certainly sleep in when you get the chance. Lots of sleep will be good for you."

"I'm feeling kind of tired talking about this pupiter stuff," he said. "Dad, when will all this begin?"

"It'll happen when it should. I'm sure that puberty will come right on time for you. God has everything planned out. The orders are laid out in your pituitary gland, which sits underneath your brain at the back of your head. It is my favorite gland. I love to say *pi-tu-i-tary*. Doesn't it feel like you are spitting when you say it?"

Michael tried it a few times, grinning.

"Well, the pituitary is the general of the gland army. When it's time to get started, he gives orders to all the other glands. When the body's glands get their orders, they begin sending out chemical messengers that give your body the directions it needs to grow. Of course, every pituitary gland is different. Some will give early commands, some later. There's nothing you can do about it. You've just got to wait until the orders go out."

"Well, since I can't go fishing in Canada with you and Jasen until I get hair under my arms, I wish that part would come early."

Michael was referring to the prize he would receive when he started getting hair under his arms.

"Don't worry, Son. You'll be fishing in Canada before you know it."

Discussion: Go back to the beginning and read through your highlighted phrases. Discuss them together.

Optional Discussion Questions

1. I first heard about intercourse when an older boy told me a dirty joke. Tell your son about the first time you heard about it, and ask him if he has heard about it before now.

2. I always thought that sex was kind of dirty and scary at first. What did you think about it? What did your friends say about it?

3. Tell your son what it was like to grow so fast during puberty. Did you ache? Were you tired?

4. It used to bug me that some of my friends could grow sideburns and I couldn't. How did you deal with stuff like this during puberty?

5. Dad, were you a late bloomer or an early bloomer? What was that like?

Closing Scripture

There is a time for everything,
and a season for every activity under heaven:
a time to be born and a time to die. (Ecclesiastes 3:1-2)

Closing Prayer

Puberty is one of those times "under heaven." Dad, take a moment to stand before your son and place your hands on his shoulders. Lift your face, pray out loud, and thank God for your son. Tell the Lord how happy you are that the Lord is making a man out of him and that you can't wait to help him in any way that you can.

Son, give your dad a big, fat hug and then pray. Tell the Lord how thankful you are for a father who is willing to help you understand what is coming in the days ahead. Ask the Lord to give your dad the wisdom and the memory he needs to share what it was like when he grew up so you can learn.

when girls enter the picture

As you can see from my discussion with Michael, puberty's main work is to prepare your body to create sperm, have sexual intercourse, and produce your own children someday. Don't forget that the halftime adjustments were designed to make a man out of you, and having kids is certainly a big part of being a man.

But puberty does far more than equip us to produce sperm. It also changes the way we look at girls.

Maybe you've noticed the fairer sex. Maybe you've thought, *Why do girls look so nice all of a sudden? My heart just races when I'm around some girls. What's up with that?*

I sat behind Janet all year in my eighth-grade science class. She was really growing up fast, and I couldn't keep my eyes off her, especially her chest. I got A's in science, but I'd make up phony questions to ask her, pretending I needed her help. I'd tap her on the back just so she'd have to turn around to talk to me. An added benefit was seeing her lovely profile.

I loved to hear her giggle and see her eyes sparkle. She just took my breath away! I'd never felt like that about girls before. What was happening? God's halftime adjustments were simply kicking in.

While I kind of liked these new and exciting feelings, in other ways I found this whole boy-girl thing rather annoying. I was the quarterback of my football team, and when I'd ask receivers to stay after practice to work on timing patterns, they'd say, "Sorry, I've got to get showered." I knew they wanted to get going so they could talk to the girls after they showered.

I hated that. These same guys used to play pickup football and basketball games until sundown every night, with nary a thought for girls. Now they were putting girls ahead of football, and I couldn't understand that. I didn't know it at the time, but my friends' attraction to girls was very normal and very necessary. I talked to my older son, Jasen, about this once.

GIRL TALK

When Jasen was around eleven years old, he and I went through a book on adolescence together that had a big section on girls. "You probably still think girls are kind of dumb. Right?" I asked as a way of introduction.

"Well, I don't really think they're *dumb,*" Jasen replied. "I mean, I've noticed in school that they get the same kinds of grades we do, so I know they're smart. It's just that I think girls are *weird.*"

"You could be on to something there," I responded.

I took the opportunity to point out that if God hadn't given us the appetites for girls at puberty, none of us would ever choose to live with someone as weird as a girl. "How many marriages would happen if guys felt like you do toward classmates like Jennifer or Megan?" I watched Jasen nod his head.

"Jasen, did you know that God created our emotions—our anger, our fears, and our attractions—in a kind of chemical base? Our desire for girls, in many ways, is a product of these chemicals called hormones. This was God's answer to the 'weirdness' of girls so we'd like them anyway."

As the days passed, we went deeper into this girl thing, and then we came to this passage in the book we were reading together:

> Now let me describe for you the feeling that sex will bring in the next few
> years. Boys will become very interested in the bodies of girls—in the way
> they're built, in their curves and softness, and their pretty hair and eyes.
> Even their feminine feet may have appeal to boys during this time.

Things had finally gone far enough for Jasen. This was over the top. He said firmly, "Even if this attraction thing *does* happen to me [which he was clearly not conceding], I'm *not* going to find their feet attractive!"

But things got even heavier for him during the discussions that followed. As Jasen and I kept reading, we came to the part where the author described what sexual intercourse was all about—how a man inserted his stiff penis into the vagina of his wife and how they both got this tingling feeling all over them.

"You and Mom do *this?*" Jasen interrupted.

"Well…yes, Son. I do— I mean, yes, we do."

"Oh, *yuck!*" he cried out as he rocked and fell to the floor laughing.

As we moved through the text, I casually mentioned that some couples actually do this intercourse thing two or three times a week.

"What?" he squawked with amazement. "How often do you and Mom…do this?"

Now it was my time to be surprised. I certainly didn't expect this question, but I deflected his question like the finest goalie. "Listen, Son, I knew a couple that did this two to three times a *day.*"

"A day!" he gasped and burst into the sort of belly laugh you get during a good night of *America's Funniest Home Videos.*

You may be laughing as well. This whole attraction and intercourse thing can be funny and amusing and confusing all at the same time. Perhaps you're like Keenan, who listened patiently as his dad explained the details of intercourse to him. When he was finished, Keenan responded, "Okay, I see. Now, do you have to set up a doctor's appointment to do this?"

Or maybe you're like Jon, a student in middle school, who insisted that since his parents were no longer interested in having more children, they must no longer be having sexual intercourse. I know his parents. Jon is mistaken.

As parents, we sometimes laugh at these stories. But this was serious business to us back then at your age, just like it is to you now. At first we couldn't understand how this sexual intercourse thing could also be pleasurable—after all, it sounds like work. But once puberty completes its course, and you've waded through enough school-bus conversations, movies, and shower-room boasts, the truth begins to emerge. And the truth is that there is more to this intercourse thing than making babies, and that tingling feeling—called an orgasm—is more than a little bit fun. And while it may not seem possible now, once puberty's work is complete and you are fully attracted to girls on every level, you will have the ability—and maybe the desire—to experience sexual intercourse before marriage.

The trouble is, while you may soon have the desire to do so, you won't have a right to do so. God says that sex is to be saved for marriage.

And so the battle is on. How can you handle all these new feelings and attractions appropriately without breaking God's standards? You'll find out as you read this book with your dad. The important thing is to be very honest and open with your father as your body begins to change.

HONEST FEELINGS

For example, let me tell you about Caleb, who, when he turned twelve years old, felt as though a shower nozzle labeled "Hormones" had been turned wide open onto his head. Stuff was happening inside his body, but he couldn't understand why he was experiencing certain feelings. All he knew was that he had some urges that were difficult to control. The young boy then did a very courageous thing. He approached his father one day and said, "Dad, sometimes I feel like taking off my clothes and standing in front of a girl naked."

That was an honest expression of feelings and an accurate description of what it felt like to be a twelve-year-old boy. Will you have those same feelings? Perhaps, but I wouldn't worry about it. These changes feel stronger in some boys than in others. Besides, the point of all this is not to scare you, because there is really nothing to be scared about. Hormones aren't like some demon that possesses you and makes you do what you don't want to do.

On the contrary, attraction to the female body is a natural, God-given desire. It will become natural for you to want to hang around girls. Very soon you'll find a girl's beauty tugging at your eyes for attention.

The temptation, however, is to go beyond a natural and normal look. That means viewing a girl more as an extremely interesting collection of body parts rather than as a precious child of God. You'll be tempted in many ways to play with these natural desires and attractions to girls in some wrong ways.

We want to help you understand the temptations and deal with them in an effective way. But we are getting ahead of ourselves. First, let's explore a few more mysteries that you'll face when you land on Planet Pupiter.

> Discussion: Go back to the beginning and read through your highlighted phrases. Discuss them together.

Optional Discussion Questions

1. Dad, tell about that girl in eighth grade that you couldn't keep your eyes off of. Did you notice that you were looking at girls differently back then, or can you only see it now, thinking back?

2. Did you find the whole boy-girl thing annoying like I did? If not, what did you feel?

3. Do you remember the hormones turning on overnight like a spigot or was it gradual?

4. Dad, did you have pimples as a young man? dandruff? a ridiculous hairstyle that you thought was cool at the time? Have any pictures to prove it? Pull them out.

5. Ask your son what he is thinking about girls these days.

Closing Scripture

> My lover [husband] is radiant and ruddy,
>> outstanding among ten thousand.
> His head is purest gold;
>> his hair is wavy
>> and black as a raven....
> His mouth is sweetness itself;
>> he is altogether lovely.
> This is my lover, this my friend....

I belong to my lover,

    and his desire is for me....

Let us go early to the vineyards...

    there I will give you my love.

The mandrakes send out their fragrance,

    and at our door is every delicacy,

both new and old,

    that I have stored up for you, my lover.

        (Song of Songs 5:10-11,16; 7:10,12-13)

Closing Prayer

The sexual relationship is lovely in marriage, and as you can see above, wives are as passionate for their husbands as husbands are for their wives.

Dad, take a moment to pray that God will use this book and your discussions together to paint a wonderful picture of sexuality for your son. Pray that even though we'll be talking more about controlling our sexual urges in this book than the wonders of it, he'll see that nothing we have is more wonderful than our sexuality when it is kept in its proper place.

Son, ask the Lord to open your heart to understand all that He wants you to know about your sexuality and how you might use it to honor Him. Ask Him to help you walk like Jesus in every way.

what's happening?

When you go through puberty, you can bet the bank that you'll be asking yourself these two questions:

- Am I normal?
- Do my friends know more about this than I do?

Let's start with the answers. If you're wondering if you're normal, the answer is yes. You've got nothing to worry about. *Every* guy goes through puberty, and while it seems strange when it happens to us, it really isn't. As for your friends knowing more about puberty and sex than you do, the answer is maybe.

MYSTERIES EXPLAINED

I imagine that you're already taking showers after PE with the guys. Maybe that makes you nervous, especially if puberty is still around the corner and you're showering with guys who could use a shave on their rear ends! It's certainly normal to feel nervous undressing with other guys and walking into a community shower naked as the day you were born.

I remember the first time I got undressed in front of a bunch of guys at a summer football camp. My dad knew an old coaching buddy who ran a football camp at Cornell College in Mount Vernon, Iowa. I was just a seventh grader, but Dad talked the coach into letting me attend his camp even though it was for high-school players only. I was a pretty good player for my age, and Dad thought the experience would be great for me. Let me tell you, I was excited to train with the big high-school guys. The first day we did drills, I thought I was in heaven.

When the final whistle blew late that afternoon, the coach yelled for us to huddle up around him. "Okay, gentlemen, here's what's going to happen this evening," he said. We listened as he told us where to go and when to be there, and then, with a glint in his eye, he bellowed, "Good job, men. Now everyone into the pool for some skinny-dipping!"

Everyone whooped and hollered after hearing that. We tore off toward the pool, thinking it would be really cool to get away with skinny-dipping. After all, this was a football camp, and there weren't any girls around. Like everyone else, I pulled off my sweaty clothes and jumped into the cool, refreshing water. Then I climbed out of the pool and headed for the diving board. That's when four high-school players suddenly surrounded me. They began pointing below my waist and howling, "Bald eagle, bald eagle!"

Bald eagle? That's right. I was the only guy in camp who didn't have any hair around my penis. I was bald as an eagle because I hadn't reached puberty yet, so I rushed away, totally humiliated. Can you guess who wore a bathing suit the rest of the week?

Maybe you've heard the same stinging laughter. In my case, I was younger than the rest of the guys, so I hadn't developed yet. You might be a late bloomer, desperately wondering when in the world things will start humming for you. It doesn't matter—in either case, you are right on time for you, and there is no sense in being concerned or humiliated. When General Pituitary gives the order to start, things will start for you.

Of course, pubic hair is not your only locker-room concern. The size of your penis is another issue. Puberty will present you with a bigger, slightly darker penis, and there is no getting around it… Like it or not, your penis is on parade when you take a public shower. With furtive, sideways glances, you can check out how you stack up against your school chums.

Should you feel guilty looking around? Don't. Everyone else is looking too. While it's rude to stare, it's also perfectly natural to compare. It seems to be a big concern on everyone's mind at puberty. I can remember a guy named Tanner who played on my eighth-grade baseball team. His penis was dark as mud and seemed to hang to his knees. I'm telling you, it was *long*.

I didn't know what to make of it, so I asked my best friend, Brian, for some answers. He didn't know anything either, but he was funny. "Man, Tanner could tie a knot in his, and it would still be longer than both of ours put together!"

I laughed with him, but I was secretly worried about that at the time. I shouldn't have been. After all, let's be men and talk straight about this. There are only two things that a penis must be able to do in life. First, when you unzip your pants to go to the bathroom, your penis must reach out far enough so that you can go to the bathroom without wetting your pants. I've never known a guy who couldn't get this job done.

Second, your penis must be able to stand up far enough to be able to deposit the sperm during sexual intercourse. Those are the only two required things. And to put your mind at rest, no matter how big or how small a penis looks in the locker room, it will be adequate in size to get that second job done.

How do I know?

When I was a freshman at Stanford University, I enrolled in a human sexuality class where I learned that all erections are about the same size, no matter what size a penis might be in the locker room. So no matter how you compare with the others taking showers, you will be just fine. I've never found a single area in life where the size of a guy's penis counted for anything. If you've been worrying about it, you can stop now.

I sure wish someone had told me this in junior high so I didn't have to worry about it. I mean, there were plenty of other things happening to me, and I could have used one less worry. Besides, my penis was giving me enough problems as it was—it seemed to have developed a mind and life of its own. How so?

Erections, for one thing. They completely mystified me! Mine stood up and down without rhyme or reason. It was as if the circuitry was shorted out somewhere after God made the adjustments during puberty. My sensors had simply gone haywire.

I could be riding along in the backseat on my way to Grandma's, absently gazing off across the cornfields in the distance, and *boom,* an erection would pop up. I could be lounging in the family room with a friend watching an explosive, intense war movie, and *boom,* I'd get one. I could be sitting in the congregation on Sunday morning listening to the pastor's sermon, and *boom,* there would come another one. Why? I hadn't a clue.

It was quite annoying, but it could also get downright embarrassing. I remember sitting in church with an erection when the pastor said, "Okay, now let's all stand and turn to number 210 in our hymnals. Sing with all your might!"

Of course, I couldn't sing with all my might. All my might was focused on trying to hide that lump in the front of my pants with my hymnal. I just hated that, and I suspected something was wrong with me. Turns out nothing was wrong. I was normal, and that happens to a lot of guys. That'll probably happen to you, if it hasn't already. But cheer up! I've got good news for you. As you get older and your circuitry matures, this stops happening.

There was another issue, however, that drove me crazy and left me even more confused. Sometimes I'd wake up from a dream and find something wet and sticky on the front of my underwear. Turns out the sticky stuff was something called semen—the fluid that carries and deposits our sperm during intercourse.

What was this thing that happened? Officially, it's called a nocturnal emission. But somewhere in a dank, smelly locker room, some kid decided to call it a wet dream, and that name stuck. Not everyone experiences this, but I did quite often.

When your testicles create sperm, the sperm are transferred to storage sacks in your body. As the sacks fill up, they sometimes simply overflow into the bladder, and the excess passes out with your urine. This makes room for new sperm production, and you usually don't even notice this. Sometimes, however, you get an erection in your sleep at night, and the excess is released in that way. Either way is perfectly natural, and if this has happened to you, you are not weird. You are normal.

If you've been thinking that your penis has a mind of its own, relax. You are growing up, and your body is simply growing and changing. If none of this has happened yet, that is fine too. Now you know what to look for, and you can feel comfortable talking about it with your dad when it does happen.

> Discussion: Go back to the beginning and read through your
> highlighted phrases. Discuss them together.

Optional Discussion Questions

1. Erections always made me wonder if I was normal. Dad, what made you wonder if you were normal?

2. Tell your own PE shower sagas. What did you feel like, having to shower with the guys? What did you see?

3. Have the guys started joking around about sex yet? About penises?

4. Dad, did you ever worry about your size and whether everything was growing right?

5. Tell your son a story or two about what it was like to get an erection at the wrong time.

Closing Scriptures

Teach them to your children, talking about them when you sit at home and when you walk along the road, when you lie down and when you get up. (Deuteronomy 11:19)

A time to gain,
And a time to lose. (Ecclesiastes 3:6, NKJV)

Closing Prayer

Puberty is your time to gain and your time to lose all at the same time...a time to *gain* hormones and a time to *lose* your footing a bit.

Dad, place your hands on your son's shoulders and ask God to help you consistently talk to your son about these issues. Thank the Lord that He chose you to be your boy's father at this time, and tell the Lord out loud how much your son means to you.

Son, ask God to give you a courageous heart so that you can ask the questions that come up. Thank the Lord out loud for all that your dad means to you.

does everyone else know more than I do?

It's easy to feel bewildered about this puberty stuff, isn't it? Everything is new, especially if Dad and Mom haven't talked to you in much detail about these things. This story from a single mom in North Carolina shows that it's easy for new things to sneak up on you during these days.

Lisa had to go out of town for the weekend, leaving her boys to fend for themselves for a couple of days. She was running late, and as she was stuffing her last bag into the car, Kyle, her thirteen-year-old seventh-grader came up to her and said, "There's a dance at the school on Saturday night. Can I go?"

As Lisa climbed into the car, she replied without further explanation, "Yes, you can go, but no dancing." Then she turned on the ignition and zoomed down the road.

Arriving back on Sunday afternoon, Lisa said, "So, Kyle, how'd the dance go?"

"I don't want to talk about it right now."

Lisa thought, *Uh oh*. Like any mother, her intuition was especially tuned to her children's frequencies. She spotted a moment where she needed to go deep with her son.

A bit later, she gathered Kyle and his older brother, Brandon, to talk about the dance.

"Tell me what happened, Kyle. Was it that bad?" she asked.

"It started out so well, Mom. I was just hanging out with the guys—you know, talking and goofing around. But all the other guys were dancing from time to time. I didn't dance, of course, because of what you said. Before long, though, they began teasing me, pushing me to get out on the floor. One guy said, 'What in the world are you coming to a dance for if you aren't going to dance?' Everyone laughed pretty hard at that one."

"Kyle, I'm so sorry."

"Mom, they got on a roll and kept saying that kind of thing over and over, and I didn't know what to say. You told me not to dance, but I didn't know why. It *did* seem weird to go to a dance and not dance. I thought the same thing myself when you were heading out in the car and told me I couldn't dance. I couldn't understand why you would say that."

Lisa nodded. No quarrel there. Before she could comment further, Kyle said, "I was fine until they got the girls involved. One of the guys told a couple of the girls what was up, and they spread it around that I needed some prodding. Girls began coming up one after another to ask me to dance. Since I didn't have any real good reason to tell them, and I didn't know why I shouldn't dance, it became harder and harder to resist. Besides, it was kind of starting to cause a scene, and I was really feeling uncomfortable."

"So what happened?"

"Mom, they wore me down, and I finally just gave in and went out onto the floor with one of the girls."

Kyle's mother thought for a moment before saying, "I am so sorry I didn't take the time to explain it to you in detail, Kyle. I really put you in a bad position, and I was wrong to do that."

"Mom, I should have obeyed you anyway. It's not your fault."

"Maybe so," Lisa continued, "but God didn't leave us on earth without explanations. He gave us His Word, but He also gave us His Holy Spirit to help us understand everything in between the lines. I should have followed His example and explained my thinking before I left, but I was in a hurry. What I would have said is that when you are out on the dance floor, it's very easy to have some girl's breast rub up against your chest in a provocative way."

Kyle's eyes got a bit wider, and he nodded knowingly. Lisa knew she was on the right track.

"See, these girls who were pushing you were aggressive girls, and they were trying to teach you a thing or two. They probably meant no real harm. But at your age, when her chest rubs up against yours, it will most likely stir things up in you, and you might just get an erection right on the spot."

Kyle's eyes got wider still, and he nodded with even more vigor.

"You see, Kyle, that's why I told you no dancing. There is a lot of sensuality that comes with dancing, and I was just trying to protect you. I only wish I'd explained this to you sooner."

Before long, the discussion closed, and Kyle went to the dining room to catch up on some homework. Later that evening, however, Kyle really thanked his mom for being open with him about these things. He didn't want to try to figure out life on his own. None of us do, and it was wise for him to talk with his mom and especially thoughtful to thank her.

It is normal to be ignorant about these things at first, and there is no shame in that. After reading the first few chapters in this book, you know that an erection is your body's way of preparing for sexual intercourse. But how in the world would you know that *any* sensuality could do this, even on the dance floor?

It's no fun to be in the dark about these things, especially when you are with a bunch of friends on a Saturday night like Kyle was. What's worse, when you feel ignorant, you worry that someone else might notice your ignorance and laugh at you.

But let's step back a minute. Some guys may have developed earlier than you, so they began asking questions long before you did. Naturally, they have a head start in learning about these things. Others may have even started experimenting with sex already, although it is flat-out wrong. They, too, will naturally know more than you do. Should you feel bad for knowing less than these guys?

The answer is no.

Sometimes, of course, you'll feel bad anyway, because it always feels a little bit funny when people tease you. But if you know that it's normal for a young Christian man to know less than everyone else, that should help you deal with it. Take heart because you're certainly not alone in this.

A friend of mine was laughed at once because he didn't know what French kissing was (which, by the way, is when you stick your tongue into a girl's mouth when you kiss her). But his ignorance was actually a mark of his character and purity, virtues to be honored in a young Christian man. You have to accept knowing less than those around you. Not knowing as much as your friends is not just a sign of your purity but, in truth, it's a sign of your emerging manhood. It means you've been standing strong by God's principles.

I remember the time I asked my son, who was ten years old at the time. "Michael, do you know what pornography means?"

I could tell by his expression that he hadn't a clue. "Well, I talked to your brother, Jasen, about this when he was your age, so I guess it's time to talk to you about it too."

Michael shrugged his shoulders as I began my explanation. "Well, the *graphy* part of the word means 'printed page.' The 'porno' part of the word refers to 'naked people.'"

"So?" he asked. He hadn't put two and two together.

"So pornography is pictures of naked girls that people print and sell to others to look at."

Mere words could *never* describe his reaction. I can assure you that he was as appalled as anyone I've ever seen at any time.

"People print pictures of naked women?"

"Yes, I'm afraid they do," I offered.

"You mean people make a living doing this?" he asked. My son was simply dumbfounded.

"Yes, they certainly do. A mighty good living, I'm afraid."

"Why isn't that illegal?" he exclaimed.

Michael's reaction came from a pure, innocent mind, and I hope yours is just as innocent.

It is normal to be ignorant about these things at first, and don't be surprised or concerned when you are different. God's people are *supposed* to be different from everyone else:

But among you there must not be even a hint of sexual immorality, or of any kind of impurity, or of greed, because these are improper for God's holy people. Nor should there be obscenity, foolish talk or coarse joking, which are out of place, but rather thanksgiving. (Ephesians 5:3-4)

We need to accept the fact that we will be different and at times not know as much as others on these issues. Accepting the fact that it is okay to know less than your peers is your first line of defense in your battle for sexual purity.

Why? Your concern with what others think of you is probably a bigger threat to your sexual purity than all your new attraction to girls.

My son Jasen noticed it in himself. Remember, he once told me, "It's just that it's been harder and harder for me to say no to my friends lately. I've been kind of scared—it's been harder for me to stand up to them."

Maybe you've noticed the same thing in your own life, and you find that you are dealing with peer pressure in a huge way for the first time in your life. If so, that is natural. But it is also an obstacle to your sexual purity, because your peers can pressure you to say yes to sex when you know you shouldn't, just like Kyle's friends pressured him to dance when his mom told him not to. You need to be aware of this pressure in order to stand up to it.

> Discussion: Go back to the beginning and read through your highlighted phrases. Discuss them together.

Optional Discussion Questions

1. Dad, did either of your parents ever talk openly to you like Lisa did to Kyle? Were there rules that you didn't understand then but you understand now? Did you go behind their backs and pay an embarrassing price for it later?

2. Tell your son what it was like to get laughed at for not knowing enough about sex. Ask him if he's ever been laughed at like this.

3. Dad, if you could live life over again, would you have wanted to learn what you learned in the locker room a lot later in life? What did you get into as a result of all this talk that you wouldn't have gotten into otherwise?

Closing Scripture

> Therefore come out from them
> > and be separate,
> > says the Lord....
> I will be a Father to you,
> > and you will be my sons and daughters,
> > says the Lord Almighty. (2 Corinthians 6:17-18)

Closing Prayer

Innocence is the mark of a real man, the mark of those who will "come out...and be separate."

Dad, kneel with your son and repent of your own oversophistication, and ask the Lord to cleanse you by the washing of the Word and His Spirit. Commit out loud to the Lord, with your son as your witness, that you want the Lord to restore your innocence wherever possible and that intimacy with God is your first goal.

Son, tell the Lord that you accept who you are. Ask Him to keep you from rushing to become sophisticated and familiar with the vulgar, sinful ways of this world. Ask Him to help you stay innocent, so that you will always know great intimacy with Him.

the Ps in the pod

As we said earlier, God makes the Triple-P halftime adjustments early in your teen years because He knows what's waiting for you in the second half. This is a fun time to be alive because, as you get older, your parents will be giving you more and more freedom—as long as you can show that you can responsibly handle it.

Of the three adjustments, puberty gets all the headlines. You're going to shed that baby fat and slim down as your muscles gain more bulk and definition. If you exercise the way you should and watch what you eat, you'll be a strong young man in no time. This happens because your body starts receiving massive doses of the hormone testosterone during puberty.

Puberty gets so much attention that we sometimes forget about the other two adjustments. For instance, Michael told me that after he viewed the sex education film in his fifth-grade class, his teacher opened the floor to questions from his classmates. Michael wasn't bashful about raising his hand. "The movie said lots of things will be happening to our bodies," he began. "What happens to our brains?"

"Nothing, Michael. Nothing at all," replied his teacher.

Nothing could be further from the truth. Over the next few years, you will experience even *bigger* changes in your brain than in your body. These changes will allow you to *think* and to *act* like a man. Of course, you can't see these changes in the mirror, so they'll be hard to notice. You may not even notice how your thinking changes, but it will.

If this sounds scary to you, don't be afraid. These changes simply give you the ability to dream big and the courage to pursue these dreams. There's nothing scary about that!

So let's direct our attention to the other two Ps and find out what changes they bring about. The first one is what I call the Piaget Effect, which is named after the Swiss thinker and psychologist Jean Piaget. It seems that Mr. Piaget discovered that the human brain changes dramatically around halftime, somewhere around eleven years of age. He said that when this happens, young men (and women) can think abstractly for the first time about such things as God, the meaning of life, why we have rules, and relationships with others.

Abstract thinking is a fancy phrase that simply means you are no longer limited to thinking logically about *things.* Now you can think logically about *thoughts* and *philosophies,* especially your own thoughts. You've probably been wondering why you were put on this earth or why your parents are so strict or if you're really liked by your friends. If so, that means this P is doing its work. You are thinking abstractly when you ask yourself these questions.

Abstract thinking helps launch the effects of the third P of your halftime adjustment—your search for your identity and your place in life. This is what I call the Pride of Life, a term that comes from the Bible that expresses concern with how others see you and how you see yourself. My daughter Rebecca, who is thirteen, is well into her search for her identity. I recently found her staring absently off into the distance.

"Watcha thinkin', girl?" I said.

"Oh, just wondering about stuff," she said. "Like what I want, and what I like. I was thinking about Jasen and Laura—I envy them. They seem to know just where they're going. I can't seem to figure out where I'm going at all. Did you ever feel that way?"

"Yes, I did at one time," I confessed. Have you felt this way? Looking inside at yourself is called *introspection,* and it's a natural part of your halftime adjustments. If you envy older brothers or sisters because they seem to know where they are going, don't worry. They didn't know where they were going at your age, either. Chances are, they felt a bit lost along the way at times too.

You'll find your place in life naturally, as you try new things and make decisions along the way. Sure, you may find yourself a bit lost and unsettled at times, but if you're like most people, finding your identity is fairly gradual and uneventful and will be made up of the many daily choices that you make along the way. It's usually not traumatic at all.

But there *is* a side of this pride-of-life adjustment that can be quite traumatic at times. Maybe you can relate to how Rebecca once described her feelings to me.

"In fifth grade, everyone was accepted, simply by being a member of the class," she said. "It didn't matter if your clothes were old-fashioned or you were homely or you got bad grades. You belonged. Everyone was your friend and you were everyone's friend, and really, no one made fun of each other or tried to be different. Nobody cared about popularity.

"That began to change in sixth grade. People began to break into cliques, and all of a sudden some of my friends who used to talk to me and used to have me over for sleepovers hardly ever talked to me anymore. It's in full swing now that I'm in seventh grade. I see so many kids without friends, and so many people getting cut off from everyone else. Like me."

Then, with a tear dripping out of the corner of her eye, she said, "I just wish it could go back to like it was. I just want everyone to like everyone again."

Have you noticed the cliques at your school? Have you had trouble breaking in with the right crowd? If so, you probably long for a return to the old days when everyone was a friend and everyone was accepted.

The reason why that's not going to happen is because you and your classmates are going through the Three Ps. In a sense there's nothing wrong with that because this is part of the transition from being a kid to becoming a young adult, and you're learning to think for yourself and associate with others you want to be with. But sometimes it hurts, and sometimes you'll feel lonely.

We're telling you this so you can recognize what's happening and gain experience in life. Later in this book, we'll share more of our experiences with this stage of life, and hopefully, your dad will too. You can draw upon our experiences and learn to deal with the confusing times that middle school and high school inevitably bring your way.

But for now, there you have it—the glories of the Triple Ps. They deliver great things to your doorstep, don't they? Deeper attractions, deeper dreams, and a deeper sense of self—all are gifts from God to make a man out of you. Why? So you can form healthy relationships with girls. So you can stand courageously for what you believe in someday. So you can serve God purely and love Him deeply. God isn't hoping you'll become just any kind of man when He makes these adjustments and gives you these gifts. He's hoping for a God's man.

Most of us would settle for being a man's man. Have you ever known a guy whose beard is so heavy that he uses two blades to shave in the morning—one for each side of his face? I have. Jim played on the Stanford rugby team and always returned with a bloody face...smiling, no less! After graduation, he left the country to fight as a mercenary, or paid soldier, with a foreign army. If I ever knew a man's man, Jim was the guy.

But God cares nothing about that. When God looks around, He's not looking for what everyone else calls a man's man. He's looking for something better and tougher from you—a God's man. His definition of a man—someone who hears His Word and acts upon it—is clear, and you've been given everything you need to become just that through the Three Ps.

But though the Three Ps open the door to true manhood, they bring along some obstacles that can shut that door again as quick as a wink. Let's take a look at the flip side of the Three Ps in our next chapter.

> Discussion: Go back to the beginning and read through your highlighted phrases. Discuss them together.

Optional Discussion Questions

1. Dad, have you noticed the effects of the Piaget Effect and the Pride of Life happening in your son? Tell him what you've seen.
2. I remember spending hours as a teen lying on my bed, staring at the ceiling, and thinking a lot. Dad, tell your son what you used to think about during such times.
3. Reflect on how you found your place in life, and tell your son about the key moments along the way.
4. Ask your son if he's noticed changes in how much his friends care about popularity.

5. I can remember vividly the canyon growing between the haves and the have-nots in middle school, especially in eighth grade. Dad, were you a have or a have-not in terms of popularity?

Closing Scripture

Every year his parents went to Jerusalem for the Feast of the Passover. When he was twelve years old, they went up to the Feast, according to the custom. After the Feast was over, while his parents were returning home, the boy Jesus stayed behind in Jerusalem, but they were unaware of it.... When they did not find him, they went back to Jerusalem to look for him. After three days they found him in the temple courts, sitting among the teachers, listening to them and asking them questions. Everyone who heard him was amazed at his understanding and his answers. (Luke 2:41-43,45-47)

Closing Prayer

Notice Jesus' age—He was twelve. Jesus was growing like the rest of us grow. The halftime adjustments had done their work, and Jesus was thinking abstractly, listening to the teachers and amazing them with His own insights.

Dad, pray out loud and thank God that you are seeing these same changes shine forth in your son. Ask the Lord to make you patient with the changes and to reveal to you how you must change your own attitudes and ways in order to grow closer to your son.

Son, ask the Lord to open your eyes to these changes in you as they unfold so you can see how they are affecting those around you. Ask the Lord to help you grow in wisdom. Commit to godliness at all times.

flip sides

While you've been given everything you need to become a man, there's a strange little flip side to the Three Ps that you need to keep in mind.

What's a "flip side?" Back in the Middle Ages when your dad and I grew up, we had really great music, but we didn't have CDs. We had records, or what we called LPs.

Like CDs, our LPs were plastic disks with music recorded on them. But unlike CDs, the LPs had music recorded on both sides. When you finished listening to the music on one side, you turned it over to the flip side to hear the rest of the tunes.

It was very common to like the music on one side better than the other. If the music really rocked on one side, we called it the good side. A weak flip side was forgotten because it was a drag to listen to.

Here at halftime, of course, we aren't dealing with LPs. But we *are* dealing with the Three Ps, each of which has a good side we love to hear about and really look forward to. But it's the flip sides that drag us down and away from real manhood.

Take puberty, for instance. Puberty, as you've heard, increases your attraction to girls and enables you to have children. You will be experiencing a natural, God-given attraction to the female body, and there is nothing wrong with that.

But like Darth Vader in *Star Wars,* these attractions can take a turn to the Dark Side, where you can no longer see girls as precious children of God. Instead, you see them more as lovely collections of body parts and little else. If you allow this to happen, you may experience the same things that Derek did as he zeroed in on girls' bodies:

> I was raised in a Christian home by two wonderful parents; however, our family never mentioned anything about sex and gave me no guidance on the issue. My older brother and I would joke about it occasionally, but that was it. This didn't bother me until I was in junior high when my two closest friends and I dove into one father's stash of *Penthouse* magazines. Soon we were watching his dad's large collection of pornographic videos. Then I got my own stash of *Penthouse* magazines I had stolen from his dad and some *Playboy*s that I stole from the grocery store.
>
> By high school, I was playing on sports teams, enjoying a close group of friends, and receiving excellent grades. Certain people called me things like "the chosen boy," because I seemed to have it all in terms of what's important in high school. But they didn't know me. They didn't know that I snuck around looking at those *Penthouse* magazines, which really warped my view of women and hurt my relationship with God. After a while, I considered Christianity to be merely a bunch of rules—rules I gladly left behind. I didn't know God anymore.

Derek knew in his heart of hearts that what he was doing was wrong. Worse yet, these attractions, turned to the Dark Side, were not leading Derek into real manhood as they were intended to.

When Derek decided to stop looking at pornographic magazines, he did so because he knew it was wrong and because it gave him the wrong idea of what women are really like. Taking that step really changed his life, said Derek, as he continued his story:

> I feel so free now, and do you know what is most amazing to me? I feel much more like a *man*. I had been tricked into thinking that pornography and pre-marital sex made me a man, but I was wrong. Real manhood is standing before the devil and denying him his way into your life. Now I feel like a real man, fighting not only for my own purity but also for my girlfriend's purity,

as well. I desperately want to show her true love and to guard her spiritually, like a man should.

FEEL LIKE ARGUING THESE DAYS?

The Piaget Effect has a dark flip side as well. Learning how to think for yourself isn't so easy to deal with either, although this change in your body is designed to help you stand and think independently of your parents. The trick is to do what your parents ask you to do and not act as though you know it all, because that's disobedient to God.

Have you been more argumentative with your parents lately? If so, I'd bet a pile they have noticed it too. Go ahead. Ask your dad if he's noticed this change in you.

You see, you're changing from a fairly pliable grammar-school kid to a some-times feisty, argumentative teenager who can marshal facts and ideas to build your own case.

When my son Michael turned eleven, as Piaget might have predicted, he changed almost overnight as that abstract thinking kicked in. He became more argumentative. He slowed in responding to our requests. His temper developed a quicker fuse. The Piaget Effect had arrived with a crash!

"Michael, that's not right to say that!" Mom might say.

Michael's retort? "I don't care! I can say what I want."

There's another thing we noticed: Michael's favorite phrase suddenly became "I don't care."

Have you seen such changes in yourself? One night our family waited to meet Jasen at Iowa State University so we could take him out to a good Chinese restaurant off campus. We waited for him at Memorial Union, where the main hallway had benches lining one wall. Four Stoekers sat on the benches waiting for Jasen to arrive. Not Michael. He had to be different. He spied a waist-high shelf protruding from the opposite wall, so he decided to lie down across it until Jasen arrived.

It was early on a Saturday evening, so practically no one was around. The shelf was sturdy, and Michael really couldn't hurt it. I was indifferent to his perch, so see-ing him lying on his side didn't really rev my engines.

Nonetheless, it really wasn't appropriate to lie sideways on a shelf in the main hall. That's why I didn't argue with my wife, Brenda, when she said, "Michael, you probably shouldn't be lying up there." You know mothers. When they say you "probably should not" be up there, they mean you *should not* be up there.

"I don't care!" Michael replied. "This is fun!" Then he smirked like he was the Cat in the Hat.

My engines roared to life at this one, and I immediately cleared the shelf of Michael and cleared the air of his attitude. Jasen meandered in shortly thereafter, and we headed off to eat. Nothing more was said about the incident.

After chowing down, our family dropped Jasen back at Friley Hall and took off on the forty-five-minute drive back home to Johnston. Somewhere along that drive, God convicted Michael about his recent attitude.

Shortly after we hit our driveway and closed the garage door, Michael slipped quietly up to Brenda to apologize. Then, with tears in his eyes, he asked, "Mom, do you think Dad and I could go out tonight? I really need to talk to him."

When she told me that Michael needed to talk, I nodded that I would. "And please, do a good job!" Brenda pleaded. "He's driving me crazy tonight."

Grabbing pairs of shorts, we decided to head over to a nearby gym to goof off. On the drive over there, I simply said, "Okay, Michael, what's up?"

His voice cracked a little, and he sounded confused. "Dad, I don't understand what's happening to me! I keep saying sharp things to you and Mom and Beck, and I keep getting into trouble all the time."

"Do you know why you're blurting all these things out?" I asked.

"I don't know. I can't seem to help it. They just pop out, and I can't stop them. We had that talk about puberty, Dad—do those hormone things have something to do with this?"

"Yeah, Son, hormones probably are a part of it, along with a bunch of the other changes going on in you right now."

"You mean that abstract thinking thing you told me about?"

"No doubt about it, Michael. You're becoming a man. That's what all this stuff is about, you know. Your body is changing so that you can make babies and be strong enough to defend your family and work hard to support them."

"Oh."

"But, Michael, you have to remember something. You need a lot more than a strong body to do this father thing. You need to be able to think for yourself and stand on your own. All leaders need to be able to do this, and God is changing your brain so you can be a real man. Right now, you are starting to think on your own. That's what all this sharp talking is all about. You are suddenly stretching your wings, and you're not just accepting everything we say without question. If you don't like something, you say it. Of course, that's a bit irritating to your mother and me, but we understand. We can't always let you get away with everything you blurt out because some of it is wrong. But we understand."

"Thanks, Dad."

"Hey, pretty soon you'll stand like a man, and you'll be making good choices. And then a really cool thing happens. People will look up to you because you are a real man, and everybody can tell it."

"Nobody is looking up to me right now," he said.

"True enough. The best way I can explain it is that you just aren't used to all this thinking on your own."

"But, Dad, I know I'm hurting Mom and Beck!"

"Sure, you're upsetting some things around here, and you need to get things under control, no doubt. But this change is actually a good thing. Whenever you are good in the future, it will be because you've listened to God and you've chosen to be good."

Arriving at the club, we gathered our stuff as we got out of the car. Pausing a moment, I said, "You know how you felt guilty tonight and you just had to come talk to me?"

"Yeah."

"That was the Holy Spirit speaking to you through your conscience. He wanted you to know that you are hurting people. Once He pointed it out, you responded to Him and went to Mom to apologize. You chose to obey Him. That is a great sign, Son! Do you want to know the best part? You can choose to follow His voice whenever you want to, because He is living in you and gives you all the help you need to live His way."

"Thanks, Dad."

I wasn't mad at Michael. How could I be? I knew that he was seeing the world in a whole new light and that he was flush with excitement and wanting to share whatever popped into his head. He just had to learn to think through what he would say before he said it. That's what abstract thinking is all about.

FLIPPING YOUR PRIDE

Yes, it's true—the pride of life has a dark flip side too. Jasen arrived home from high school one afternoon annoyed to the max. "I hate the way those jocks swagger around, snapping towels and picking on everybody," he sputtered. "They lose a football game by thirty points and act all week as if they won by fifty! They bug me so much sometimes."

The jocks think that everyone *wants* to watch their every move. It's too bad that their brains are fogged over from their feelings of self-importance. But the pride of life can puff up any of us. Learn to spot it in yourself and try not to let it happen to you.

Sure, you're searching for your identity and a place to fit in, but the trick is to not value your place in life over your place in God. And that is tricky because in your desire to fit in with your friends, you may "go along to get along."

You might go watch some of those popular teen movies that show couples having sex on the screen—or performing other sex acts. You might be asked to join your buddies in the basement, where a stash of *Hustler* magazines is waiting. You might be in your best friend's bedroom as he calls you over to check out these unbelievable pictures of naked women on the Internet. You might get teased in the locker room by one of the guys saying, "How do you know your equipment works if you've never tried it?" If you aren't careful, your friends will rule your decisions far more than God. That's the dark side of the pride of life, and that certainly takes you nowhere near real manhood!

Besides, it's dangerous to play it both ways when you're trying to get along and be popular. Who are you hanging out with, and who are you listening to? My daughter Rebecca once said, "Dad, earlier this year I had the chance to get into one of the popular cliques. But right away I felt uneasy. If you're in one of the popular cliques, you don't have much freedom. If someone in the group dislikes a person, you have to dislike her too. You've got to think and behave like the rest of the group continually, even if it seems wrong. So," she concluded, "being in the popular groups is kind of like being in a prison."

THINK WELL

As you can see, your halftime adjustments come with no guarantee that you and your friends will think or look anything like a God's man at all. The dark flip sides of these adjustments can do us in.

Yes, this adolescence thing can sure get confusing, but one thing is always true, and it can serve as your own personal North Star to guide you on your journey: God. He already knows who you are and where you fit.

He wants you to become a real man as badly as you do, but He knows it won't happen overnight. Your maturation takes place over a period of years, giving you the time to make your own adjustments and get used to the new you. Although everything seems to be happening at warp speed, you've got time to determine your own identity and become the man God wants you to be.

God's halftime adjustments will make you manly automatically, without any work or effort from you. But it will be your *decisions* that will make you a God's man. So you've got to begin making good choices early, especially when these flip sides urge you to go their way instead of God's. You needn't worry. You have everything you need to walk His way:

> His divine power has given us everything we need for life and godliness
> through our knowledge of him who called us by his own glory and good-
> ness. (2 Peter 1:3)

All right! Those flip sides don't have to mess us up after all. I wish somebody had shared this message with me when I was your age, because I stumbled for a long, long time until the Lord rescued me from a prison of sexual sin. You won't believe what happened, as you'll soon read about in the next chapter.

Discussion: Go back to the beginning and read through your highlighted phrases. Discuss them together.

Optional Discussion Questions

1. If you still have some LPs tucked away, show your son the side you always listened to. Then explain why you ignored the other side.

2. I remember watching my sisters mature right before my eyes. Dad, did you notice these changes as they occurred in your siblings (or cousins or friends)?

3. Ask your son if he's seen these changes in himself, like Michael did. Have you seen changes, Dad? Tell him what changes you've seen.

4. As I passed through middle school and high school, I remember getting more and more puffed up about how I could debate and think on my feet. Dad, when was your swagger most prominent?

5. I was in the popular cliques in middle school, but then I opted out and went my own way in high school. Which did you do, Dad? If you opted out, what did it cost you?

6. Tell your son how proud you are to see him growing up.

Closing Scripture

I will sing of your love and justice;
    to you, O LORD, I will sing praise.
I will be careful to lead a blameless life—
    when will you come to me?
I will walk in my house
    with blameless heart.
I will set before my eyes
    no vile thing.
The deeds of faithless men I hate;
    they will not cling to me.

Men of perverse heart shall be far from me;
　I will have nothing to do with evil.
　　(Psalm 101:1-4)

Closing Prayer

Dad, pray a blessing of peace and holiness over your son. Ask the Lord to guide his steps and make him a warrior for purity and a soldier who keeps his promises.

Son, pray that same blessing of peace and holiness over your father. Ask the Lord to guide his steps and make him a strong warrior and trustworthy soldier, too.

my story

I was quite a little thief when I was a kid. My first caper was stealing an oversized Tootsie Roll inside the Mee-Too store in Marion, Iowa. I casually stuffed that Tootsie Roll into my coat pocket while the cashier was taking care of Mom. No one was ever the wiser.

At home, Dad was clueless as well. He had a little china sugar bowl on his dresser in which he would toss his pocket change at the end of the day. That china bowl always looked full to me, so when my light fingers pinched a couple of coins, I never thought Dad would notice that anything was amiss. That's the way things stayed for a long time until the day when my best friend Tommy Burton and I had places to go and things to do and snacks to buy. A simple coin or two wouldn't cut it. We needed a small handful for the big adventures that we planned to carry out.

The dark day of reckoning dawned the following morning when the shadow of a six-foot-three-inch, 250-pound, former national wrestling champ towered over me—his 75-pound, third-grade weakling son. I felt like the sun had been totally eclipsed!

"Tell me the truth!" my father demanded. "Have you been taking money from this change jar?"

The color ran from my face, and my mouth went dry. Too scared to speak, I began to shake my head no. But suddenly I thought better of adding lying to the charges against me. Bursting into tears, I cried out, "Tommy and I both stole your money!"

At first, Dad simply scowled at me. Then with a fierceness in his eyes that I never saw again, my father hissed through gritted teeth, "If I ever catch you stealing again, I will beat you black and blue until you are almost dead!"

Was Dad exaggerating to scare me? Maybe, but I wasn't going to call his bluff to find out. All I know is that I was so scared that day that I promised myself I would never, ever steal anything again. I kept that promise. I haven't stolen anything since, and that's probably because my father put the fear of God into me at a very young age.

When I grew up and became a young man, however, I didn't have anyone to put the fear of God into me about how I should treat girls when I went out on dates. It wasn't long before I wanted to help myself to their bodies, just like I helped myself to Dad's quarters, nickels, and dimes that filled a small china bowl. Because of the changes that were going through my body during puberty, I wanted to be close to girls, touch their bodies, kiss their lips, and explore as much as they would let me.

It wasn't because I didn't know better. I did, just like I always knew better than to steal from Dad, even before that Sunday morning when he caught me.

And it wasn't because I hadn't made a decision to treat girls the right way. I had. Earlier I told you that when I saw my Mom crying over the pressure of making the money to raise us, I vowed that I'd never do anything again to make her cry. Mom also used to cry because Dad had left her to date and have sex with other women. When I saw those tears, I vowed that I would never hurt any girl like that. I would treat them with honor and respect, and I vowed to keep sex special for marriage.

But while I kept my promise to never steal again, I didn't keep my promise about sex. Because of the changes in my life at halftime and the attraction to girls we spoke of in the last chapter, it was a much harder promise to keep because the temptations were far greater.

Have you ever been on a real muddy, slippery hill? If you stay right at the top, you are pretty safe. But if you take even a baby step down the side, you can slide quite a ways down the hill before you can stop yourself. With each baby step you seem to slide a mile, and before long, your few small, slippery steps have taken you all the way to the bottom.

Impurity is like a slippery slope. If you stay at the top of Purity Hill, everything is fine. But sometimes you might think, *Well, everyone else is doing it, so I will too* or *We are so in love, what can it hurt?* Those small steps with girls or with pornography may seem like no big deal at the time, but before you know it, you'll be sliding down the hill like the Jamaican bobsled team, and you won't be able to do anything to slow yourself down. That's what happened to me. As you'll see in my story, I took another baby step or two down that slope each year as I grew older. Before I knew it, I had hit rock bottom.

But let's begin my story at the top. Because of my vow to treat girls right, I was pretty careful around girls early in junior high. I'll never forget the time when as a seventh-grader I was the star fullback on the Linn-Mar Junior High football team in Marion, Iowa. Since I was such a hot football player, I got invited to all the best parties, including one at Kathy Johnson's house on a Friday night, a very hot ticket indeed. I felt great!

As I entered the house, Kathy's parents directed me downstairs to their basement rec room with a cheery "Have fun!"

So far, so good. But as I started down the stairs, I could see that the lights were quite dim. I wondered how anyone could have any fun with the lights so low.

As I hit the last stair, Janice jumped out and blocked my path like a big tarantula. Janice was developing *real* early, and she had a *very* curvy body. That made her a bit scary to me on any day, but she was especially scary now as she slyly grinned and brushed her body against mine. Nodding toward the bedroom to her right, she purred, "Wanna play school? I'll be the teacher, and you can be my pet. I'll teach you everything you need to know. Good students really learn a lot in my class."

Time-out! I wasn't ready for this. Then my eyes adjusted to the dark basement, and if I looked closely, I could see my classmates paired off and making out in assorted nooks and crannies. *What in the world? How can they kiss in front of everybody? Isn't that embarrassing?*

Janice, meanwhile, was still wondering if she could "school" me, and I could tell that her first lesson plan would take us well beyond elementary kissing. I hadn't even smacked with a girl before, so I stalled for time. "Uh…uh…I like Amy now," I stammered.

This was news to Janice and to my host, Kathy, who had come by to greet me. They looked at each other with Cheshire cat grins. "Oh, you *do*," said Janice. "I think we can do something about that, don't you, Kathy?"

"Oh, I think you're right, Janice." The two girls disappeared, and I was grateful. I hurried and found a corner to hide in to catch my breath, but there was to be no peace for me *that* night. They returned in a heartbeat with Amy, who was wondering what all the fuss was about.

"Here, Amy. Fred just told us that he likes you."

I wanted to crawl in a hole. I had never even talked to Amy before. She had to be the cutest girl at Linn-Mar, but I'd never had the nerve to talk to her, so we weren't exactly exchanging notes between periods.

"Ah, hi, Amy." I said awkwardly. What do you say to a dazzling girl? I had no idea. I suppose I could try to say something and try to kiss her...she was clearly open to that, but it seemed weird to kiss out in the open and in front of everybody.

Saying nothing and doing less, I must have seemed the biggest bore in the world to Amy. I—Mr. Star Fullback—left Kathy's house about fifteen minutes later that night feeling demoralized and like an idiot. I didn't like that feeling, and I wondered if I shouldn't get with the program a bit more on this girl thing. I didn't want to look stupid in front of my friends again. My promise to stay pure didn't look quite as important as I walked home that night because of how embarrassed I was in front of my friends—I was edging toward that slope of Purity Hill.

Eighth grade brought new frontiers for me. I had asked Mom if I could move to a bigger school so I could get stronger competition in sports. As the new kid on the block, my only connection was with the guys on the football team. The locker-room talk was just what you'd figure, and what I heard the other guys say in the showers really stirred my imagination. Don bragged about his times in bed with Tracy and how much she loved having sex with him.

I listened with big ears because I sat behind Tracy in math class. After hearing about her times with Don, you can only imagine what I was thinking as my eyes bored into her back during class. As Don bragged on and on in the showers each day and as I got to know Tracy better, I began thinking too much. *What would it be like to be with Tracy like that?* That thought excited me.

You could say that that was my first step off Purity Hill. Not that I had ever done anything with Tracy, but in my mind, I sure did. I never stopped to think about whether it was right to think such thoughts. The thoughts came on their own, naturally, and they felt good inside because they were *my* thoughts. But those thoughts changed me and my purity, and I would soon find out where such thinking leads.

Of course, shower talk wasn't the only thing influencing me in junior high. When Dad divorced Mom, he moved into a bachelor pad, where he hung a giant velvet picture of a nude woman in his living room. I couldn't help but take in this mural-like painting whenever we played cards during my Sunday afternoon visits.

When Dad asked me to clean up around the place, I never knew what I'd find. One time, while emptying the trash can in his bedroom, I came across a photo of his girlfriend—nude. Dad's place is where I also discovered his copies of *From Sex to Sexty,* a publication filled with dirty jokes and sexy comic strips. He left them out in the open for me to read, along with his *Playboy* magazines, which were filled with pictures of nude women. That was his coffee-table reading. It felt wrong to read them, but I wanted to be a man like my Dad, so I ignored my feelings. I didn't want to seem like a dork. But this baby step also caused huge sexual feelings to churn deep inside me.

Eventually, the feelings began bubbling over in confusing ways that I didn't understand. For instance, Marianne sat beside me in my eighth-grade French class. She wore tight jeans and a jeans jacket to class every day, and she had long straight dishwater blonde hair streaking down her back. She wore a perpetual scowl of rebellion across her lips, and she liked to hang out and smoke with her cool friends after school. That didn't impress me since I wasn't into the smoking crowd.

So why did my heart tremble whenever I looked at her? There was something about Marianne's denim-clad curves that nearly caused me to drool on myself during class. Nearly every night I had dreams about kissing her, though I *still* hadn't kissed a girl in my life. Some mornings, I'd wake up with something wet and sticky on my underwear after a dreamy episode. *What's up with this?* I hadn't a clue.

What was happening was that I was having lustful thoughts. When you lust for something like I did, you really want it badly. I was lusting for Marianne, and those thoughts were feeding my dreams at night. It felt wrong and dirty somehow, but I wasn't about to come right out and ask *anyone* why. Besides, I was enjoying it somehow. Those dreams felt really good, and I was always excited to see Marianne slide her little bottom into her seat the following day.

Those lustful thoughts over Tracy and Marianne were born out of the flip-side effects of puberty, and they were changing the way I thought about girls. I should have been putting those lusts in their place. Instead, I was letting them run freely in my mind.

By the ninth grade, Don was still bragging in the showers about his times in bed with Tracy every weekend. I was now on some activity and leadership teams with Tracy, and I was having more and more contact with her, which caused me to long for her in a lustful way. I couldn't tell anyone this, but in my mind, I had held her in my arms countless times already.

One night after a meeting at her house, she asked me, "Did you hear Don and I broke up?"

Actually, I had heard. News travels fast in school corridors. "Yeah," I said. "I guess so."

"I was wondering if you could stay after the meeting tonight so we could talk about it."

"Well, okay," I said, being a nice guy. But what was there to talk about? She had broken up, right?

After the meeting, we slipped out into her backyard under the cover of darkness. We found a bench to sit on. After some small talk, she admitted that she'd been attracted to me ever since our eighth-grade math class. We kissed. Then she untucked her shirt and pulled it up a little. My eyes popped out. "I'm lonely," she said. "Would you help me feel better?"

I felt paralyzed, but since Tracy was so sexually experienced, she took matters into her own hands. She reached for my right hand and placed it on her left breast. I should have resisted, but I didn't. It all happened so fast. In the span of a few minutes, I kissed my first girl full on the lips and then touched her breast.

That evening when Tracy made herself available, I just went along. I had no real defenses. I hadn't thought through what I would do in a situation like that. Now there was no time to think about whether it was right or wrong to feel Tracy's breast. I just did it. It seemed like a small thing, really. She asked for it, and we'd already done it a million times in my mind…it couldn't be wrong, right?

Why do I share all this? Think back to how all this started.

I made a promise to stay on top of Purity Hill. But in the eighth grade, Don had told me how great sex was with his girlfriend, Tracy. Then I got into those pornographic magazines at Dad's house, and then a girl let me feel her breast, and then...

They were all little steps, but when added together, I'd slid miles from the peak of that hill. Sure, I'd heard the truth in church: "Fred, God wants you to wait until marriage. He wants to spare you from emotional pain and save you from getting a sexually transmitted disease. God wants to save you from becoming a parent of a little infant boy or girl before you're married."

I knew that God reserved sex for marriage, but I didn't know how to defend my place atop Purity Hill. No one told me that my fear of looking like a dork would lead me to take small steps with girls so that I could look cool. No one told me that the lustful thoughts in my bedroom would make it so easy to go ahead with Tracy in her backyard. No one told me that pornography changes the way you look at girls and makes it hard to respect and honor them when you are alone with them. I had no idea that those choices could have such an impact in my life.

That's why your father is going through this book with you right now. Your dad wants you to know that not only does God care very much about how you're growing up to become a young man but He also has plans for you, as He says in Jeremiah 29:11, "to prosper you and not to harm you, plans to give you hope and a future." Engaging in sexual conduct before you're married can mess up all those plans for reasons I've just described.

That's why it's very important for you to keep yourself as pure as you can—because you never know how far you'll slide with the first step off the hill. Don't look at those magazines with pictures of naked women! Don't go on the Internet and look at those XXX-rated Web sites! Don't dwell on what girls look like with no clothes on! There's a great verse in the Bible that sums up God's feelings in this area:

Flee from sexual immorality. All other sins a man commits are outside his body, but he who sins sexually sins against his own body.
(1 Corinthians 6:18)

Looking at pornography and playing with a girl's body are examples of sexual immorality. Don't sin against your own body! You're hurting yourself and those around you.

Sadly, like I said, I never heard that advice. I subjected myself to so much emotional pain and wasted so much time chasing after sexual thrills. But you are at the point in life where you can decide what kind of young man you want to be. Isn't that exciting? Choose well!

And remember, there is really no such thing as a small step on a slippery slope. Every step, even a small one, can take you miles down the side. Choose to be sexually pure from now until you marry that special person God has waiting for you.

Yes, marriage is a long way off, but if you drive a stake into the ground at the top of the hill and hold on, you will never regret what you did or what you decided during your teen years.

> Discussion: Go back to the beginning and read through your highlighted phrases. Discuss them together.

Optional Discussion Questions

1. Dad, describe the scariest time your father caught you doing something wrong. Did you make a promise to stop? Son, what is *your* scariest memory of your father?

2. Dad, what were your earliest steps off Purity Hill like? What made you lose your balance?

3. As you watched your friends take their steps off Purity Hill, what were you thinking?

4. Was there a scary "tarantula" in your grade who had developed early like Janice? How did you feel when you looked at her?

5. What was it like to go to your first parties, dances, or group dates? Did they turn out like you expected, or was it weird or even disastrous like mine?

6. Do you remember the shower-room talk? Tell your son what other things in your world were churning up your sexuality back then. Did your father have porn magazines in the house?

Closing Scripture

In the course of time, Amnon son of David fell in love with Tamar, the beautiful sister of Absalom son of David.

Amnon became frustrated to the point of illness on account of his sister Tamar, for she was a virgin, and it seemed impossible for him to do anything to her. (2 Samuel 13:1-2)

Closing Prayer

When we lust with our eyes, we get burned. It has always been this way.

Dad, thank the Lord out loud for His Word. Thank Him that it is still relevant today, and thank Him that He never shies away from the topic of sexual sin.

Son, ask God to help you watch over your steps on this slippery slope. Thank Him for stories that reveal the danger ahead for you. Commit yourself to learning from the mistakes of others rather than your own.

the eyes have it

As you approach Planet Pupiter, nothing will abort a smooth landing more quickly than pornography. Even if your interest in girls is pretty low, looking at images of undressed women can grab your eyes and heart and mess up your life badly. So whether your interest in girls is high or low, you need to listen closely to what we have to say about our male eyes.

Why are the eyes so difficult to control? Because we are men, and we're made that way. It's the way we're built.

Before Brenda gave birth to our fourth child, I was certain that the child would be a boy, our second son. I was *so* certain that I told her and a few close friends that it was a done deal—we were having a boy.

As delivery day neared, the pressure rose. "Why did I tell everyone?" I whined. "What if it's a girl? What if I'm wrong?"

With the start of Brenda's labor pains, the pressure seemed to double every minute. Finally, standing under the bright lights of the delivery room and watching Brenda bear down in the last moments before birth, I knew the moment of truth was near.

The baby came out face up. *Good,* I thought. *I'll have a perfect view.* Anxious, I gently urged Brenda, "Come on, sweetheart. Push a little more."

The shoulders emerged. Just a few more inches, I thought. And then? *Arghh! What are you doing, doctor?* He turned the baby toward himself at the last moment, just as the hips and legs popped out. Now I could only see the baby's back. *C'mon, c'mon,* I cried inside.

The doctor and nurse said nothing. It was maddening! Steadily and efficiently they dried the baby, suctioned the throat, and slapped a silly little cap on the newborn. When the doctor finally presented our new child to me, the legs were flopping apart. Immediately I looked down; I just had to know.

"It's a boy!" I exclaimed. Yep, most definitely, I thought with a smirk. *He's got the right equipment.* But as you'll see, that "equipment" comes hard-wired with certain qualities that make it very tough to stay sexually pure.

WE DO HAVE THESE TENDENCIES, GUYS

Eleven years have passed since Michael was born, and just like your father would say to anyone who would listen, you and Michael both are definitely males. Because you're male, there are natural tendencies within you that make you *very* interested in looking at the female body. It's this part of maleness that I want to address in this chapter because it relates to how you may struggle with the lust of the eyes.

Perhaps—depending on your age, of course—you aren't aware that your eyes give you the ability to sin just about any time you want. All it takes is a long, lingering look at the clothed, partially clothed, or unclothed female body, and you can receive a jolt of sexual pleasure. Of course, if you've already seen pornography, you may already understand the pull of the female body through the eyes. (Did you know that the average guy in America sees his first pornography by age eleven?)

When you stare too long at a girl's shape, you begin thinking sexy thoughts and what it would be like to see her without clothes and that sort of stuff. That's what we call lusting. When you lust, you are sinning. Remember, we're talking about long, long looks, not glances. It's not a sin to look at a girl. It's a sin to *lust* after her, as we'll get into in a minute.

Remember, guys are turned on by female nudity in any way, shape, or form, so there's this desire to do more than glance or have a short look. We are so attracted to the female body that it doesn't matter if we know her or not. You can get turned on from a photograph of a nude stranger or just by staring at the tight sweater of one of your classmates at school. It doesn't take much to flip the visual ignition switch when it comes to viewing the female anatomy.

Girls seldom understand this because they aren't sexually stimulated in the same way. Do girls get turned on when they see the guys' swim team walking around in their bright blue Speedos—the ones with the telltale bulge? I hate to burst anyone's bubble, but the answer is a resounding no! The ignition switch for girls is tied to touch and relationship—not to the guy's body.

It's just the opposite for us. We like to look at breasts—and the bigger the better. That's why I feel sorry for you these days. You've got it tough walking the halls between classes. Given what the sight of partial nudity and nudity does to the pleasure center of your brain, and given the fact that it's pretty easy to see a lot of skin and tight tops when you're at school these days, it's no wonder that your eyes and mind resist control. (And it would help if our female friends would dress more modestly.)

That's why God gave us an unusual command when it comes to sexual sin and lust of the eyes:

> Flee from sexual immorality. All other sins a man commits are out-
> side his body, but he who sins sexually sins against his own body.
> (1 Corinthians 6:18)

This is an unusual command from Scripture because this particular sin is unique. The apostle Paul said sexual sin is different from other sins, which is what I told Jasen back when he was eleven. "Jasen, it's hard to describe the effects of pornography, but it is like taking drugs," I said that evening. "You know how your teachers warn you about drugs?"

Jasen nodded his assent that evening. He had heard those DARE cops talk about drugs in his classroom, so he understood the comparison.

"When we look at women without clothes on, there is a chemical reaction that happens in our brains that is much like the reaction the brain has to taking cocaine. There were studies showing this way back when I was in college. I'll never forget watching some of my rich Stanford friends blow thousands and thousands of dollars on cocaine in just a few days over spring break. They just couldn't get enough."

"Wow," said my son.

"You got that right, Jace. But listen. I've never done cocaine, but I *have* viewed pornography, and once I did, I was hooked and wanted to see more and more, just like those guys with their drugs. It was a brutal habit to break, Son, and I just don't want you to make the same mistake that I did."

Why is looking at pornography such a hard habit to break? It's because men receive a chemical high from looking at pictures of nude women. A hormone called epinephrine is secreted into the bloodstream when your eyes lock onto images of naked women. Pleasure chemicals bathe the limbic pleasure center in the brain, and because it feels good, you want to come back for another look. It's just like drug addicts' wanting another hit of their favorite drug.

Jesus understood all this because He created us. That's why he said:

You have heard that it was said, "Do not commit adultery." But I tell you that anyone who looks at a woman lustfully has already committed adultery with her in his heart. (Matthew 5:27-28)

For married men, lustfully thinking of another woman is the same as committing physical adultery, according to Jesus. That's true for you, too. If you look lustfully at a girl, then that's the same as having sex with her. Looking at a woman and thinking about sex really *is* the same as doing it when you think about it. The strong wash of chemical pleasure when you lust with your eyes is similar to experiencing the real thing with a girl. You will have to trust your father and me when we say this, but it's true.

When the apostle Paul said that those who sexually sin actually sin against their own bodies, he was referring to how your body craves more and more when it sins by lusting after women's bodies. The eyes have it—they keep searching and hunting and lurking for you. They want to see more naked women.

All this may sound a lot like the effects of drugs to you. Well, it *is* a lot like that, because you get addicted to those pleasure highs, and your mind and body crave more. But the difference is, if you have a drug problem, theoretically you can walk away from drugs. You don't have to buy them and take them. Not so with lusting with the eyes because you can't walk away from your eyes. And that's the main difference between this sin and other sin—the ability to sin is right inside you, embedded in your eyes and mind.

Here's the way it works: You don't actually need a date with Lisa to get sexually excited about her. You can steal some looks and get some real pleasure from where you are sitting in class. This is why the lust of the eyes is so dangerous to your purity. Think back to my story. If I hadn't been thinking about Don's boasts in the showers while sitting behind Tracy in math class, I'd never have fallen for her charms in the backyard later. Had I not lusted after Marianne in French class, I wouldn't have had wet dreams about her. The ability of the male eyes and mind to draw sexual pleasure from almost any female body explains why sexual sin is so common.

Your buddies might say, "Look, women are a good part of God's creation! God wouldn't have made them beautiful if He didn't want us to feast on their beauty." I've heard that old argument. But just because God made someone beautiful doesn't mean He wants you to take a taste of her or stare at her rear end. God made the fruit of the tree in the middle of the Garden of Eden *very* beautiful. Would you like to ask Eve if its beauty made it all right to look at it and not eat it? I didn't think so. God asked her not to eat the fruit, and He's asked us not to lust over girls.

GAME PLAN

So you're probably wondering what you can do to keep your eyes from parking on Tara's well-proportioned chest or Tammy's cute behind.

Well, you're going to have to figure out a way to control where your eyes look and how your thoughts process those images coming into your brain. While it's true that you can't walk away from your eyes, you *can* train them to straighten up and fly right.

I'm not going to lie to you, though, and this is the hard part—training your eyes to behave themselves and look away when something inappropriate appears does not come naturally.

For instance, you shouldn't fixate your eyes on a girl's body when you think nobody is looking. First of all, you should look away because it's the right thing to do. But now you also understand the chemical high that comes from staring at sexy girls.

That goes for sexy magazines and Web sites, too. With these, you cannot only turn your eyes away, but you must also *walk* away, leave, depart—whatever. After all, odds are that sooner or later someone's going to say, "Hey, guys, check out this magazine my big brother gave me."

That's what happened to Jasen when he was in high school.

Several of his friends brought a *Hustler* magazine to school, and let me tell you, that's one raunchy magazine. His buddies called Jasen over to have a look.

What would you do if one of your friends said he had a great magazine in his locker that he wanted you to see? And you knew he wasn't talking about *National Geographic* but probably some skin magazine. What would you do? You must decide *right now* because you will be asked to have a look sometime before you graduate from high school.

Jasen had already made his decision and knew what he wanted to do. He didn't have to experience the addictive draw to know he wanted no part of that. He said, "No thanks, guys," and kept on walking to his next class. He *walked away* because he did not want to sin against God by looking at that terrible magazine.

"I kept right on walking, just like you said I should," he told me.

"That's great, Jasen," I said, and believe me, I was impressed. "I'm really proud of you for doing that."

You can make your dad proud as well. Hey, you can make God proud too by turning your back on a magazine or Web site that you know you should not look at.

You can choose to think like God's man. Your heavenly Father is calling you to act like a mature man by saying no, even this early in your life. When He calls us to "be perfect...as your heavenly Father is perfect" (Matthew 5:48), He's asking you to rise above your natural tendencies—the impure eyes and the fanciful mind. God is calling you to rise up by the power of His indwelling presence and walk away when you're asked to view pornography.

Back in Old Testament days, Joab commanded the troops of Israel. Once, before an important battle, he addressed the troops by saying, "Be of good courage, and let us play the men for our people" (2 Samuel 10:12, KJV). What did Joab mean? He meant, "We know God's plan for us. Let's rise up as men and set our hearts and minds to get it done!"

You can do the same and flee sexual immorality when it comes your way. It can be done. You have great role models from the Bible who led godly lives despite great temptations. We're going to take a closer look at one named Job in the next chapter.

> Discussion: Go back to the beginning and read through your
> highlighted phrases. Discuss them together.

Optional Discussion Questions

1. Share with your son one of the first times you remember lusting with your eyes.
2. Tell your son about one of the first movies that tripped a trigger of lust in you. (Mine was *Mahogany,* starring Diana Ross). Don't share the vivid details—just talk about the confusion it caused in you.
3. Tell your son what happened the first few times you saw some form of pornography. Did you walk away from porn like Jasen or did you get hooked? Where did you first see it and with whom?

Closing Scripture

If my steps have turned from the path,
     if my heart has been led by my eyes,
     or if my hands have been defiled,
then may others eat what I have sown,
     and may my crops be uprooted. (Job 31:7-8)

Closing Prayer

Job knew that the lust of the eyes would warp your heart and tempt you to put your hands where they don't belong.

Dad, commit to the Lord that you will work with your son as a team to defend his eyes as well as your own. Commit to be accountable in this to the Lord and to your son.

Son, commit to the Lord that you will follow Joab's lead and begin to "play the man" in your fight against the enemy. Thank the Lord that you have role models in the Bible who prove that you can both flee and fight in your battle to win.

manly eyes

I know what you're probably thinking after reading the last chapter: How does God want me to look at girls? When does a glance turn into a stare? How do I deal with my eyes and mind and body?

For answers, let's look at how a guy named Job handled the same set of questions a long, long time ago. Job, you'll soon see, was a great role model for sexual purity. His story unfolds in the Old Testament, where in the first chapter of the book that bears his name, we see God bragging about Job to Satan:

Have you considered my servant Job? There is no one on earth like
him; he is blameless and upright, a man who fears God and shuns
evil. (Job 1:8)

Was God proud of Job? You bet! He applauded His servant's faithfulness in words of highest praise. If you walk in purity, blameless and upright, He'll speak just as proudly of you. You can learn from Job.

How did Job stay so sexually pure? In Job 31:1 we see Job making this startling revelation: "I made a covenant with my eyes not to look lustfully at a girl."

A covenant with his eyes! You mean he made a promise with his eyes to not gaze upon a young woman? It's not possible. It can't be true.

But it was true, and he must have been successful, or God couldn't have called him blameless and upright.

Making Your Ocular Covenant

When I first gave serious consideration to Job's example, I thought upon his words for days on end. My mind first turned to the word *covenant.* What was that? I learned that a covenant was an agreement between God and man. We promise to do something, and God promises to do His part. So how would I go about making an agreement with God? If I did make a promise to God not to stare at women's bodies, could I be counted on to keep my word?

Day after day my mind returned to this covenant concept, trying to intellectually grasp it. Then it happened. I remember the moment—the exact spot on Merle Hay Road in Des Moines—when everything broke loose. Minutes before I had failed God with my eyes for the thirty millionth time, staring and lusting at a pretty female jogger as I drove past her. Boy, did I take a good look at her glistening body, so shapely in her jogging outfit. As soon as I passed by and she was a distant figure in my rearview mirror, my heart churned in guilt, pain, and sorrow. Driving down Merle Hay Road, I gripped the wheel, and through clenched teeth I yelled out: "That's it! I'm through with this! I'm making a covenant with my eyes. I don't care what it takes, and I don't care if I die trying. It stops here. It stops here!"

That's when the Lord gave me a concept that I call bouncing the eyes.

Bouncing the Eyes

You probably agree with me that your eyes are built to *look toward* the sexual and not *away* from it. That's how your eyes were made. But like Job, you need to train your eyes to immediately *bounce* away when they come upon a sexy image—much like the way you jerk your hand away from a hot stove. Here's what you want to do:

**When your eyes look toward a female's body parts,
they must bounce away immediately.**

But why must the bounce be immediate? Because that's the fastest way. That keeps a glance just a glance. You don't want that glance to linger one millisecond longer.

Granted, a glance is different from staring open-mouthed until drool pools at your feet, but a lingering glance can be more than enough "eye juice" to give you that little chemical high, that little pop. In our experience, bouncing away immediately is clean and easy for the mind to understand and doesn't give it any wiggle room.

But girls are all around me! How am I going to do that without living in a cave? Obviously, you can't live in a cave like Fred Flintstone. You see girls every day. You probably talk with them and laugh with them, especially the pretty ones. This is not only natural; it is very normal.

But for a Christian young person, it is not normal to stare at their bodies like some slobbering dog, like I did with Marianne and Tracy. The apostle Paul says we are to treat all girls as we would treat our own sisters. This truth is the key to looking at girls the right way:

Treat…younger women as sisters, with absolute purity. (1 Timothy 5:1-2)

But the apostle Peter takes it one step further. Though he was writing to women here in this verse, it is very instructional for us as well:

Your beauty should not come from outward adornment, such as braided hair
and the wearing of gold jewelry and fine clothes. Instead, it should be that of
your inner self, the unfading beauty of a gentle and quiet spirit, which is of
great worth in God's sight. For this is the way the holy women of the past
who put their hope in God used to make themselves beautiful. (1 Peter 3:3-5)

God wants girls to concentrate on their inner beauty, not their outer beauty. If He wants girls to concentrate on their inner beauty, what do you suppose God wants us guys to concentrate on in the girls around us? Answer: their inner beauty.

But this won't happen naturally. That's why God pointed it out in Scripture…you'll have to *choose* to do this. Left to nature, our eyes will naturally look for the girl's *outer* beauty. We care more how she *looks* than how nice she is.

You needn't feel guilty about this, because that's how we're made. This is that dark flip side of puberty that comes with the territory. Still, you *do* have to understand how you are made and adjust your habits accordingly if you expect to please God in the way you approach His daughters. He looks at the heart and the inner beauty of His girls, and He wants us to do the same.

Though I (Steve) was a Christian, I didn't even try to do this when I was young, and it really messed up my life. Almost every day when I was in high school, I would review the naked pictures "filed" in my brain, which I had collected by looking at pornography. It wasn't long before I got a little tired of the same old pictures, so I added some to the collection. They were easy to find in certain magazines. The more magazines I looked at, and the more I added to my mental collection, the more it felt like women weren't real people to me. I didn't see them as fully human; they were just something to give me physical pleasure. All I was concerned about was their physical features. Psychologists call this the *objectification* of women. When you do that, you feel free to treat them any way you want. That means when you start dating later, you won't respect a girl the way you should. You'll see her as just something to give you physical pleasure, and you'll use her body for yourself with no concern about how she feels. That's no way to treat a sister.

Remember, that's what happened to me (Fred), too. Though I had vowed to treat girls well and to save sex until marriage, in the end I was treating them as my own personal toys. I was not thinking normally about girls from God's point of view at all. When I finally committed my life to Christ, it was years before I re-learned how to look at women properly.

But you don't have to let that happen to you. If you treat girls purely the way you would your own sister, and if you don't allow your eyes to run freely over their bodies, you'll have the right view of girls and treat them with respect.

Garrett told us this story:

My eyes used to roam over every girl I saw. Honestly, I'd never really guarded my eyes before or even thought about it. I watched any movies I wanted, and I looked way too long at the girls at school, but I really didn't think those things affected my life. But after my mom read your book and told me about it, I began to wonder. So I paid more attention to my eyes over the next day or so, and I found that they were collecting more sexual gratification than I'd thought.

I started bouncing my eyes, and since I've stopped doing the old "up-downs" with my eyes, it's really changed the way I look at my girlfriend, Tracy. I really *did* start seeing more of what was inside her heart instead of what was outside. In fact, I began seeing all girls this way.

Garrett now has a healthy, godly view of women because he began looking at them as sisters. Another friend named Patrick said it another way: "I like to look at girls from the inside out and from the neck up." They are both paying attention to what their eyes are doing.

Are you paying attention to what your eyes are doing? Garrett said he used to watch any movie he wanted. What about you? Hollywood releases sexy teen movies regularly, and they're filled with sexual innuendo, girls taking their tops off, simulated sex acts, and tons of racy behavior. They know that if they get you excited and you start talking about the movie at school, your friends will buy tickets to see the movie too. They care more about making money than they care about your purity.

Everyone knows that PG-13 movies can be all about sex and that R-rated films show nude couples having sex, but you also have to watch out for certain PG movies these days. The PG-rated *Dead Poet's Society* sports a long closeup of a *Playboy*-style foldout. The PG-rated *Runaway Bride* has no nudity, but the film has plenty of sensual joking that is way out of bounds. The jokes get you thinking about sex when you shouldn't and get you thinking that sex is a big joke and okay to play around with.

There are ways you can begin to protect yourself. You can find out what the movie's all about and what the sexual content is by going online and typing in "Christian movie reviews" into your Google search engine. Holly McClure at crosswalk.com will tell you what's in the movie. Focus on the Family's *Plugged In* will give you the straight scoop, as will Screenit.com.

Or you can ask your parents to subscribe to a Christian movie review magazine, such as *MovieGuide* or *Preview Family Movie*. Remember that you can't make an informed decision until you're informed.

You've got a decision to make. You can't visually feed on the same films your school chums watch and expect to stay sexually pure. Does this mean that you have to give up going to the movies or transfer to an academy for aspiring monks? Of course not. Still, you do have to discern what is right to see. Do you want sexual purity and deeper intimacy with God, or do you want to be one of the gang, squeezing in purity only when it's convenient?

Sometimes you don't have a choice about what's playing. On-screen sexualized content can even be found in your classroom. Teachers sometimes show a movie as a reward, and *blam!*—there's the teen couple getting each other hot and bothered. You can't watch a football game without being hit on by those beer commercials featuring a bunch of bikini beauties and guys making sly, suggestive comments.

Whenever that sexy stuff comes on the screen, you should bounce your eyes away. If you're in the classroom, look to the floor or to the blackboard. If you're at home watching an NFL game and one of those sexy commercials comes on, use the remote control and zap it. When you're armed with a remote, you can do anything! *Phasers set to kill, Worf.* (If your father hogs the clicker, as dads love to do, have him zap the beer-and-bikini commercials for the both of you.)

Or you can simply look down or bounce your eyes. My eleven-year-old, Michael, is into watching college and NFL football, but he immediately looks away to the floor whenever a sexy beer commercial pops up. He began doing this before I'd talked to him even once about it. He's simply picked it up from seeing how Jasen and I react when that stuff comes on the tube. If you are with a group of guys, you don't have to make a big deal out of it. Just look away. You can tell when it's time to look back at the screen by the change in music accompanying the commercial.

You know, all these sexy images in the media aren't normal. There was a time when you couldn't show unclothed women in a movie, but then Hollywood chipped away at that standard. There was a time when television shows and commercials couldn't be as sexually suggestive as they are today. But bit by bit the standards changed.

So what you're exposed to isn't normal, but don't worry. You can still stay pure and normal if you follow God's plan. God says it *is* normal for a Christian teen to make a covenant with his eyes (Job 31:1) and not to lust after girls. It is normal that you don't have even a hint of sexual immorality in your life (Ephesians 5:3). It is normal that your conversations should not contain a trace of coarse language or filthy jokes (Ephesians 5:4). It is normal that you don't leer at breasts and let out a low whistle when you see pretty girls walking down the street. It is normal to avoid sexy movies.

Don't you want to be normal in God's eyes? Of course, you do. So don't listen to what others say—listen to what God says.

> Discussion: Go back to the beginning and read through your highlighted phrases. Discuss them together.

Optional Discussion Questions

1. Read the first chapter of Job about how God bragged to Satan about "my servant." Dad, does God brag to Satan about your sexual purity?

2. Dad, have you made a covenant with your eyes? Tell your son what it was like to make that covenant.

3. When you met your wife, was her inner beauty the first thing you saw? How about today? Tell your son about the best parts of his mom's inner beauty.

4. Talk about your family standards for television and movies. Take your son to the computer and show him how to use Christian Web sites to research the content of movies.

5. Ask your son, "Would you consider you and me to be good role models of purity to those around us?"

Closing Scripture

Turn away my eyes from looking at worthless things,
And revive me in Your way. (Psalm 119:37, NKJV)

Closing Prayer

Dad, ask the Lord to revive you in His ways and breathe new life in your spirit as you turn your eyes away more than ever before.

Son, ask the Lord to revive you in His ways and breathe new life into your spirit as you make a covenant with your eyes. Ask Him for more intimacy when you worship Him.

self-control

Choices.

You can win your battle for sexual purity, but your choices will play a big role in the fight. Either you can choose to be sexually pure, or you can choose not to be. Will you choose to control your roaming eyes? What choices will you make with the rest of your body?

"I've been a Christian since the age of nine," said Ryan, "and I've been sexually active since I was twelve. Now I'm in my late twenties, and I'm on the Internet constantly viewing the worst kinds of pornography. Though I'm a Christian, it's always two steps backward and one step forward due to my sexual sin. I regret the things I do but then go right back to them."

Ryan is bound, bogged down by his own choices—choices he made at your age. You are young, but your choices today will be just as crucial to your purity and your future.

You probably aren't used to having so much riding on your decisions. Up until now, your parents have made most of the decisions about what you see or do. It has been *their* good choices that have protected your life and spiritual growth.

But God has begun to make an independent man out of you, a young man who can hear His Word and do it. With the halftime adjustments come the darker flip sides, the temptations to lust with the eyes and to listen to your friends more than to God—in short, the temptation to hear His Word and *not* do it. Your choices in the face of these flip sides will determine whether you move into real manhood.

Why? Because of the law of sowing and reaping, a natural law as strong as the law of gravity. The word *sowing* means to plant seeds, and the word *reaping* means to harvest the crop that grew from those seeds. Even your kid brother knows that if you want to grow sweet corn, you don't plant tomato seeds. You need to plant corn seed if you expect to see cornstalks rising in your backyard.

This is true of all life. Michael Jordan used to work on his basketball game year-round—shooting, dribbling, lifting weights, and watching videos of himself and his opponents, often eight hours a day. Self-control and discipline were the seeds that he chose to plant in his life and career, and his great skills on the basketball court were the predictable harvest he reaped.

Of course, the law of reaping and sowing works both ways. Laura came home from the high-school weight room one time chuckling at what she'd just seen. It seems that some of the most gifted athletes in her school—those with dreams of college scholarships dancing in their heads—weren't that interested in pumping iron. "Dad, those guys crack me up," she said. "They hung out in the weight room for more than hour, telling jokes and taking water breaks even though they barely did any weightlifting at all."

Without making an effort to plant seeds of self-control, these young athletes will harvest little strength. It's guaranteed. The price they pay for their lack of discipline in the weight room shows up in their physical condition—that's how muscles work.

The same is true of sexual purity and manhood. Your brain's pleasure center releases pleasure chemicals when you stare lustfully at girls or at pornography. If you fail to plant self-control in your eyes, you will pay the price at harvest time. It's guaranteed. That's the way your body works. Let's return to Garrett's story for a minute:

My eyes used to roam over every girl I saw. I watched any movie I wanted, and I looked way too long at the girls at school, but I really didn't think those things affected my life.

It didn't matter that Garrett really didn't think those things affected his life. They still did, because he has the same pleasure center as any other guy, and his eyes work like any other guy's. Planting very few seeds of discipline in his life, Garrett harvested a predictable, dismal crop of struggles with sexual sin.

Then, reversing course, Garrett heavily planted seeds of both self-control and discipline:

> I started bouncing my eyes, and since I've stopped doing the old "up-downs" with my eyes, it's really changed the way I look at my girlfriend, Tracy. I really *did* start seeing more of what was inside her heart instead of what was outside. In fact, I began seeing all girls this way.

This strong bumper crop was predictable too. Good harvests come from good seeds. It's built right into creation.

Sometimes we think that our poor crop is a direct punishment from God. But God isn't looking for a chance to nail us. When we sin sexually, God doesn't jump from his throne in a rage and bellow, "Okay, now you've done it! I'm going to give you an addiction you'll never squirm out of!"

No, in most cases He doesn't do anything to punish us at all. Instead, He allows the natural laws of sowing and reaping to do their work. When problems crop up for us, they usually grew naturally from our own choices.

God's will for us is sexual purity, no question. He told us that clearly:

> It is God's will that you should be sanctified: that you should avoid sexual immorality; that each of you should learn to control his own body in a way that is holy and honorable, not in passionate lust like the heathen, who do not know God. (1 Thessalonians 4:3-5)

But while He's very interested in His *own* will regarding sexual immorality, He's even more interested in what *our* will is. Why? Because our will and our choices regarding sexual sin reveal our love for Him. I can assure you that our love for Him means everything:

Whoever has my commands and obeys them, he is the one who loves me.
He who loves me will be loved by my Father, and I too will love him and
show myself to him. (John 14:21)

Our obedience puts a smile on God's face and a song in His heart, and that
should be worth more than anything we possess. God has a deep hunger to see our
love for Him displayed in our sexual purity. Knowing this should make good
choices easier.

Of course, good choices alone will not carry the day in this battle. God has a
huge role in your sexual purity too. Only God can author holiness in a young
man's life. Christ died and won the victory for you and me, breaking the power of
sin in our lives and giving us the ability to choose well:

His divine power has given us *everything* we need for life and godliness
through our knowledge of him who called us by his own glory and goodness.
Through these he has given us his very great and precious promises, so that
through them *you may participate in the divine nature and escape the corrup-
tion in the world caused by evil desires.* (2 Peter 1:3-4)

Christ's new life is placed in us at salvation, and this life works unceasingly
toward holiness. When that new life is placed in us, growth and wisdom appear
immediately, without effort on our part. Let me explain how this can happen.

When I was at Stanford University, I memorized the dates my favorite pornographic magazines would arrive each month at the campus drugstore so that I
could be among the first to buy them. Deep down, however, I knew looking at
these pictures wasn't right, and I didn't particularly like how they dominated my
life. The trouble is that I was hooked. I loved looking at these pictures, and I knew
no way to stop.

About a year after graduating from Stanford, I was working in the San Francisco Bay Area when the Lord grabbed my attention around sundown one fine
spring evening. I realized that I needed to repent for the sins I had committed and
turn my life around. As the sun dipped below the horizon, I prayed and gave my

life *and* my future to Him. A few weeks later, I was offered a job back in Iowa, and I jumped at the fresh start. On my cross-country drive home to Iowa, something happened that showed me how Christ had moved into my life and begun cleaning house.

It happened when I stopped in Steamboat Springs, Colorado, to visit a couple of Stanford buddies. The father of one of my friends owned a ranch just outside Steamboat, so I was looking forward to grabbing a few days of relaxation and a Rocky Mountain high as I passed through.

When I arrived, I needed to make a pit stop, so I headed straight for the bathroom. When I opened the door, I found the walls papered with *Playboy* centerfolds. As I surveyed the landscape, I was instantly repulsed.

The feelings of revulsion shocked me. Why would I be shocked at seeing *Playboy* centerfolds? After all, we're talking about Fred Stoeker here, the guy who'd memorized the dates when porn magazines hit the local drugstore. I'd never been repulsed by a centerfold in my life—just the opposite, in fact. But my newfound revulsion demonstrated that Christ was already at work in me.

It is through God's power that we have been saved, and it is through His power that we are free to live holy lives. God, through Christ, fulfilled His responsibility to help us with our sexual purity at Calvary.

But the Lord didn't stop there. He continues to fulfill His responsibility by sending the Holy Spirit, who guides us into truth and relentlessly points us toward Christ. One example of the Spirit's work today is the book you are holding in your hands, which He is using to train and guide you with your dad's help.

With God's training, the Holy Spirit cultivates His fruit in our lives:

> But the fruit of the Spirit is love, joy, peace, patience, kindness, goodness, faithfulness, gentleness and *self-control.* . . . Those who belong to Christ Jesus *have crucified* the sinful nature with its passions and desires. (Galatians 5:22-24)

If you submit to the Spirit's work, self-control will grow in your life, and you'll crucify the passions that lead to sexual sin.

Believe me, you will be tempted to ignore your responsibility in this battle for sexual purity. But you must never forget that you yourself have a role in crucifying these passions. God asks *you* to "not let sin reign in your mortal body" (Romans 6:12). God asks *you* to "make every effort to be found spotless, blameless and at peace with him" (2 Peter 3:14). God asks *you* to purify yourself from everything that contaminates your body and spirit. God asks *you* to perfect holiness in your life out of reverence for Him (see 2 Corinthians 7:1). Finally, God asks *you* to "flee from sexual immorality" (1 Corinthians 6:18).

You have every right to feel encouraged! You have help in this battle. God will help you, and the law of sowing and reaping can work in your favor. Show your love for God by being God's man. Begin by planting good choices today so that you can reap sexual purity tomorrow.

> Discussion: Go back to the beginning and read through your highlighted phrases. Discuss them together.

Optional Discussion Questions

1. Think of a guy you know with a history like Ryan's (see page 187). Tell your son about him.

2. When I was young, all my discipline and self-control were directed at sports and schoolwork. I never thought about applying self-control to my sexuality. Tell your son where you directed your self-control in high school.

3. Tell your son about a time when the changes Christ brought to your life became obvious to you, like my trip home through the ranch in Colorado.

4. The Holy Spirit convicts and tells the truth, but He is never harsh. Tell your son how much we should cherish that voice of the Holy Spirit in our lives. Tell him how much you cherish it and why.

5. Run through the list of the fruit of the Spirit. Tell your son which fruits are strongest in him and why. Ask him which ones he thinks are strongest in you and why.

Closing Scripture

> May the God of peace himself make you entirely pure and devoted to God; and may your spirit and soul and body be kept strong and blameless until that day when our Lord Jesus Christ comes back again. God, who called you to become his child, will do all this for you, just as he promised.
> (1 Thessalonians 5:23-24, TLB)

Closing Prayer

Dad, pray this second Scripture passage over your son. Lay your hands on his shoulders and pray that the God of peace will make your son entirely pure and devoted to Him, and that his spirit and soul and body will be kept strong and blameless until that day when our Lord Jesus Christ comes back again. Ask Him to keep His promise and do all this for you.

Son, have your dad kneel and put your hands on his shoulders. Pray this Scripture passage over your dad as he did for you.

The Birth of a Man

This section is for thirteen- to fifteen-year-old sons who are clearly within the grasp of puberty or heading out the other side.

Part 2 defines our defenses against the darker flip sides of our Triple-P adjustments that arrive with early adolescence. These flip sides are called lusts by the apostle John:

> Do not love the world or the things in the world. If anyone loves
> the world, the love of the Father is not in him. For all that is in the
> world—the lust of the flesh, the lust of the eyes, and the pride of
> life—is not of the Father but is of the world. And the world is pass-
> ing away, and the lust of it; but he who does the will of God abides
> forever. (1 John 2:15-17, NKJV)

We deal with all three of these lusts in this book. The lust of the eyes is dealt with in chapters 9 and 10 of part 1, while the pride of life (lust for independence from parents and a lust for acceptance of peers) and the lust of the flesh (lusts in relationships with girls) are dealt with here in part 2.

If you and your son read through part 1 together when he was eleven or twelve, we suggest that you review chapters 7 and 9–11 as a refresher before embarking on part 2.

If your son is thirteen or older and you have not yet gone through part 1, we would suggest returning to part 1 to go through chapters 6–11 before embarking on part 2. Of course, you may start all the way back at the beginning of part 1 if you like, although some of the material may be elementary for your son.

my story: the sequel

Tears were pouring from my eyes.

And the day had begun so well too. Rolling out of bed and throwing open the curtains to a gloriously blue May day in the San Francisco Bay Area, I felt on top of the world. One year out of college, I was a young stockbroker raring to go and ready to grow. I had big dreams.

Big dreams were nothing new to me. As a quarterback on the football fields of my high-school frontier, I had lived out my dreams as the valedictorian and athlete of the year at 4-A powerhouse Thomas Jefferson High School in Cedar Rapids, Iowa.

After graduation I saddled up and headed west to a new frontier, riding into the campus at Stanford University to settle into stately Soto Hall. As an Iowa boy, I was amused that Stanford was affectionately known as the Farm. Listen, I know farms, and this was like no farm *I'd* ever seen. In fact, all I saw were big cities, big beaches, big mountains, and big times. At Stanford I began living out big dreams, and I would never be the same again.

On this particular day in May, I stood on the edge of yet another new frontier—one with another view of unlimited horizons. I was riding hard, striving to make my mark in the business world. This day had been no exception. Except for a lunch of burgers, fries, and a Coke and a couple of quick games of dice with the guys, I'd been pushing all day, skipping dinner and making phone calls well into the evening.

It was late now, and everyone else had gone home. I was beat, so I decided to wrap it up. As I straightened up my desk for the next day, I casually glanced out my west window and froze. Unfolding before my eyes was an unbelievably grand California sunset. As a reward to myself for a long day of work, I decided to kick back in my chair and take it all in before locking up and heading home.

Lacing my fingers behind my head and propping my feet on the credenza under the window, I leaned back in my chair with a satisfied sigh. Life was good.

But suddenly this pleasant scene was shattered by an intruder…the Lord Himself. I don't know how He did it, but He interrupted my world, breaking into that moment to replace the sunset with a view of how hopelessly ugly my life had become. My satisfied sigh turned to sorrow and despair, and tears began streaming down my face. The picture was so awful that even today my eyes well up whenever I think back on it.

With my gaze locked on that scene, I really had no choice about my next move. Immediately, I turned and reversed the course I'd been on, praying, "Lord, I'm ready to work with You if You're ready to work with me." Things have never been the same since.

Hold it a minute! I thought things were going so well? So did I. I've often asked myself how I could have sunk so low without really noticing. And you must be wondering what could be so ugly that it could bring a young, strapping Stanford graduate to tears and then to his knees? The answer: My sexual sin, or to be more precise, the pornography and the girls. I was really hooked on both.

How did this happen? It wasn't because I was a bad guy or anything. In fact, I was one of the nicest guys around, as everyone who knew me at that time would have told you.

It wasn't because I didn't know any better, because I did. Though I'd never personally committed my heart to Christ's ways, I'd grown up going to church on weekends. My pastor even saw something special in me, once drawing me aside with my best friend Brian and telling us that we would both be pastors one day. (And he wasn't far off, either. Brian is now an accomplished pastor near Minneapolis, and I'm an author serving the Lord.)

It also wasn't because I hadn't made a decision to stay sexually pure, because I had. Earlier, I told you that when I saw my mom crying over the pressure of making the money to raise us, I vowed that I'd never do anything to make her cry. I couldn't face adding any more pressure in her life, and I wanted to be a dependable man to help shoulder some of the load she was carrying.

But I had seen other tears, too. I'd see Mom sob because Dad had left her to date other women and have sex with them. When I saw Mom's tears, I vowed that I would never hurt any girls like that. I would treat them with honor and respect, and I vowed to keep sex special for marriage.

So I was a nice guy, I knew better, and I promised myself to stay sexually pure throughout my life. If I was all these things and still fell so deeply into sexual sin, how can you be so sure it won't happen to you?

It can, you know. Not all of a sudden, of course. You won't wake up one day and say, "Hmm, today I think I'll take a dive off Purity Hill and sail all the way to the bottom." That's rarely how it works.

No, if you slip, you'll slip because you took a small step or two on the slippery slope. If you don't take measures to stop sliding, you'll slip all the way to the bottom as well, where you'll wonder how you ever managed to slide down Purity Hill so fast, just like me.

You know what it's like to stand atop a muddy, slippery hill. If you stay right at the top, you're pretty safe. But if you take even a baby step down the side, you can slide quite a ways before you can stop yourself again. With each baby step you seem to slide a mile and, before long, you can end up all the way at the bottom.

Impurity is like a slippery slope. If you stay at the top of Purity Hill, everything will be fine. But sometimes you might think, *Well, everyone else is doing it, so I will too* or *We are in love, so what can it hurt?* Those small steps with girls or with pornography may seem like no big deal now, but before you know it, you'll be sliding down the hill like the Jamaican bobsled team, and you won't be able to do anything to slow yourself down. That's what happened to me. Before I knew it, I hit rock bottom.

THE LONG, SLIPPERY SLIDE

Obviously, I did not slither all the way down that hill after I got to Stanford. No, my slide picked up speed in high school. Do you remember the part of my story about Tracy and how I kissed her and touched her on our first "date"? Well things never really clicked with Tracy after that, and we went our separate ways.

I didn't have my first real girlfriend and take my next step down the hill until my sophomore year. Her name was Calley, and she really stole my heart! She had long blonde hair and a cute silvery smile because she wore braces. Calley had this certain way of standing next to me and patting my chest with the flat of her hand. I felt so strong and so happy when I was with her.

I was kind of shy, but she was outgoing and the center of all the popular people. I got to go with her to the first big party of the year, and it wasn't long before she grabbed my arm and led me to a make-out corner. What had happened to my aversion to kissing in public? I didn't even question it this time, proving I'd already slid pretty far down the hill from my once-pure perch at the top. Besides, I was certain this had to be real love.

But I didn't know much about love—and anything I *did* know was from what I picked up in the movies. After that glorious night, I wanted to express my deep feelings for her with something romantic, something in writing. I wrote her a note telling her how much I loved her. I even naively dropped the hint that I would love to be married to her some day; I did this to show her that my passion was no average passion.

A buddy of mine took her the note between classes. For fun, he watched her open it next to her locker. When she came to the part where I talked about marrying her, Calley laughed out loud. "He cannot be serious," she told my friend. "What a weirdo."

It didn't take long for this story to get passed through the school halls. For the next few days, Calley told anyone who would listen what a big dork I was. We never really spoke again, though I tried to call her several times. As you can imagine, I was absolutely crushed by this experience, and I swore off girlfriends until I was forty years old.

Ah, but that oath didn't last long. I had enjoyed a taste of the forbidden fruit. I had kissed in dark corners, felt a girl, and looked at tons of pornography. All seemed like small steps at the time, but they were adding up.

Not as much as they could have, though. I'm grateful that my passion for football kept most of my sexual yearnings in check. I dedicated myself to football, and after my solid senior year as quarterback of the J-Hawks, I received full-ride scholarship offers from the Air Force Academy and Yale University.

I had bigger dreams, however—playing PAC-10 football, even if it meant trying out for the team as a walk-on. I wouldn't settle for anything less. Before long I stood before my locker at Stanford University, staring in awe at the familiar white helmet with the red *S* and the name Stoeker taped across the front. Strapping on my helmet and chin strap, I proudly raced onto the field in my attempt to win a spot on the Cardinal. I was sure everyone in the country would know my name when I tossed long rainbow passes into the end zone.

In one afternoon that dream shattered into a thousand pieces. I was one of eight quarterbacks trying to make the Stanford team. From the corner of my eye, I saw Turk Shonert, a blue-chip recruit from Southern California, throwing thirty-five-yard bullets! Two other quarterbacks zipped the ball through the air as if it were on a string.

I, along with Corky Bradford, an all-state quarterback from Wyoming, stared in disbelief. There was no way either of us had the skill level to compete with these blue-chippers. When my football dreams died that afternoon, I turned my attention to…women, or more specifically, pictures of naked women.

As I settled into college life without sports, my churning sexuality broke through every dike, and I was soon awash in pornography. I actually memorized the day of the month when my favorite soft-core magazine, *Gallery,* arrived at the local drugstore. I'd be standing at the front door at opening time, even if I had to skip class to do it.

While I waded into porn waters up to my neck, I somehow kept sexual intercourse on some higher moral ground. From where I stood, making love was something *special* that you saved for when you were married. I still felt that way after I returned to Iowa following my freshman year. I got a summer job on a roofing crew to make some quick, big cash, and I began dating an old friend named Melissa, entering a relationship that quickly mushroomed into a heavy love affair. When I wasn't pounding nails on someone's roof, Melissa and I spent endless hours together. Just before I got set to return to Stanford for my sophomore year, we decided to spend a secluded weekend together at Dad's property on Shield's Lake in southern Minnesota.

Beneath a bright, full moon on a crystal-clear night, we lay down to sleep with a cool breeze blowing gently over us. The setting was romantic, and I was getting more excited by the minute. I quietly reached for Melissa, and she knew exactly where I was headed. Melissa looked up at me with a deep sadness in her big brown eyes, the moonlight framing her innocent face. "You know that I'm saving myself for marriage—hopefully ours," she said. "If you push forward with this, I want you to know that I won't stop you. But I will never be able to respect you as much as I do right now, and that would make me very sad for a very long time."

Who did I love more—her or me? My head spun. My desire and passion pounded away as I gazed into that sweet face glowing softly at me. We became silent for a long time. Finally, I smiled. Snuggling in next to her, I dozed off to sleep, passing her test with flying colors. Little did I know that it was the last test I'd pass for many years.

When I left Melissa behind on my drive back to Stanford University, a deep loneliness settled in. Far from home and with few Christian underpinnings, I wandered aimlessly through my days, feeling sorry for myself. Then one day during an intramural football game, my eyes caught sight of a female referee. She looked like a grown-up version of my childhood sweetheart, Melody Knight, who had moved to Canada when we were in the third grade.

I was in love! Since there was nothing holding either of us back, it wasn't too long before we were in bed making love. I was tired of being a virgin after spending so much time thinking about sex. Besides, I was having sex with the girl I *knew* I would marry.

Sadly, the flame of our relationship burned out as quickly as it ignited, but sadder still, this small step led to many more steps down the hill. The next time I made love, it was with a girl I *thought* I would marry. The time after that, it was with a good friend that I thought I could love and *maybe* marry. Then came the pleasant coed I barely knew who simply wanted to experience sex before she left college.

Each seemed like a small step. Yet within twelve short months, I'd gone from being able to say no in a secluded camper on a moonlit night to being able to say yes in any bed on any night. Later, just one year out of college in California, I found myself with four "steady" girlfriends simultaneously. I was sleeping with three of them and was essentially engaged to marry two of them. None knew of the others.

But then God stepped in with that devastating interruption of that spring sunset, showing me what I had become. He took me back to the top of Purity Hill, and that is where I'm going to stay for the rest of my life. I hope to see you there as well.

> Discussion: Go back to the beginning and read through your highlighted phrases. Discuss them together.

Optional Discussion Questions

1. Dad, tell your son what your life was like before you became a Christian. Or, if you were saved at a young age and drifted into sin, tell him what your life was like just before you recommitted your life to Him.
2. Dad, did you know better growing up? Can you remember making a commitment to sexual purity? If so, was it because of church, or was it for some other reason like the tears of a mother?

Closing Scripture

Keep yourselves from sexual promiscuity.
    Learn to appreciate and give dignity to your body, not abusing it, as is so common among those who know nothing of God. (1 Thessalonians 4:3-5, MSG)

Closing Prayer

I was one of those who knew too little about God, abusing my body like countless others around this world.

Dad, put one arm around your son's shoulders and reach your other hand up to God, reminding God that this is your precious son that you are so very thankful for. Ask God to use these book times to give your son true knowledge of God and a sense of appreciation and dignity regarding his body.

Son, ask God to help you stand upright in His image, especially in the area of your sexuality. Ask Him to help you appreciate and understand what it means to give dignity to your body.

sloppy promises

Why do I share so much of my story? Think back to how all this started.

I made a promise to stay on top of Purity Hill. But in the ninth grade, Don had told me how great sex was with his girlfriend, Tracy. Then I got into those pornographic magazines at Dad's house, and then a girl let me go up her shirt, and then I hooked up with a Stanford girl, and then...

They were all little steps, but added together, I slid miles down from the peak of that hill. Sure, I'd heard the truth in church. I knew that God reserved sex for marriage, but I didn't know how to defend my place atop Purity Hill. No one told me that my fear of looking like a dork would lead me to take small steps with girls so that I could look cool. No one told me that the lustful thoughts in my bedroom would make it so easy to go ahead with Tracy in her backyard. No one told me that pornography changes the way you look at girls and makes it hard to respect and honor them when you are alone with them. I had no idea that those choices could have such an impact in my life.

That's why your father is going through this book with you right now.

It's one thing to make a promise. It's another to know how to keep that promise, and when it comes to our sexuality, we can get very sloppy with our promises indeed. Even Christians.

But you weren't even a Christian back then! It'll be different for me.

That's a good point, and maybe it *will* be different for you. And maybe I could be excused for being sloppy with my promises to treat girls well because I hadn't committed to Christ.

After all, there is definitely a difference between having the new life of Christ in you and not having that life in you. After asking Christ to take over my life in my office that night in Palo Alto, I stood up and walked out of the office, not yet fully realizing what I'd just done. But God knew, and in the first two weeks, it seemed as if the heavens moved everything in my life. In no time I had a new job back in Iowa and a new life ahead of me. And I left the girlfriends behind!

See? You were okay from there, right? Not on your life. I was still sloppy with my promises for some years before God finally got me back to the peak of that hill. After moving back and settling into an apartment in Ankeny, Iowa, my nights were monotonous and long. A man accustomed to entertaining four girlfriends isn't used to having his nights free!

In no time, thoughts of Janet began to swirl in my imagination. She was an old friend from high school, and I'd been enamored with her for years. Back then, I'd been too busy with football to start a relationship with her, but I'd often dreamed of sleeping with her.

I soon tracked her down and—what luck! She was still single and living in Omaha. I called her, and after some cheerful banter, she invited me to meet her at her favorite dance bar. Need I say more? After closing time, we found ourselves alone in her apartment. One thing led to another, and we slipped out of our clothes and into her bed. We began kissing, but a strange thing happened: I couldn't get an erection! *That* had never happened before. Deeply humiliated, my head spinning, I slunk out to the parking lot and slumped into my car.

Then I clearly heard the Spirit whisper into my heart, "By the way, I did that to you. I know it hurt you, but this practice can't be tolerated anymore in your life. You are Christ's now, and He loves you." He didn't have to say it twice—on the spot I made a commitment to save intercourse for marriage. But even then there were other areas of my sexuality that remained well out of His control for many years.

Surprised? You may be, but once you're just a few years older, you won't be surprised by such stories in the least. Lots of Christians are sloppy with their sexual promises, living in the same bondage to their sexual sin as non-Christians. Check out Ryan's story:

Gina and I led the youth worship group together, and we were both involved in the Wednesday night meetings. Because of our leadership positions, we were involved in many activities together. We also had some pretty intimate prayer times, just the two of us. I found I spent a lot of time thinking about her, fantasizing and wondering what she'd think if I grabbed her and kissed her. I figured those thoughts were harmless. She was pure and from a strict family. I didn't think she'd see anything in me anyway.

But I thought about it all the time, how I would reach out, how I would take her in my arms. It was almost as if we'd done it many times already. One night we were the last two to leave after cleaning up on a Wednesday night, and we were standing in the parking lot. That's when my mental games became a reality. Before I knew it, we were in the back of my mom's van, naked and scared, wondering what we'd just done.

Since then, we've been having intercourse constantly for about six months, leading worship and prayer times like always, but living in such hypocrisy. I can't imagine we have any real leadership or power in the Spirit realm. I feel like a fool and a failure, but how can I stop? We can't figure out how.

Ryan's story began in his thoughts—the same way mine did in middle school, and it ended similarly too. And yet he had the new life living in him the whole time. How can this be?

We can all say no to that new life, and we can all choose to be sloppy with our promises to God. And when we do, we lock ourselves into the same prison as everyone else, even those who've never *heard* of the new life of Christ.

Having the new life in you makes a huge difference, and freedom isn't possible without it. But it isn't the fact that you have a new life in you that finishes the job…you also have to listen to the voice of the Holy Spirit and walk like Christ walked. That is what makes the difference.

How did Christ walk? There's a great verse in the Bible that sums up God's standard in this area:

But among you there must not be even a hint of sexual immorality, or of any kind of impurity, or of greed, because these are improper for God's holy people. Nor should there be obscenity, foolish talk or coarse joking, which are out of place, but rather thanksgiving. (Ephesians 5:3-4)

Looking at pornography and pushing a girl's boundaries are examples of sexual immorality. Young Christian men shouldn't look at pornography. They should *avoid* every hint of impurity, just as this passage says.

You are at the point in life where you can decide what kind of young man you want to be. When God looks around, He's not looking for what everyone else calls a man's man. He's looking for something better and tougher from you—a God's man. His definition of a man—someone who hears His Word and acts upon it—is clear.

Are you sexually pure today, or have you taken baby steps off the peak of Purity Hill, at least in your thoughts?

No one else may know the truth, but God knows. So does Satan, the enemy of your soul. If you aren't sexually pure, your enemy has you in the cross hairs, and he's laughing as he readies to tempt you into taking a few more steps. He knows there is really no such thing as a small step on a slippery slope. Every step can take you miles down the side, even small ones.

You need to be God's man and drive a stake into the ground at the top of the hill and then grab that stake and hold on.

> Discussion: Go back to the beginning and read through your highlighted phrases. Discuss them together.

Optional Discussion Questions

1. Dad, did you know how to defend your place on top of Purity Hill back then?

2. If you could live life over again, would you have preferred to learn what you learned in the shower rooms later in life? What did you get into as a result of all that locker-room talk?

3. Discuss together whether you've each noticed the difference between having the new life in your life and not having it.

4. Dad, were you sloppy in your sexual practices? Did you know back then that God's standard was not a hint?

5. Were there areas of your sexuality that stayed out of God's control for many years?

Closing Scripture

So I advise you to live according to your new life in the Holy Spirit. Then you won't be doing what your sinful nature craves. (Galatians 5:16, NLT)

Closing Prayer

Dad, pray out loud with your son as your witness. Ask the Lord to sharpen your spiritual ears to hear His voice in your life. Ask Him to reveal the areas in your life where you have said no so often that you can't hear Him anymore. Commit to do anything He asks you to do.

Son, reject the cravings of your sinful nature and commit to the Lord that you will live according to that new life in you. Tell Him you love Him dearly and that you desire a deep closeness with Him that grows from that yes in your heart.

what's independence?

On a recent Friday I had finished speaking before several hundred people in Cedar Rapids, Iowa, when a pleasant woman approached me. I could tell something was on her mind.

"My son really liked your book *Every Young Man's Battle,*" she began. "He's in school today, but I'm going to pull him out of class so he can come and hear what you have to say this afternoon."

"That's very nice of you, ma'am, but why—"

"Because I need *someone* to talk to him," she said. "He doesn't listen to me anymore. He's sixteen—you know how they are!"

Hmm. That's a pretty common attitude among teens, and it isn't really surprising. After all, Jean Piaget said you should be thinking independently from your parents by now. But there's a difference between thinking independently and *acting* independently, which can get on everyone's nerves. Let me illustrate that difference.

Tim, a friend from church, told me a story about a trip to the video store with his teenage daughter Caitlin. "As we neared the store, Caitlin said, 'Okay, Daddy, this is what you are going to do. Drop me off at the edge of the parking lot, away from the door. Then park and watch while I go in. You can't come in until two other customers come in after me, so no one knows that we're together. When you come in, don't come over by me or look at me.'"

He kind of chuckled but went on, "And when she wants money? She doesn't ask. She comes up and begins tapping on my chest, much like you would tap buttons on an ATM, and then she just holds out her hand."

I appreciate Tim's honesty, because it likely hurt him to tell me that story. Maybe you've asked Dad to keep his distance when you go to the mall together. If so, that's not at all uncommon since teens naturally draw away from their parents in their search for independence. But it's *how* you handle this newfound desire for independence that demonstrates how much you are maturing.

Sure, the Three Ps gave you the increasing ability to think independently and find your identity. But with that came the flip side, that darker temptation to pull away from your parents.

God clearly wants you to grow up as a well-adjusted, independent young man. When God took you into the locker room of life at halftime, He knew you still had another full half of football to play—a time when you will mature and be tested in the heat of the game. But He also knew that you would be inexperienced and would need an older teammate to show you the ropes.

Many teens fail to see that they haven't played the second half yet—meaning they lack the experience to make good decisions. Instead, they got a taste of independence late in the first half, so they are ready to ditch Dad and Mom as soon as the second half rolls around. That's not a good idea, especially because you'll need your parents' experience to make up for where you are lacking.

Most teens see independence as putting distance between them and their parents. You know what I mean—when you think like this, you want to be your own man and set your own course and you want to buzz around town without Dad and his curfews. When Dad speaks, you don't want to hear it.

But that's not what God calls independence, and that's not the kind of independence He hoped you'd step into in the second half once He'd completed His adjustments in you. You see, authority means a lot to God. God loves order, and where there is no respect for authority, there is no order. Here's what Jesus said about submission to authority:

> The teachers of the law and the Pharisees sit in Moses' seat. So you must
> obey them and do everything they tell you. But do not do what they do, for
> they do not practice what they preach. (Matthew 23:2-3)

This is amazing! Jesus called the Pharisees all sorts of names—vipers, hypocrites, wicked, blind guides, whitewashed tombs, and sons of hell—elsewhere in the Bible, but He still believed His disciples should obey the Pharisees, because obedience is right. The same goes for you regarding obeying your dad and mom:

> Children, obey your parents in the Lord, for this is right. "Honor your
> father and mother"—which is the first commandment with a promise—
> "that it may go well with you and that you may enjoy long life on the
> earth." (Ephesians 6:1-3)

If independence has anything to do with distance at all, it lies in moving *closer* to your dad, not farther away. To God, independence means rising up and taking your place side by side with your dad, standing shoulder to shoulder with him as a man.

That's a whole new way of looking at it, isn't it? But doesn't it sound good? If you think normally like this about independence, your move into manhood will be exciting to your dad, because soon you'll become more than just a son to him. You'll become one of his closest brothers in Christ. That's what God had in mind for the second half.

Wait a minute. How do I get independence from my father by obeying? That doesn't sound like freedom and independence.

But it is.

When you do what your father wants you to do or asks you to do—and it's okay to ask questions—you are showing how you are maturing before his eyes. That's the way you become a man—by recognizing the authority figures in your life. When you listen to Dad, even though you're feeling more and more independent, your relationship will become closer than either of you can imagine. Real independence means listening *more* and talking *more* with your dad, eye to eye. This is the kind of independence God approves of.

It's important to think for yourself and express your views openly and clearly, but you don't have to draw away from Dad. You can have a great relationship with him even as you seek your independence. Just be sure to do what he asks of you in the meantime.

One of the best ways to show that you're willing to do what he asks is by going through this book with him. And you know what? I guarantee you that your relationship will grow closer by the time you finish the last chapter. Doing book with Dad is a great way to form a lasting partnership with someone who really cares about you.

That's what happened to Jasen and me when we went through this experience. Today, at the age of nineteen, he seems like a brother to me, and it's because we did book together. He matured along the way. I'll never forget the time when Jasen—he must have been twelve or so—raised an important topic with me. He felt that I was being too harsh with him regarding a disagreement he had with his younger sister Laura. Since Jasen had been a good son who listened and did what I asked, I was receptive to hearing him out when he felt he was getting a raw deal. We opened up, man to man.

I had to admit that my son made some sense. I *had* reacted too strongly when he and Laura got into an argument, and upon further review, I reversed my call, just like an NFL referee.

I've also witnessed how mature Jasen has become with his friends and whom he chooses to hang out with. I once asked Jasen how he went about picking such good friends.

"Dad, I make it a point to make friends with the least popular kids. I used to be made fun of for that a lot, but that probably doesn't surprise you."

"No, it doesn't. But tell me—why do you pick the least popular kids?"

"Because they're nicer, Dad. We have a lot of fun."

That's so cool. Believe me, when a father hears *that*, he's going to give his son as much independence as he can. I never gave Jasen a curfew during high school. He told me when he thought he would be coming home, and if that sounded reasonable, I said, "Go for it." Whenever I asked him to do something around the house, he never gave me any trouble. He just did it, as the Nike ads say. Consequently, Jasen had more independence than any teen I knew. But he had earned it with his maturity.

Maturity doesn't happen overnight. It grows out of good choices. One day you'll think totally for yourself, but for now, until your maturity fully develops and until you have enough life experiences to crunch through your wonderful new thinking processes, it's not a bad idea to listen to your dad. He's gone through adolescence himself, so he's going to have more experience. Listen to him. Learn from him.

Don't be too proud to admit you're inexperienced at life. Your dad was once young and inexperienced, and so was every other man on the planet. He won't think you're a doofus.

Sure, maybe he's behind the times on a few things today. So what if your father isn't a pro on the Internet or doesn't know an MP3 from a 3PM? The fact is that he knows you better than anyone else, and he wants the best for you. He knows the mistakes he made growing up, and he knows that he doesn't want you to experience the same pain he has. That's the way I feel. One of my great desires in life is to raise godly sons who won't get caught up in the sexual sins that I committed in high school and college. I want to spare them the pain I went through.

Your dad and I may be fossils, but we know every rock and curly swirl in the rapids on Adolescence River. Why would you want to put distance between you and your river guide?

If your dad cramps your style with what you think are a bunch of stupid rules, ask whether you can talk to him man to man. Calmly explain your side, but ask him to explain his point of view. If you demonstrate maturity and have two-way communication, your dad will see that you have a good head on your shoulders. Chances are he'll change or relax the rules because we fathers don't want to control our sons—we want you to learn to control yourself. Check out this verse:

> You are all sons of the light…. Since we belong to the day, let us be
> self-controlled. (1 Thessalonians 5:5,8)

God doesn't want to control your life, either. He wants you to control your own life using His weapons. God is a strong God, and He wants you to be a strong man.

> Do everything…so that you may become blameless and pure, chil-
> dren of God without fault in a crooked and depraved generation, in

which you shine like stars in the universe as you hold out the word of life. (Philippians 2:14-16)

Having a strong relationship with your dad is one of the best ways to ensure that your emerging sexuality is integrated well into your Christian life and that you can stay independent from sin.

And remember this as well: Your relationship with your dad is connected to your ability to say no to pornography. Research shows that the closer you are to your dad, the easier it is to stand against your lusts and temptations.

Your dad wants to be there for you, listen to your questions, share some of his stories, and be your best friend. Isn't that why he's reading this book with you?

If your dad is not around, take heart. You have your mom, and you have your youth pastor, not to mention your Father in heaven, who calls Himself the Father of the fatherless. Stand with them, shoulder to shoulder, as you seek your independence as a man.

> Discussion: Go back to the beginning and read through your highlighted phrases. Discuss them together.

Optional Discussion Questions

1. Dad, did you ever pull away from your parents?
2. Ask your son if any of the guys seem embarrassed to be seen with their parents. Do they go to great lengths to avoid being with them in public? Does that seem strange to him?
3. Ask your son if there has been a time recently where he felt you were unfair. Talk about it.
4. Ask your son if there is a family rule that he feels is unfair. Dad, tell him about some of your parents' rules that you thought were unfair. Do they seem so unfair now, when you are looking back through the eyes of experience?
5. Dad, talk about your relationship with your father. Tell your son how it has affected your ability to stand up against your lusts through the years.

Closing Scripture

Children, obey your parents in the Lord, for this is right. "Honor your father and mother"—which is the first commandment with a promise—"that it may go well with you and that you may enjoy long life on the earth." (Ephesians 6:1-3)

Closing Prayer

Son, you take the lead this time. Have your dad kneel and put your hands on his shoulders. Thank God again for your father and commit to staying obedient and drawing closer to your dad during your teen years. With your dad as your witness, ask the Lord to point out to you whenever you are failing in this commitment to Him and promise to make necessary changes.

Dad, commit to God that you will be a father who listens when your son respectfully challenges you. Ask God to help you hear so that you might be a better father and friend.

we aren't perfect

God wants you to move in closer to your father so you can benefit from his experience. Trouble is, not all his experiences were good. He grew up in the same sexually charged culture that you're growing up in. He, too, likely took a few too many steps down Purity Hill, and now he may be so used to his old ways that he doesn't even notice what he's doing.

This is called a *blind spot,* and because we are sinners, we all get them from time to time. The problem is, they are *blind* spots, which means we can't see them and we can't always see that they're hurting those around us. The solution? We need someone close to tell us that he can see something we can't see. Real men do that for each other, especially fathers and sons. But daughters help out too!

God once used Rebecca to deliver a message to me as only God can deliver the mail. Now fourteen, Rebecca is a soft-hearted, loving girl. She's always been especially tender-hearted and sensitive toward violence. Even a single gunshot on the television can really shake her.

One Saturday night a number of years ago, I was watching an episode of *Walker: Texas Ranger.* The show starred martial arts champion Chuck Norris as a good-guy Texas Ranger putting a Far Eastern–style hurt on the baddies each week. If you've never seen it, I'll add that the show had its fair share of gunshots as well.

Well, Rebecca wandered into the family room during a big-time chase scene. A car turned sharply and slammed on its brakes, spinning sideways to a stop. Men dove from the cars and began firing away. Rebecca jumped with a pained squeal, clapped her hands over her ears, and ran out of the room.

Annoyed at her antics, I scornfully muttered under my breath, "I've never seen such a sissy."

Instantly, God stopped me in my tracks. *That is how I created all of my children to react to violence…with horror. She hates violence like I do. You're the one who is wrong, Fred!*

Broken inside at my callous reaction to my daughter's soft wisdom, I repented on the spot in humility. After praying, I realized I was very happy that my little girl's character spoke to me. As she's gotten older, I've given her the freedom to address blind spots she sees in me, because I want to get rid of them as quickly as I can.

The bottom line? We fathers aren't perfect, and because we can have blind spots, sometimes we'll trip up our sons in their battle for sexual purity without really knowing it. In tears, Jimmie once told his mother, "It's hard to be a Christian with Dad, because he wants me to watch TV with him, and it's always the stuff you don't like, Mom. He always gets mad at me if I won't watch these shows with him."

Now fifteen, Jimmie is struggling with his purity, especially around his father. And yet Jimmie hasn't spoken to his dad about this because he's afraid of losing the relationship.

I understand Jimmie's fear very well because of my relationship with my own father after the divorce. But as I've grown older, I've learned something else that you can begin learning now: True relationships are built upon open and honest conversations. If your dad is tripping you up, you have a right to talk to him about it, as long as you are respectful. But understand this—I know full well that dads don't always want to listen to what you have to say.

It was never easy for me to talk to Dad about the things he did that hurt me. At first, this was because he was my hero. One of my most vivid memories is of something that happened during a seventh-grade track meet held on a fine spring afternoon behind Linn-Mar Junior High School. My track-and-field discipline was the shot put. Dad was late for the meet, so between throws I watched anxiously for him to appear over the bluff that rose up gently from the parking lot.

Suddenly, there he was! Striding boldly across that low rise, Dad's light hair was striking against a bright yellow jacket that we had given him for his birthday a few weeks before. A former national wrestling champion, he walked with a jock's flair. Smiling, nodding confidently to acquaintances as he cruised my way, he was *the* box-office star of my universe. I stared helplessly with admiration. He was a superman among mere mortals, and he was *my dad*. I adored him.

But later, talking to him was hard for another reason. My father left Mom for another woman, and I had lost all that respect for him through the divorce. Worse yet, even though I was growing up and now able to reason and think on my own, he'd shown no interest in listening to my ideas about anything. That drove me crazy, and I wanted to push him away further.

But I couldn't push him away. My father had changed jobs and began to have more time around town during the week. So now Dad not only came to my football games on Friday nights, but he also regularly dropped in on my football practices to boot. Instead of cheering me on or even watching passively from the sidelines, he yelled at me like he was the second coming of Woody Hayes. He constantly ripped me for the slightest mistake. If I threw an interception and hung my head a little, he'd bark, "Get your head up!" If I fumbled a snap, he'd shout, "Get your head out of your rear!"

I don't mean to dishonor him, I'm simply telling you what he did. It got so bad that my coach had to bar him from practices. This wasn't easy for my coach since he and my father were old college buddies, but he stepped up and told him, "Look, Fred, this is disrupting your son and the whole team."

My coach couldn't protect me after Friday night games, however. That's when Dad would lay into me and deliver a verbal blitz that caused me to run from the pocket. He would chase after me by naming all the mistakes I had made. After one tirade I got so nauseous that I vomited into my baseball cap.

I felt like my dad didn't know me and didn't care to get to know me. I resented how his affair with another woman had smashed his marriage into smithereens and that he'd introduced me to pornography, which caused me huge problems in my twenties.

While I loved my father, deep down I knew he'd traded a life with me for a life with a mistress. That spelled betrayal to me. And now, as I was seeking independence to stand with him man to man, I knew that he didn't accept me as a young man or as an equal.

I was just plain scared to talk to my dad about his mistakes in our relationship because of his big, blustery ways. Perhaps your relationship with your father hasn't been very good. Maybe he isn't part of your life and you're reading this book with your mother or an uncle or a mentor. People—even fathers—aren't perfect, as we've already said.

If that's the case, there's still hope for the both of you. God can work mighty miracles in our lives. Christ is in the business of changing people, and perhaps your father's decision to do book with you is the first step toward rebuilding your relationship. If you've had a rocky time with your dad, please show him mercy. He probably means well.

I believe my dad meant well, and I'm sure he loved me. I'm also sure he thought bellowing at me at football practice and showing me his *Playboys* was the best way to make a man out of me. He was just blind to the truth. That's why I eventually chose to show mercy to Dad, and we were finally able to build a relationship we could both enjoy before he died.

One of the reasons Steve and I have written this book is so that you and your dad can learn to talk about things that are really hard to talk about, like sex. We believe that once you can talk to your dad about sex, you can talk to him about any ol' thing.

Our hope is that by having come this far in the book, your dad is already beginning to see that you really *are* becoming a young man and that your thoughts on these issues are worth hearing.

You won't have real independence from your dad until you can both talk openly about what you believe, especially when one of you is hurting the other. You need this kind of independence.

It isn't easy to know where to start on such things, so I've put together a list of questions at the end of this chapter to help out. It isn't easy to go through questions like these, but I've done it myself, and it is really helpful for a very simple reason: Dads need someone else to point out their blind spots.

Your dad wants to be a great father. How about letting him ask you the questions below to help him out? (If your mother is going through this book with you, she can ask the questions as well.) Would you be brave enough to answer them honestly? I think you are. Please don't forget that my intention is not to put anybody on the spot here but to get the discussion ball rolling.

> Discussion: Go back to the beginning and read through your highlighted phrases. Discuss them together.

Optional Discussion Questions That a Parent Can Ask a Son

Before asking the questions, shake your son's hand and promise to listen to his answers without shifting any blame to him.

1. Is there anything I do in public that drives you crazy?
2. Is there anything in the way I treat you that makes you scared to get closer to me?
3. Am I harsh with you? Is there anything in the way I speak to you that makes you feel angry or like a little kid?
4. Do you feel that I've studied you through the years and that I know you well?
5. Am I doing anything that is making it hard for you to keep your sexual purity?
6. If there were one thing you could change in the way I treat you, what would it be?
7. Do you feel that I forgive you when you do something that I feel is wrong? Do you think I'm quick to ask forgiveness when I hurt you?

I know—these are tough questions to discuss. But if you and your father can get on track now, you won't have to wait twenty years to work out your differences, like I did with my father.

Closing Scripture

> Fathers, don't aggravate your children. If you do, they will become discouraged and quit trying. (Colossians 3:21, NLT)

Closing Prayer

Son, again take the lead and lay your hands on your dad's shoulders as he kneels. Pray to the Lord, forgiving your dad for anything he has aggravated you with in the past. Ask the Lord to bless your dad as he considers your answers to his questions.

Dad, now lay your hands on your son's shoulders and ask the Lord to forgive you for anything you've done to exasperate and aggravate your son. Commit to change and to listen to your son's appeals without being defensive.

normal or warped?

Have you ever been to a major-league baseball game and watched the first batter use his cleats to obliterate the chalk lines of the batter's box?

That's exactly what's happening to our culture regarding sex. The line marking the difference between right and wrong has been swiped at so much that only traces of chalk remain. I'm sure that many of your friends—especially if you attend a public school—won't have any concerns about being sexually experienced in one way or another. In fact, when given the chance they will probably boast about doing those things.

If you aren't careful, you'll find yourself thinking the same way. As a young man thinking broadly with your abstract thinking processes, you are making all kinds of decisions for yourself for the first time. If you are anything like my kids, you're intoxicated with your new mind and all the fun you are having with your new freedom.

But as with all intoxication, your vision can be blurry and your thinking skewed. Why? First, as we said earlier, you'll often lack the life experiences necessary to come to the right logical decisions. Oh, your mind works just fine. It just doesn't have all the experience it needs to work with.

You likely won't have the depth of Bible knowledge to make sense of things from a Christian perspective, either. That makes it harder to sort out the truth from the many contrary voices in the world around you.

Of all the flip sides, this is the one you'll ignore the most. This is nothing to be ashamed of, however. Your dad and I have both been through it, and this is just part of learning. But you do need to accept and understand this weakness, or your thinking will be warped before you know it.

Look, I'm not pointing fingers. It is quite clear from my story that I wasn't thinking normally at your age. I stared at Marianne in French class and lusted over Tracy at leadership meetings, all the while thinking I was cool and sophisticated. But I was wrong, and you've seen how foolish I acted during my teen years.

You'll be prone to making mistakes, like I was. You won't be accustomed to the attractions you have for girls because you don't have much experience with the opposite sex. As you stretch your new wings of independence and begin making more decisions, you need to be aware that your inexperience may cause you to make bad decisions. So humility will be the key. You need to understand that you won't always understand. To whatever extent you lack humility on this point, to that extent you could stumble.

This is a time to be open with your struggles and ask others what they think. That was never easy for me, because I was too proud. I could have used the insights of others to help me prepare for what was coming, though, and you could too. Listen to the advice from your father and from other adults you respect—like your youth-group pastor. Their experience will help steer you right.

If you don't listen, you might get fooled like I did. Wrong things can really seem sensible and logical when you aren't thinking normally. When I was going to drive-in movies and messing around sexually with girls for fun, I was thinking, *Sex isn't wrong for everyone. Besides, God is really only concerned about sexual intercourse—everything else is okay.* It sounded sensible to my young mind, but it wasn't true or sensible at all. God *isn't* just concerned about premarital intercourse, but I didn't dig too hard into the Bible to find out how concerned He really was about *any* sexual immorality. You can't depend on your own logic alone.

In the coming years, you will be tempted to do things sexually with a girl, and sometimes it may seem to make sense. But God is asking you to respond differently than your classmates. He's asking you to think normally about these things—you know, to think like Christ.

IT'S ALL NORMAL

What exactly *is* normal these days? It's easy to think it's what *you* consider normal and what your friends consider normal. But the Bible warns us that people will try to tell us that what is good (like saving sex for marriage) is actually bad (because if you save sex for marriage, you won't be sexually experienced when you get married). You will have to be careful not to be sucked in by that thinking because it's out there in subtle ways. For instance, kids who are virgins are usually portrayed in movies as nerds and outcasts—definitely not the cool kids. I once heard from a sixteen-year-old boy named Chad who told me that he got caught up in all this good and bad and what's normal stuff. Here's what he had to say:

> Reading *Every Young Man's Battle* really opened my eyes. My girlfriend and
> I broke up two weeks ago, though it wasn't very easy. Both of us wanted to
> serve God, but we couldn't keep from having sex, and that sin caused decay
> in our relationships with God and with each other. We both wanted to be
> together and serve God together, but the guilt and distance we felt from God
> was too great.
>
> I never thought of sex as being wrong—as a matter of fact, I was raised
> to believe it was normal. Everyone seems to do it. But after reading what you
> wrote in *Every Young Man's Battle* and listening to what God was trying to
> tell me, I now understand that it is *not* normal for a Christian to have sex
> before marriage.

Chad found out that thinking normally means thinking like God thinks. We learn what God thinks by reading the Bible. Those who don't read the Bible are more likely to get confused about what's normal, and they may start doing things that, after a while, start to seem okay. It's like going to see an R-rated movie every week. After a while, you're going to say, what's the big deal? That's because you've desensitized yourself to all the sex and violence splashed on the screen—so much so that it now seems normal to you. That will hurt your relationships with girls down the road.

Pornography is like that too. If you keep looking at pornography, you get used to looking at it and stop feeling guilty about viewing it. That shouldn't be normal, but that's what happens.

According to God, it's normal for a Christian guy to "keep his way pure" (Psalm 119:9) and to set "no vile thing" before his eyes (Psalm 101:3). It's normal for a Christian teen to avoid lusting after girls (see Job 31:1). It's normal to have no "hint of sexual immorality" in his life (Ephesians 5:3). Normal teen conversations should not contain a trace of coarse language or filthy jokes (see Ephesians 5:4). Normal teens don't leer at breasts and wink at each other with a low whistle as the babes prance by. They don't rent *Titanic* and watch Kate Winslett drop her robe and stretch nude across the couch, and they stay away from watching the sexual escapades found in the *American Pie*–type films.

You will find in the next few years, however, that many Christian kids will be virtually indistinguishable from non-Christian kids. Everyone pretty much watches the same movies, listens to the same music, tells the same dirty jokes, and shares the same attitudes about premarital sexual activity. I hope that you'll be different, and not like Tyson, who's in my daughter's youth group. He recently declared to me, "It's no secret. Most guys just want to have sex or get some kind of action when they go out. They don't care about the relationship part of things like the girls do. Guys like to see girls with little or nothing on, that's the bottom line. Even we Christian guys."

Even we Christians. Hmm. If you were to ask me what surprises me most about Christianity, it would be that so few Christians live any differently than anyone else. The sad thing is that other Christian kids may mock you. Even worse, they may laugh at you and say, "Why are you being so straight? That's weird." When that happens, you will feel great pressure to conform to what everyone else is doing. Knowing that you are the normal one should give you the strength to stand up for what you believe.

WARPED THINKING

Hopefully, you're beginning to see that it's pretty easy to get warped in your thinking. But just to make sure, let's unpack a few really bad ideas that others will try to talk you into…the Top Five countdown of the hottest warped records we play in our heads.

5. Sex Is Such a Beautiful Creation of God's—and He Wants Us to Enjoy His Creation. Since We're Both Willing, How Can It Hurt?

This statement seems enlightened on the surface, and there is a lot of truth in it. Sex *is* a beautiful creation of God's—no argument there. I want my sons and daughters to experience all the beauty and wonder of sex. I want them to love sex and to have as much sex as they want, but just not right now.

I'm not being mean. I'm not being old-fashioned. I'm being smart and thinking normally. My experience gives me an edge, because I know it really *can* hurt, no matter how willing you are.

Reasons? We don't need the Bible for this one. Even secular magazines reveal the link between premarital abstinence and sexual satisfaction in marriage. As far back as 1975, "a study of more than 100,000 women by *Redbook* magazine found that those who had been sexually active at age 15 [were] more likely to express dissatisfaction with their current marriage and their current sex life." Worse yet, a survey of *Christianity Today* subscribers found that "those who had engaged in sex before marriage were more likely to commit adultery than those who had no premarital sexual experience." I don't care how enlightened you are; it can't be right to place such a ticking time bomb of pain into a girl's life like this. God can't possibly want you to enjoy the beauty of His creation at the expense of one of His precious daughters.[1]

4. We Love Each Other So Much, and We Are Going to Get Married in a Couple of Years Anyway. Why Wait?

I used to say that myself. And I had sex with three girls in a row whom I thought I was going to marry. The point? You don't know that you will marry someone until you marry her. And if you do jump the gun, you most likely *won't* make it to the altar.

Why? Having sexual intercourse short-circuits the natural development of

---

1. Found at www.marriageproject.org/fs0015.html.

relationships. At the beginning of a relationship, you naturally focus on the wonder of your girl's outer and inner beauty, and you spend your time digging into her
personality and dreams and thoughts. Once you leap past this stage and into sex,
however, your natural focus is to get it on again and again and again, so the growth
of the relationship is stunted. Researchers have found that relationships *should* go
through a twelve-step process, starting with "eye to body" and progressing all the
way to intercourse. If you jump over those several stages (such as "hand to hand,"
"hand to shoulder," "hand to head"), it detracts hugely from intimacy. There has
been no nurturing nor even a foundation built, and the relationship will likely
crumble.[2]

Abby told me, "I'm eighteen now, and I'm trying to get over a four-year relationship with Keith. I really thought we would get married someday. We had
known each other our whole lives, and I always had such a huge crush on him!
When I turned fourteen, my dream came true, and he asked me to be his girlfriend. We had a lot of fun together, and our relationship was wonderful until we
made the worst decision of our lives—to have premarital sex. Dumb, dumb, dumb!
Everything just went downhill from there. He crushed my heart two months ago
when he broke up with me out of nowhere. I didn't know what to do or where to
go. I just wanted to die."

If you *want* your relationship to last, then the last thing you want to do is have
premarital sex.

3. Sex Is a Rite of Passage Where I Come From. You Aren't a Man Until You've Done It with a Girl.

Growing up in the hallways and locker rooms of life, it often seems as though sex is
all that older kids ever talk about, and they seem to want everyone else to experience it too. Sex is your ticket into manhood, or so it seems.

But if sex isn't the ticket, what *is* the Christian guy's rite of passage into manhood? Jesus grew up on earth. What was *His* rite of passage when He was your
age and going through His halftime adjustments? Do you remember how He went
with His parents when He was twelve to the Feast of the Passover in Jerusalem?

---

2. Dr. James Dobson, *Love for a Lifetime* (Sisters, Oreg.: Multnomah, 1987), 32-4.

It's a great story of how He was obviously thinking for Himself and got caught up in discussions with the religious scholars at the temple and stayed behind when His parents left for home. When His parents finally found Him and His mother asked just what He was doing, Jesus responded respectfully, "'Why were you searching for me?' he asked. 'Didn't you know I had to be in my Father's house?'" (Luke 2:49).

Being about our Father's business is our rite of passage into manhood. That's where it's at. We must seek and defend God's purposes for our lives, not seek some passage into manhood in the sight of our peers.

2. The Bible Doesn't Say That Sex Is Wrong; It Only Says That Adultery Is Wrong.

Let's take a look at Ephesians 5:3-4 again:

> But among you there must not be even a hint of sexual immorality,
> or of any kind of impurity, or of greed, because these are improper
> for God's holy people. Nor should there be obscenity, foolish talk
> or coarse joking.

Please, let me ask you a question: If joking about sex is wrong for a Christian, how can sexual intercourse be okay?

The answer is obvious, and many will concede that premarital sexual intercourse is wrong but will concede no further limitations. A few years ago, Brad told me, "I know intercourse is wrong before marriage, but anything short of that is fine. I love to get up under a bra."

We get a glimpse of God's thoughts in Ezekiel 23:3, where God, portraying the waywardness of His chosen people, used the picture of unmarried virgins in passionate sin: "In that land their breasts were fondled and their virgin bosoms caressed."

Waywardness is the sin most detested by God. In looking for a metaphor to show us His feelings, He chose this one because it, too, is detestable, and He knew it would help us understand His feelings about waywardness. The Bible is quite clear here that "getting up under a bra" is out of bounds.

1. I Don't Feel Guilty About Looking at Porn or Lusting After Girls,
so It Must Not Be Wrong.

Again, this sounds reasonable on the surface, but it's flat-out warped thinking when you dig a little. The Bible teaches that it is very possible that when you've done something wrong for so long, you've numbed your conscience and can no longer tell if it is right or wrong:

> In fact, both their minds and consciences are corrupted. They claim to know God, but by their actions they deny him. (Titus 1:15-16)

Paul also told us the Law was given so that we would understand right from wrong, so that we could know when we've missed God's mark. He said that, without it, we really couldn't know right from wrong.

> Indeed I would not have known what sin was except through the law. For I would not have known what coveting really was if the law had not said, "Do no covet." (Romans 7:7)

Based on the truth of Paul's words, we can't go by whether we *feel* guilty or not, because our natural feelings can't tell the difference between right and wrong. We must go by God's mark, and God's mark is clear—there must not be even a hint of sexual immorality in our lives. If you don't feel guilty about something, it doesn't necessarily make the practice right. It may simply mean your thinking is warped.

EXAMINATION ROOM

Sex should be pure as a prayer and as holy as worship. It is not a pastime to play with your friends, like shooting hoops or jumping on the GameCube. When you make love, there is a connection made with another's soul. It is a connection that God intended for you to make with your bride, a connection that will defend the relationship against the world and against the hard times to come.

I've had intercourse with many girls, and when I think back on each one, there is a soul-connection with every one of them that I wish was not there. I was a fool, warped in my thinking.

To prevent us from becoming foolish, Paul exhorts us to examine ourselves:

Examine yourselves to see whether you are in the faith; test yourselves. Do you not realize that Christ Jesus is in you—unless, of course, you fail the test? (2 Corinthians 13:5)

One criterion in your examination is to see if you are growing in the knowledge of the Word and whether you are quick to conform to its truths. Without examination, it's too easy to follow our warped thinking and to easily hurt and rob others, as Marty did.

I had intercourse at age sixteen, but only once with one girl. I had no idea how strongly that could affect someone until I met my current girlfriend. When she found out that I was not a virgin, she cried. Sometimes she still cries about it. It hurts to see her in pain because of something selfish I have done.

Commit to thinking normally and with honor so that you'll bless those around you. Knowing that you are the normal one should give you the strength to stand up for what you believe. It also helps to find other kids who share the same values as you. Hang out with them.

The Bible says that normal Christian teens will "flee the evil desires of youth, and pursue righteousness, faith, love and peace, along with those who call on the Lord out of a pure heart" (2 Timothy 2:22). Notice what I call the action items in that verse. You should *flee* the evil desires of youth. That means to run, scoot, vamoose, or hightail it away from danger. The other action item is to *pursue* righteousness, faith, love, and peace. That means to search, go after, hunt, or seek those godly qualities. If you pursue those things, you won't have any problem staying normal and avoiding warped thinking.

> Discussion: Go back to the beginning and read through your
> highlighted phrases. Discuss them together.

Optional Discussion Questions

1. Ephesians 5:3-4 is God's standard for sexual purity. Tell your son what this standard means to you today. Did you understand this standard when you were a teen?
2. Tell your son about your own rationalizations that seemed sensible because of your inexperience.
3. When I grew up, I didn't think that premarital sexual activity was wrong. What was it like for you?

Closing Scripture

Do not be conformed to this world but be transformed by the renewal of your mind, that you may prove what is the will of God, what is good and acceptable and perfect. (Romans 12:2, RSV)

Closing Prayer

Dad, ask the Lord to help you and your son examine your thinking together, as a team. Invite Him to reveal any warped thinking so that your minds might be transformed to think like Him. Thank the Lord for your son and pray that God will paint a wonderful picture of sexuality for him. Pray that even though we've talked so much more about controlling our sexual urges rather than about the wonders of it, your son will see that nothing is more wonderful than our sexuality, when kept in its proper place.

Son, commit to the Lord to join your dad in examining your thinking and ask the Lord to sharpen your dad's memory of stories and statements that reveal warped thinking in either of you. Ask the Lord to make you accountability partners in this ongoing examination.

who loves ya?

Joe, a high-school freshman, couldn't wait for football season to start. Sure, Hell Week—the two-a-day practices under a broiling sun in August—was the toughest thing he had ever done, but he loved the camaraderie of being with the guys and being part of a team. There was something about getting on all fours and pounding each other into the freshly cut grass that formed bonds with other guys.

When the exhausted players returned to the locker room at the end of the day, the talk naturally turned to girls. Joe told the guys about Lynn, whom he had started going out with during the summer.

"Is that *all* you've been doing—going out with her?" asked one of the linemen, and the rest of the team joined in his laughter.

"Well…yes," replied Joe, who felt embarrassed. They had kissed some after going to the movies, but that was it.

"Then you mustn't be much of a dude!" said the lineman.

"Or a ladies' man!" yelled out the starting quarterback and team leader. Everyone laughed again, and Joe wished a big hole would open up so that he could disappear.

Over the next few weeks, Joe got teased every day about whether he was "doing stuff" with Lynn. He wondered if he should make something up to get them off his back, but then there would probably be follow-up questions: *What was she like? Did she say anything?*

Hey, if everyone else on the football team was having sex, then it stood to reason that he should too. After all, wasn't he a member of the Warrior football team—the squad that newspapers were picking to go to the state playoffs? And he had heard the cheerleaders saying that he was cute.

So Joe made his move, just like a linebacker keying off the quarterback. He slowly but surely broke down Lynn's resistance, increasing the pressure bit by bit with each date until the time he was over at her house on a Saturday afternoon, and her parents had gone to the mall with her sister. They were totally alone, and nothing was stopping them. So Joe ran his play and, after two weeks of pounding, Lynn's defenses were exhausted. She was putty in his arms as they went all the way.

Now he had something to really talk about in the locker room, and when he intimated that he and Lynn had had a hot time in her bedroom, he received looks of admiration and war whoops from his teammates. He was now one of them.

But something happened. Joe felt guilty about what he had done. Lynn, he noticed, wasn't herself any longer, and she was pulling away from him. The more he thought about it, having sex with her had been a huge, huge mistake that couldn't be swept under the rug.

Joe had stepped off Purity Hill, but did you notice something? It wasn't the sexual lust of the flesh that did him in. It was the lust of the pride of life, that deep desire to receive acceptance from his teammates. Either lust can lead to the same result. And once he started sliding down the slope, he realized how stupid he had been to pressure a girl to have sex with him.

Talk about making a bad choice: Joe had chosen to listen to his friends, not to what God said about premarital sex.

NOTICEABLE DIFFERENCES

Doing things for the approval of others. You won't receive a lecture about it here. Sure, it would be easy for me or your father to simply say, "Don't listen to your friends. Listen to what God says."

But we went through high school too, and we understand how much you want to be liked and accepted by your peers. This desire stems from the Three Ps working overtime and from a growing need to win acceptance from your peers, whom you sometimes deem to be more important than your parents.

But your problem really goes far deeper than that. You may want to fit in and be accepted in the worst possible way, but you are desiring something that's really not possible. Which is why we want to make an important point: If you're walking normally with God, you'll never fully fit in with your friends at school. That's what *really* needs to be accepted…by you.

You're just too different, because you are normal and they aren't. It's a shame because the differences weren't that noticeable in elementary school before the Three Ps did their thing, but once you hit junior high and high school, it's a whole new ballgame. Suddenly, everyone is noticing things like beauty, clothes, athletic skill, smarts in the classroom, what type of vacations kids take, what part of town they live in, and what type of car they drive to school. Your peers and friends are keeping score, and you know it.

And when the score is totaled up, you know how popular you are. It can be a vicious cycle. When I asked my daughter Rebecca what it takes to be popular at her middle school, she replied quickly, as if she'd answered this question a million times: "I'd have to be going out with someone, although I don't know why that's important. I notice they are always going out with guys but then are breaking up again so soon afterward. I'd have to wear Old Navy clothes all the time. I'd have to wear my hair down, and I'd have to be especially vain about it on picture day! I'd have to be flirty, and I'd have to be up on all the cool music and movie stars."

That's what you gotta do if you want to be popular. But what if you believe in God and go to church and take your relationship with Christ seriously? From what I've seen on school campuses, not too many kids take their faith seriously these days. Far too many say to themselves, "How far can I go and still look like a Christian?" Faking your walk with God to get on the good side of your friends and classmates is much too prevalent today.

There are reasons, of course. Jordan told me, "My classmates really push me over the edge. They think it's cool to tease and make fun of people—including me. I recently changed my class schedule, and now I'm in classes with a bunch of the popular kids. Ugh. I can't stand them. First, it's health class with the stupid popular people, and then I take PE with another bunch of dumb jocks who think they are so cool." In the face of all this, Jordan might be tempted to tip right-side-up values upside-down so that he can fit in.

So I'm going to ask you a blunt question here, and it's one I want you to think about: Are you faking it at school? Does anyone know you're a Christian?

I think your father would agree on this, but whom you choose to hang out with is very important if you are to keep from faking it. We think you should hang with people who think like you and have the same set of values. In other words, hang with other Christians. If most of them are faking their walk and are telling you to get a life or get real with your faith, then at least choose non-Christians who won't pressure your values.

The trick is to choose friends who will let you live life normally as a Christian. Jasen's friends were amazing that way, though many weren't Christians. When they decided to go to a movie that they knew was out of bounds for Jasen, they didn't ice him for the entire evening. When they got back to one of their homes, they'd call him up and say, "Okay, we're back. Get on over here, bro!"

These were more than random acts of kindness from nice people. They were the results of good choices that Jasen made in picking friends.

Making good choices in friends also extends to making good choices when you start dating. If you've reached the dating years, you should date only Christians. That sounds simple enough, but I personally know how tough this can be, and it can force you to make some hard decisions at times. After I became a Christian and moved back to Iowa, I continued to maintain a phone relationship with one of my girlfriends back in California. My friends and family fully expected us to marry someday since we'd been an item for three years. Then at church I heard the pastor say that Christians shouldn't be unequally yoked with nonbelievers.

Right about now, you may be scratching your head and asking, "What does 'unequally yoked' mean?" The phrase comes from some old Bible language referring to the wooden bar joining two farm animals (like oxen) at the heads or necks for working in the field together. If two different kinds of animals were yoked together to pull the plow, such as a donkey and an ox, you'd have your hands full trying to work that plow. The yoke would weigh heavily on one animal while choking the other, or the animal with the longer stride would drag the other painfully along by the neck. This is a great word picture of what it would be like if you got romantically involved with a young girl who doesn't believe in God. You'd be working *against* each other instead of *for* each other. Believe me, in your desire to stay sexually pure, you want to be associating with someone who's on the same spiritual level as you.

Back to my story. When the pastor said Christians shouldn't be unequally yoked, this news presented a problem since I had just become a Christian and my girlfriend wasn't.

My reaction? Tell her what I just learned. So I called this young woman out in California and explained what the pastor said. "I really need you to explore this and to seek God," I said, "or I don't know how we can keep our relationship going."

"Okay, I'll read my Bible for thirty days, and we'll see," she promised. A month later, I heard from her, right on cue. "I've done what I promised," she said. "But I just can't buy into this stuff at all."

"I'm sorry to hear that," I responded. Then I quietly suggested that we should go separate ways. My college chums thought my reasoning was a tad fanatical and wondered what was happening to their old buddy. That wasn't easy to hear. Although our breakup was amicable, it still hurt to lose my girlfriend. After all, we'd enjoyed many fun times together.

Spare yourself these heartaches and stick with Christians. If you do, you will save yourself a ton of grief. Better yet, you will gain yourself a ton of blessings. Sure, I could have kept dating her so that I wouldn't look weird to my friends. And although we weren't well matched, I could have even married her, and no one would have raised an eyebrow. We'd been dating for years, and everyone was used to the idea.

But obedience to God is far better because, when we obey, we open the door for God to move in and help us. Had I not obeyed and broken things off with this non-Christian girl, God wouldn't have been free to find someone better suited to be my wife. Less than a year later, God introduced me to Brenda, and my life has never been the same. Obeying His standards frees us to live life fully and happily in His blessings.

Besides, it's dangerous to play it both ways in your life. Ask Mitchell if he would like to have a second chance with his decision to fake his walk with God. "By the end of high school, I was near the top of my class in grades, I was playing football and basketball, and I was enjoying a close group of friends. On the outside, I seemed to have it all.

"But inside, I still felt guilty after doing all the things I'd gotten involved in, like drinking and partying. Then I got involved with a girl who was not a Christian and who had been pursuing me for over a year. What she began doing to me sexually kept me from God. I couldn't break free from my lust for a long time."

> Discussion: Go back to the beginning and read through your
> highlighted phrases. Discuss them together.

Optional Discussion Questions

1. As I passed through middle school and high school, I thought I knew just about everything and was pretty cool. Dad, what did your siblings mock you about the most as you tried to be hip and fit in?

2. I used to be amused at how the jocks would lean against the lockers with their cool, slightly sullen looks, nodding casually at passing guys and winking at the girls flitting near. Did you notice such behavior back then?

3. Ask your son: What does it take to be popular in school?

4. Ask your son if he ever gets mocked at school. Tell him how you were ridiculed—and how it changed you.

5. Ask your son to name his three best friends. Ask him why he named those three.

Closing Scripture

Now we command you, brethren, in the name of our Lord Jesus Christ, that you keep away from every *brother [or sister]* who leads an unruly life and not according to the tradition which you received from us. (2 Thessalonians 3:6, NASB)

Closing Prayer

Dad, put your arm around your son's shoulder and lift your other hand to the Lord. Commit to the Lord that you will be your son's consistent friend, so that if he must lose some friends for standing up for His principles, you'll be close enough to him to pick up the slack.

Son, give your dad a hug. Thank him for being your friend as well as your father. Then, with your arm around his shoulder, ask God to bless your friendship with humility and openness for a true relationship.

the trap

Chances are that you grew up watching Disney's animated classic *The Lion King* as a young boy. Remember the young lion, Simba, in that film? If you recall, Simba turned his back on the Pridelands and everything he knew, hooking up instead with some buddies for some R&R in "paradise." *Hakuna matata*...no worries. He and his friends did whatever they pleased, whenever they pleased. The young lion had everything but responsibility.

Suddenly, Simba's evil uncle, Scar, took over the Pridelands, which caused total disarray and ruin. With everything on the line, Simba did the right thing. He turned his back on the playboy lifestyle, gathered up the troops, led them to victory, married Nala, stood regally at his coronation, and took his rightful place of greatness among the animals. In only one day, Simba moved without a hitch from being a questionable character to becoming a mature lion capable of leading others in battle. Most of us figure that's the way life will work for us as well.

You'll be tempted to follow in Simba's pawprints. *Hakuna matata*...no worries. You figure you can discover what girls are like now—and what they look like when they're naked—even though it's irresponsible and wrong. Then, once you've "grown up," you can bounce back into church, ask forgiveness, and take your rightful place in God's kingdom. That's called having it both ways.

Life doesn't work that way, just as life doesn't always imitate Disney videos. The person you become as a young man is the person you'll drag into adulthood. Your likes and dislikes—from food to music to movies—will follow you into the future. The sexual desires you feed as a teenager will be the same desires you'll want to feed when you're in your twenties.

That's why the decisions you make today *will* impact everything in your future. Careful, though: Decision making is a two-edged sword. The right decisions you make today will help you make the right decisions when you're older. Wrong decisions today get you traveling down a path that leads to more horrible mistakes tomorrow.

When you were a little kid, you probably watched *another* Disney animated classic, *Pinocchio*. In this case, real life *does* imitate this story pretty closely.

This fellow Pinocchio knew it was the right thing for all boys to go to school. One day on his way to class, however, he met some scoundrels who painted a wonderful picture of spending the day at Adventure Island, a sort of amusement park just offshore. They gave Pinocchio and his buddy Lampwick free passes for the ferry ride to Adventure Island, but neither knew that at the end of the day all the boys would be turned into donkeys and be sold to pull carts in the coal mines for the rest of their lives.

I've watched a ton of gory movies in my day, but few screams in those films have matched Lampwick's shriek of raw terror when—at the end of the day—he was turned into a donkey and his hands were turned into hooves. That's when he realized his mistake, although he never saw it coming.

You'll face pressure to visit Adventure Island—a place where boys play with their girlfriends. You may give up your values for the sake of having sex with your girlfriend. Maybe you'll think God will understand and forgive you later. He'll forgive you, all right, but your trip to Adventure Island comes with a price because sin carries inescapable consequences that will follow you. You'll have to pay the price at the toll bridge just like anyone else.

Brett's story is like Joe's and Mitchell's in the last chapter and like hundreds of others we hear. "I've been a Christian since the age of nine," said Brett, "and I've been sexually active since I was twelve. Now I'm in my late twenties, and I'm on the Internet constantly viewing the worst kinds of pornography. Though I'm a Christian, it's always two steps backward and one step forward due to my sexual sin. I regret the things I do, but then go right back to them."

The end of the day at Adventure Island has arrived for Brett as he struggles against the binding cords of sin like a donkey pulling coal cars through dark mines, day after draining day. Pinocchio couldn't help Lampwick escape, and your friends won't be able to help you escape. You'll pay a price for conforming.

But let's face it: We will also pay a price for choosing God's ways, partly because so many sissy Christians are running around today. Luke told me, "I have never kissed a girl at all, but it's hard because most guys have way lower standards than me, even at my Christian school. A lot of them have already made out, and the rest don't seem to care at all about their girlfriend's standards. I really don't want to compromise my morals, but I'm losing many friends because of it."

Luke is paying a price to follow God. The apostle Peter told us it would be this way:

> [A Christian] does not live the rest of his earthly life for evil human desires,
> but rather for the will of God. For you have spent enough time in the past
> doing what the pagans choose to do—living in debauchery, *lust,* drunken-
> ness, orgies, carousing and detestable idolatry. They think it strange that you
> do not plunge with them into the same flood of dissipation, and *they heap*
> *abuse on you.* But they will have to give account to him who is ready to judge
> the living and the dead. (1 Peter 4:2-5)

You'll always seem a bit strange to non-Christians when you act like a normal Christian. Sadly, that also goes for the kids in the youth group at times. My daughter Laura faced this while leading a morning Bible study before school. One morning a girl attacked her movie standards in front of the whole group, declaring, "It's Christians like you that give Christianity a bad name." How odd for another Christian to suggest that Laura's perfectly normal Christian behavior somehow shames Christ. If you run into this sort of thing, you'll probably feel sorry for yourself and want to hide your Christianity. Don't do it! You must understand that everyone with beliefs gets mocked, not just Christians. Don't be so afraid of it! That's simply part of becoming a young man.

You will pay a price for faking your walk, and you will pay a price for walking your walk. You will pay a price either way, so only one question remains: Which will you choose?

To help you choose, it may help you to know that high school is not the finish line of life and won't amount to a hill of beans as you move on with your life. You'll understand this better as I finish this chapter with a story about Molly Sanders, a cheerleader at my high school.

I met Molly Sanders about the same time I sent my love note to Calley—you know, the girl who dropped me like a hot potato and told the entire school what a dork I was. I swore off girls after that episode, declaring that I wanted no part of them.

Though a cheerleader, Molly was not one of the glittering popular people. She was from my side of the school district—the wrong side. We didn't come from homes with long driveways and three-car garages and manicured lawns. Molly couldn't dress in all the latest fashions, and while above average in looks, she was not exactly a knockout. Like me, she had a slight acne problem. In the world of high-school cliques, Molly bounced around somewhere in the middle of the social scale. Homecoming neared. Having decided that girls were toxic, I couldn't care less about going.

But Molly cared, deeply. She wanted to go in the worst way. Why? For one thing, it was *homecoming*. For another, if she didn't get asked, she'd be about the first cheerleader in the history of Jefferson High left home without a date on homecoming.

Two days before homecoming, hallway gossip reached my locker. Someone told me that Molly had cried all night in her room because no one had asked her to homecoming. It was like she'd been left out to play in her cinders like Cinderella. I was touched deeply in my heart; I genuinely felt sorry for her.

While I had vowed that I would skip homecoming, I also knew I had to rescue this damsel in distress. Prince Charming—that would be me—picked up the phone and saved the day. I found the last tux for rent in the city, and she managed to pull a few things together, and Molly went from sitting in the ashes to being escorted to homecoming on the arm of the starting quarterback. We had a great time, and Molly had a soft spot in her heart for me after that, as I did for her.

Not that we started dating. In fact, we never went out together again. I know that she quit the cheerleading squad at some point, but since Jefferson High was one of the largest schools in the state, our paths didn't cross much during our school lives.

Graduation came, and we all moved on. Years later, we all returned for that rite of passage—the high-school reunion. Many of the popular cheerleaders had seemed to retire from life already. Looking a bit frayed and older than their years, the blush was off the rose.

Suddenly, Cinderella strolled in. Molly looked radiant, in full bloom. Her acne long gone and her body perfectly formed, confidence oozed from her very being. She owned a string of three or four health clubs, and she was planning further expansion in her limitless future. We talked for a few minutes, and through her eyes she shared her appreciation for the connection that we made years ago. I wished her the best, and I watched her stroll off to mingle in the glow of her glorious vindication.

Every time I saw Molly that night, all I could do was marvel and grin. By golly, Miss Molly, the pillars of high school had crumbled, and you are back on top where you belong. Way to go!

When my kids struggle with the pain and absurdity of high school, I remind them of Molly. Don't trade your values for a better rank now. High school is not the end of anyone's story, and it won't be for you. Real life begins at graduation, and every weak and flightless duckling can still soar like a swan as this thing called life really begins to take shape.

> Discussion: Go back to the beginning and read through your highlighted phrases. Discuss them together.

Optional Discussion Questions

1. Ask your son if he sees this type of trap thinking in the guys at school. Ask him to give you some examples.

2. I belonged to the popular cliques in middle school, but then I opted out and went my own way in high school. What did you do, Dad? If you opted out, what did it cost you?

3. If you opted *into* the popular groups, what did it cost you? Tell your son about the time that you may have hurt your old friends from elementary school in order to look cool with your new friends. Or describe the times you laughed with the group but felt guilty and lousy inside.

4. Tell your son about your last high-school reunion and how it proves that high school is not the finish line.

Closing Scripture

The way of the righteous is like the first gleam of dawn, which shines ever brighter until the full light of day. (Proverbs 4:18, NLT)

Closing Prayer

The way of manhood is the same. You are in the first gleam of manhood and will simply shine brighter and brighter as a man as you grow in character.

Son, ask the Lord to open your soul to this truth and to accept your position as a man among men. Ask Him to help you think like a man in spite of your inexperience and to listen carefully and humbly to the advice of other men in all things—including your relationship with girls.

Dad, ask the Lord to transform your thinking toward your son in every way, and to be among the first to grant him full standing in the world of men. Then look your son in the eye and tell him again how proud you are to have another man in the house!

treat her like a sister

When I was your age, I always thought that girls were pretty much like boys in how they thought, although I knew they looked nothing like boys when it came to their soft curves and cute hair. Was I ever wrong on that first score!

In case you haven't noticed, girls are even more different from you and me. They approach relationships entirely differently. If you don't understand that, there is no possible way you'll treat them right, especially in the area of sexual purity.

That's why I thought it would be interesting to hear straight from the source in this area, so I interviewed three young women for this chapter. What Amber, Bryanna, and Cassie say about guys and relationships will surprise you.

SURPRISE 1

Gals want guys to take the lead in the relationship. I bet you've heard a lot about equality and girls' paying their share on dates. Hey, I'm all for equality between the sexes since I'm the father of two sons and two daughters, but each of these three young women told me that she wants to go out with a guy who will take the lead, plan dates, look out for her, and take care of the check when it's presented at the end of the meal.

"I want a guy to be attentive and appreciate who I am and what I like," said Cassie. "I want him to care for me and do special, thoughtful things for me out of the blue, like presenting me with flowers, gifts, and notes. I want him to open doors and pay for our dates."

Pay for your dates? Cassie says she feels that way because she knows she is being treated special when the guy pays, so remember that when you get to your dating years.

SURPRISE 2

Girls are not that turned on by guy's bodies. You'll have to take my word on this, but girls don't stay up late at night using the Internet to look at pornographic Web sites. I think there's one magazine with pictures of naked guys—it's called *Playgirl*—but believe me, gals are not memorizing the date when the new issue arrives at newsstands like I did with *Gallery* magazine when I was in college.

Young women just aren't as visually oriented as you, and they won't think about your body like you think about theirs. Amber said, "It's inconceivable to me how guys can get turned on by looking at pornography. I can't understand that at all."

SURPRISE 3

Girls are into relationship, not sex. Having a good relationship is a huge priority for young women, so much so that many have given up their virginity over the years just so they *could* have relationships with guys who make their hearts jump. But for many young women like Amber, having sex is not even on the radar screen because they are committed to remaining pure. They want relationships, but having sex is not one of their reasons. They are more interested in having relationships in which they feel cherished.

"What can a guy do to make me feel cherished?" asked Amber. "Show that he desires to spend quality time with me, tell me why he likes me, and trust me with his thoughts and feelings. He has to honor my family and respect my body by not compromising our boundaries. He needs to be a man of his word by looking out for *my* protection and best interests."

It's the same story for Bryanna. "If you want to know what turns me on, it's when he remembers what I tell him or gives me an unexpected gift. It's when he sends me a card for no reason, gives me a hug or a little kiss, holds my hand in public, and shows me respect. I especially like it when he praises me in front of the gang."

These ladies aren't looking for a "little action." They're looking for a little relationship. Said another way, they want to be better off for having known you— that's what girls want. If you provide that, you'll be their hero. I once heard a teenage girl say sadly, "You know, I really missed the boat when I let Bill slip away. He was truly kind, and he never hurt me once."

How did Bill get it right? By following the advice of someone like Bryanna. "Girls want to be loved and cherished for the person they are," she said. "We like to be told we're beautiful with no hidden sexual agendas."

Added Amber: "Guys, you need to let girls know you care more about their heart than the way they dress."

Unlike Bill, most guys don't understand these differences. All three girls said that guys have pushed past their boundaries in the past. "When that has happened to me," said Cassie, "I've felt very resentful. I know that it made me feel used when this guy I really liked tried some things that made me uncomfortable. I asked him to stop, but he persisted. I'm still angry about it."

LEARNING TIME

So there you have it—some reactions from three young women. Based on my interviews with them and other young women, here are two vital things you mustn't forget as you approach someone of the opposite sex.

1. Honor Her by Defending Her Purity

My friend Gary Rosberg once wrote about the time he was shopping one day and saw a pair of hands that reminded him of the hands of his father, who had gone on to heaven. Gary then turned his thoughts to the hands of Jesus, noting this simple truth: "They were hands that never touched a woman with dishonor."

When I read this, sorrow tore at my soul! Oh, how I wish I could say that my hands had never touched a woman with dishonor! I really regret all the wrong things I did during my teen years, and I really wish I would have been a leader and set some boundaries in my relationships.

But remember, *setting* boundaries does not necessarily make you a leader—it's *protecting* those boundaries that makes you the leader. Cassie said, "I often feel that I care more about my purity than my boyfriend, Kevin, although he's a great spiritual leader in other areas. I appreciate how he prays for others and takes church seriously. But this spiritual leadership doesn't show up in our physical relationship, even though at the beginning he made sure that we decided together on our sexual boundaries. That's all been forgotten. Now he often pushes hard at them. When I resist, he pouts. I feel so manipulated, and I don't like that."

Would you say that Kevin is protecting Cassie's purity? No more than a wolf protecting a henhouse! He's certainly no leader.

Show a girl what a relationship with a real leader is all about. Jaden's done the job. "Jaden and I sat down the night we started dating, and I told him that we could do nothing more than kiss. I had been in an earlier relationship that had gone a little further, and it killed the relationship. It has been a struggle for us at times, but I praise God that we have kept our limits.

"We have the most incredible relationship because of it. I have the best, most respectful Christian boyfriend any Christian girl could ask for. I would challenge anyone to keep limits like this because our relationship has blessed both Jaden and me beyond belief!"

And one last word for the wise from one who knows: If you expect to guard her boundaries, avoid alcohol completely. Drinking will make you forget all about God, her boundaries, and your promises. You'll slide quickly down the slope of sexual sin.

2. Honor Her by Not Putting Down Her Values

Melanie had the beautiful face of an angel. When she smiled, her face lit up the room, and she loved God with all of her pure heart. She did not sneak into R-rated movies, and she was careful to dress modestly, especially at summer pool parties, where she wore a one-piece swimsuit instead of a bikini. Though quiet and shy, she was a blast when you got to know her, leaving the adults in the church quite puzzled. *Why didn't Melanie get any dates?* She was easily the crown jewel of the youth group.

Joe was a dark, handsome, athletic guy who had stolen Melanie's heart ages ago during the countless days spent together at church camps, picnics, and ballgames. Joe knew of Melanie's crush on him, but he tossed it aside. Caught up in the pride of life and the lust of his flesh, Joe was looking for a little action. To him, Melanie was just a dead end on his fast lane of life, and when pressed on the matter, Joe would wink and say with a grin, "She's not the kind you want to date—she's the kind you marry!"

What a put-down! What Joe's really saying is that he wouldn't want to date someone like Melanie because she wouldn't let him get away with putting his hands where they shouldn't go. He'll want a pure girl later, of course—just not right now while he has his chance to have some "fun."

Like so many other foolish teens, Joe's careless little wink reveals that the same old cunning trap has snared him. Maybe you can avoid it.

What trap are we referring to? That trap we spoke of in the last chapter… Teen guys often believe that you can do whatever you want as a teenager because it won't matter after you move into adulthood. You feel like you have a kind of Get Out of Jail Free card that erases everything you do as a teen. That's why Joe wasn't too worried when he started goofing around sexually with girls.

But those "play years" passed, and Joe's now in college looking to settle down. Sadly for him, the tables have turned. Now he has his heart set on Melanie, but she will have nothing to do with him, and that's the fate he deserves.

We said it before, but we want to say it again because it is so important that you understand this: There's no magic line that you step over from the teen years to the young adult years. When it comes to your relationships with girls, your young adult years start today. You need to make your decisions today in light of that. Otherwise, you give up your values for some fun, thinking it doesn't count. But it does.

Another point worth making is how this attitude costs the pure girls, who are ignored while they sit alone wondering why the guys pay no attention to them. A young woman named Brooke told me that the girls in the youth group who dress a little risqué (you know, spaghetti straps and bare midriffs and low-riding jeans) get all the attention. "The guys go out of their way to talk to them and even date them," she said, "but the girls who dress modestly don't get the time of day from the guys. There's no friendly conversation, no eye contact, nothing. Why not give a chance to the girl who isn't showing the most skin?"

I don't know about you, but that's embarrassing to me. I think it's horrible that Christian guys are acting this way, because that's no different from how non-Christian guys treat girls. They should get better treatment from us. You should treat all of them with honor, especially those who are walking purely and normally before God. We should be making it easy for them to obey God.

Oh, and one more thing... As a dad, I *know* you're my Christian brother and I *want* to count on you to stand shoulder to shoulder with me in this call I have from God to keep my daughter pure. But can I really trust you?

You and I both know that many Christians don't walk the talk and their word isn't worth the air they breathe in to say it. Someone's father (it could be me if you got to know my Laura or Rebecca) will be putting his entire trust in you when you take out his daughter. That's a lot of responsibility to shoulder, and I want you to be up to the task. I'm confident that, if you listen to what we're saying in this book, listen to your father, and continue to read your Bible, you won't be one of those Christians whose behavior is just like any of those friends who are taking advantage of girls.

As the father of my sweet twelve-year-old Madeline—this is Steve talking—my passion for this entire book takes on a very personal slant at this juncture. I want every father's son to know this material, because I want every guy to see Madeline as she really is, inside and out. She's not an object.

The other day Madeline asked me about boys and what I felt about a guy spending time with her alone. I was ready for the question. I told her that I would never allow a young man whom I could not trust to spend time alone with her, and the only way I could trust him was to get to know him first. So before he can hang around with Madeline, he has to hang around with me.

Why do I demand to get to know a guy before he gets to know my daughter? Because that will hold us accountable to one another as men. You know what I would like some guy to say to Madeline? "You are an amazing girl…I'd sure like to spend some time with you! I wonder if I could come over and get to know your dad a little so that he can get comfortable with me and trust me. I know how much he must care for you, Madeline." That takes courage and honor, traits that would earn my trust in a heartbeat. That kind of guy would protect her boundaries like I do.

You're Not Alone

Most girls will help you be an honorable man and respect their purity and yours. But what if a girl catches you by surprise? What if some girl charges past *your* boundaries? If my daughter didn't care about her honor, I'd still care about it. I'd still expect you to honor me anyway.

In fact, if she has no boundaries of her own, you would honor me most by keeping *my* boundaries for her. When I teach on this topic, I've had teen boys ask me, "How far can I go with a girl?"

My answer? "You can go as far with her as you would be comfortable doing in front of her father. After all, her dad is the guardian of her purity."

You and I are both men. We both understand the tingly draw of lust on our bodies. But we also know that guys stand up for each other and protect each other. I may be older than you, but we're both guys, and you owe me the honor of protecting the sexual boundaries I have for my daughter, no matter what she says.

So whether you are defending against your own lusts or hers, your first line of defense should always be what I call the Joseph Plan.

Forced to Make a Choice

Have you ever heard the story of Joseph from the book of Genesis? His jealous brothers sold him into slavery in Egypt, but while Joseph lived in this foreign land, he became a very important man and was placed in charge of Pharaoh's household affairs.

Joseph was born with good looks and a bright intellect. You couldn't help but notice him if you were around him because he had the total package. One of those who did more than notice Joseph was his master's (Potiphar) wife. She began batting her big eyes at him, and then she came out with what was on her mind: "Let's sleep together."

Joseph could have said yes. But you know what Joseph did? He refused her offer, telling Potiphar's wife that he couldn't make love with her because his master had entrusted him with everything in the entire household. Besides, he said, sleeping with her was a wicked thing and a great sin against God.

Potiphar's wife wouldn't take this rebuff without a fight. She kept offering her body to Joseph, but Joseph continued to tell her no. Potiphar's wife was used to getting her way, so now she was mad. The last time she asked Joseph to sleep with her, it wasn't a request—it was a demand! Joseph turned to run—remember how we are told to "flee immorality" in 1 Corinthians—but Potiphar's wife grabbed him, tearing his jacket off.

Joseph continued running toward his chamber, but Potiphar's wife began screaming, "Rape! Rape!" She had Joseph's jacket in her hands to "prove" to Potiphar that Joseph tried to force himself on her, so he promptly dumped Joseph into prison.

The story doesn't stop there, since God used the time that Joseph was in prison to prepare him for great service, but the lesson remains as true today as it did thousands of years ago when Joseph lived. When you're tempted, you have to get a move on and get yourself out of the situation. That's the Joseph Plan.

You can put this plan to use anytime, not just when girls come on to you. You are a guy…those special feelings you get around girls aren't just going to come on dates or when you are alone together. They can come anytime, anywhere, simply in brushing up against a girl, even when you are minding your own business.

Tyler's dad told him about the Joseph Plan, which he put to good use once when he was eating lunch next to an attractive girl. At one point during their meal, their legs touched. Tyler got all these tingly feelings when that happened, but then he remembered the Joseph Plan. Tyler moved his leg right over, gave himself more space, and the tingly feelings stopped.

Later, Tyler experienced a bigger surprise after church one Sunday night. It seems the pastor invited his family over to their house for supper after the service. While everyone ate snacks waiting for the meal to be served, Becky, the pastor's daughter, invited Tyler downstairs to the rec room to chill out for a while.

Tyler slumped wearily onto a big soft sofa and closed his eyes for a moment. To his shock, Becky plopped onto his lap, wrapped her arms around his neck, and began kissing him!

Tyler handled the situation magnificently. He smiled, gently pushed her away, and stood up. He mumbled something about getting some more chips and headed upstairs. In other words, he took himself out of the basement of temptation! The Joseph Plan prevailed again!

I tell you this story to remind you that guys are not always the aggressors. Girls these days will come on to you. If some girl puts her hand on your leg, and it's just a little too close for comfort, gently lift it away and put it back in her lap. If she loosens her shirt like Tracy did years ago for me, start looking for a way out the back, Jack. You gotta nip these things in the bud, and when you do, her father will thank you for it!

> Discussion: Go back to the beginning and read through your highlighted phrases. Discuss them together.

Optional Discussion Questions

1. List a quick Top Three differences between what men and women want from relationships. Ask your son if he's noticed these three before.

2. Tell your son how you chose girlfriends back in school. Would you change your approach now?

3. Tell your son which of your girlfriends' dads was most frightening. Why? Did this fear affect the way you handled her boundaries?

4. Dad, how much could a guy do with a daughter in the same room and still leave you feeling comfortable? Share that with your son.

5. Reflect back on your own most triumphant use of the Joseph Plan. How did that go?

Closing Scripture

> Be careful with this freedom of yours. Do not cause a brother or sister [or girlfriend] with a weaker conscience to stumble. (1 Corinthians 8:9, NLT)

Closing Prayer

Dad, lay your hands on your son's shoulders, lift your face, and ask God to give your son a passion for defense, not a passion for "a little action." Ask Him to give your son a brave heart and a spine of steel.

Son, tell the Lord you want to be a Christian in action and not just seem like one in words. Commit to God that you will not only leave every girl you date better for having known you, but you will leave every father better for having known you.

date away

You don't have to date, you know. Really, you don't have to.

Maybe that seems like a strange way to start out a dating section. When I took my ride down Adolescence River, the thought of kissing dating good-bye never entered my mind. I thought dating was as much a part of being a teen as fast cars, after-game dances, and Saturday night movies. Such time-tested rites of passage like homecoming and the prom were just part of the landscape, like the Pyramids and Mount Rushmore.

Some don't see it that way. My son Jasen hung out all over town with the girls and guys in his pack, but he never really dated anyone during high school. One evening during his senior year, we got to talking about it. "Hey, Jasen," I said casually, "I've noticed that you haven't really dated anyone yet, and here you are getting ready to head off to college. That's kind of uncommon. Any particular reason?"

He looked me in the eye and replied, "There just isn't anyone out there, Dad."

Hmmm. That makes him only five thousand times more mature than I was at his age. He's got his standards, and he's planning to keep them. He's in no hurry.

Still, I pressed in a bit more, asking, "Well, some of your friends have had steady girlfriends and all that. Have any of your friends ever asked you why you don't date?"

"Some. Jan asked me about it just the other day. But I'm glad it doesn't come up that much. The whole topic is very annoying."

"How so?"

"People are so strange about it, Dad. They are all so convinced that high school is some sort of training ground with girls. Remember Mr. Peterson?"

"Sure. Everyone's favorite teacher."

"He is one of my favorites too. But I'd often hear him talking to kids about why it's important to date in high school. I didn't want to talk to him about it, but one day he and a couple of the guys cornered me. I knew they were only concerned for me, but they piled on about my need to start dating before I went off to college. They also said it would be good practice for picking a wife.

"I stood there patiently listening, while chuckling to myself inside," Jasen continued. "I thought, *If all this practice is so helpful in learning how to pick wives, why are divorce rates so high in this country?* But I kept my mouth shut. When they kept going on and on, I finally got so annoyed that I told them, 'But *I* don't want to be practiced on!'

"You should have been there, Dad! It was really funny! They all just fell quiet and stared. None of them had ever considered that while *you* are practicing on the girls, *they* are practicing on you, using you as their own little practice field."

I admired my son's thinking. Jasen realized that you don't have to date for practice and certainly not for entertainment, either. It's more serious than that, because it has a long-term impact on your life.

Remember, as a young man you are now searching for your identity, to find out who you are. Finding your identity involves discovering and accepting who you are, learning what you expect of yourself, establishing your personal goals and values, deciding what you believe, and working out a lifestyle.

As we've seen, each decision you make today impacts the man you will become tomorrow. Obviously, dealing with dating and your sexuality is part of this process, because sex is part of who you are as a human. If you expect to find out who you are, you'll certainly have to take some serious time to think about dating and the place it should take in your life.

HOUSE RULES

It isn't a bad time to bring your dad and mom into the equation and ask them what they think. Here's what happened in our household when my daughter Laura turned fifteen. But first, a little background. One of our house rules states, "No dating until age sixteen." After Laura turned fifteen, she fixed one eye on the clock and the other on the starting gate, champing anxiously at the bit. As the months ticked by, I became concerned. She seemed too anxious to run around the dating track, and there were already some other horses circling the Stoeker homestead, anxious to run at her side. That worried me.

It wasn't that I didn't trust Laura's character, because I did. She knows and understands God's Word better than most adults. Her handicap? She was inexperienced when it comes to things like boys. If you remember, it's your inexperience that will get you into trouble the quickest as you make these halftime adjustments at adolescence.

With Laura, I needed to pass on some of the things I did right and some of the things I did wrong when I was dating. But I knew that she didn't want to hear me lecture her, so I found a book on dating that I thought we could read together.

On one of the first nights we were reading together, the author said that serial dating—dating someone, breaking up, dating someone new, breaking up, dating someone new, breaking up—can be painful because your emotions are being played with by people who are not in the least committed to you in the long run.

You've already heard the story, but that night I told Laura about Calley, my first real girlfriend. "Laura, she really stole my heart," I began, as I described Calley's long blonde hair and cute smile and how I got to go to the best parties because she was so popular. "I'll never forget how she found a make-out corner for us to have some fun. I was so in love."

"You really did this, Daddy?" Laura was shocked.

"Yes, I did, but I didn't really know anything about love or relationships at all—only what I'd seen in movies. After kissing her that first night, I wanted to express my deep feelings for her with something romantic, something in writing. I wrote her a note telling her how much I loved her, and I even naively dropped the word *marriage* into the mix to show that my passion was no average passion."

"Gee, Dad, you must have really liked her," Laura said.

"That's for sure, but let me tell what happened after I wrote that note. A buddy of mine took her the note between classes. For fun, he watched her open it by her locker. When she read the word *marriage,* it was all over. She laughed out loud, and then she told my friend to tell me I was a dork. She spread the news to all her popular friends and never really spoke with me again, though I tried to call her several times."

As I finished the story, Laura saw the pain in my eyes. She could tell that it bothered me twenty-five years later. "Laura, this book on not choosing to date is right for you. When you let your emotions out freely in situations where there is no real commitment from the other person, you can be crushed."

On another night, the book declared that, as Christians, we should always leave every person better off for having known us.

I backed up that point by telling another story. "Laura, let me describe Lindsey," I said. "This happened in the late winter of my senior year. I'd known Lindsey because she was one of the smart girls and was in many of my college-prep classes. She was also very, very nice, and she wore a cross necklace every day. I don't know why, but that attracted me somehow. She wasn't the most popular person on campus, but there was a sweetness and purity in her that tugged at my heart. She was cute in her own way, so I mustered the courage to ask her out.

"I can't remember what we did, but we ended up at her house, and at some point, we began to kiss. It was very exciting, and she seemed to like it too. Problem is, I was like most guys. I didn't want to stop there. Before long, I found my hands running down and over parts of her body that were not mine to touch."

Laura looked at me with surprise, but I plodded on.

"Suddenly, like a lion, Lindsey pushed me away, stood up, and began shouting at me. 'Who do you think you are to touch me like this? You are just like all the rest! All you care about is yourself, you pig! You don't care about me at all.' Anyway, that's the condensed version, but you catch the drift, I'm sure. Like a beaten puppy, I slunk outside to the car. I felt ashamed and lousy. Here was this girl I liked and respected so much, and yet I had done this to her. I was still in her classes every day, but I could never really look her in the eye again. It was awful, and I was glad high school was almost over."

"Wow, Dad, that's an awful story."

"Laura, the pain of that evening is hard for me to describe even today. I was confused, for one thing. I thought getting physical was at the center of relationships. That was what I knew from the movies. But the real pain came from disappointing someone that I deeply respected, someone who once respected me and now didn't. If God offered me a chance to go back and change just five decisions in my life, pushing over Lindsey's boundaries would be one of them. Sure, it was just one small night in a long life, but that one night stands as one of my biggest regrets. The sad thing is that I really have no way to make up for that, even if I could find her and tell her I'm sorry."

A few nights later, we were reading together again when I returned to this topic. "Laura, last night as I was falling asleep, I got to thinking about that story I told you about Lindsey. I thought back to all the girls I could remember dating in high school and college, and when I honestly looked at the relationships, I can't think of a single young woman who was better off for having known me. I got close to it on two of them. They once agreed together that neither one of them should have let me go because I was the best boyfriend they had ever had. That made me feel pretty good, but do you know what? Maybe they thought I was pretty nice, but I know that by Christ's standards, I even left *those* two worse off than when I met them. Maybe I wasn't as bad as some of the other creeps they dated, but that doesn't really make me any better."

"But Dad, you didn't know Christ when you were in high school," Laura interjected.

"You know me, Laura. I've never been a mean and selfish guy, even back then before I was really committed to Christ. But that should tell you something, shouldn't it?"

"What do you mean, Dad?"

"If even a nice guy like me can't say that he left a single girl better off than when he found her, that tells you something about guys and dating. You have to be careful, sweetheart. It's not that all guys are creeps. It's just that guys don't think, so they aren't too concerned about whether they leave you better off when it is all said and done and the relationship is over. I was a guy like that. I just didn't think."

PURSUING A GOAL

We often ask the wrong question during our single years, which is, "Whom do I want to pursue?" As Christians, there is a much bigger question that we ought to ask: "What does God want me to pursue for Him during my single years?"

"Laura," I said, "back in high school, football was my god. Everything I did and every decision I made was based on football. In spite of my stories, I was pretty moral. But I was moral because of football, not Christianity. I didn't drink because I knew it would hurt me on the playing field. I didn't date girls seriously because I knew they would split my focus. I wanted to be all-state in the worst way. When I got to college, my god died—I couldn't pursue football. When my god died, my morality went into a death spiral too. I'm not going to give you all the details now, but I began to really chase women to replace football in my life. If I'd lose a girl, I'd grab another.

"By the time I was one year out of college, I had four girlfriends at the same time! I was sleeping with three and essentially engaged to be married to two of them. And do you know what? As odd as this may sound, never once at Stanford did I ever ask the question, What should I be doing with my single years to prepare for life? And I don't think that is so uncommon."

I reminded Laura that in high school I was focused on my football dreams and was accomplishing things. "At Stanford," I said, "I never gave the future much thought, and in many ways, I wasted my college years."

I described how one friend went on to be a CEO at an important pharmaceutical company. Another went on to design artificial hearts. Another became a well-known international bond trader and made $85 million when his company went public.

"I could go on and on," I said. "You have a dream to become a veterinarian. You've had that dream since you were three years old. Do you think God wants you to be using your single years to advance that goal?"

"Yes," she replied.

"You need to think about what place dating should have in your life in light of your dream, just like I did with football when I was in high school," I reasoned.

"Once in college, I never asked that question, and it ruined my college career and my prospects for my adult years in a career."

PRIORITIES IN LIFE

After hearing my stories, Laura decided that dating should take a smaller priority in her life. "I've been thinking," she said, "and I can really see now that getting into a heavy dating relationship could impact my dream of being a veterinarian. I don't think it makes sense to risk my emotions or my dreams on dating right now." She added that she just wanted to go out on group dates when she turned sixteen—where a bunch of guys and girls go bowling together or hit a restaurant—and chill out on the romantic part since there's no pairing off with group dating. I beamed with happiness as a proud pop because I'm a group-dating fan.

Now would be a good time to talk with your dad about how you see the dating years shaping up. Ask him what he thinks. If he's looking for advice from us as well, ours would be this: You don't have to date, but if you do, group dating is the way to go. Group dating is a fabulous way for teens to get to know the opposite sex without all the baggage that comes from one-on-one dating. It's like the romantic part is taken off the table, but you still get to have a ton of fun interacting and talking and joking with cute girls.

There's another thing I want you to keep in mind if and when you start dating. The odds of your marrying someone you date in high school are very low—less than one in a hundred. It just doesn't happen like that these days. So think about it. The girl you take to the prom will not be the girl you marry. That means someone *else* is escorting your future wife to the prom. She may be in another city or another state for all I know. *But I want you to treat your date the way you hope some other guy is treating your future wife.*

You are a young man who will make his own decision on dating, although parents can definitely set guidelines, such as no single dating until you are seventeen years old, for example. Whatever happens, choose this goal from the beginning: I'm going to leave her better off for having known me.

If all of us could do that, we'd sure live in a much better world.

> Discussion: Go back to the beginning and read through your
> highlighted phrases. Discuss them together.

Optional Discussion Questions

1. Dad, did you see dating as some sort of training ground? Describe what you hoped to learn from your dating experiences.
2. What were some of the things you did right and some of the things you did wrong when you were dating?
3. Did you leave any girlfriend better off for having known you? If so, describe how she was better off.
4. Tell your son about the biggest regret you ever had in the dating arena and why.

Closing Scripture

Therefore come out from them
and be separate,
says the Lord....
I will be a Father to you,
and you will be my sons and daughters,
says the Lord Almighty. (2 Corinthians 6:17-18)

Closing Prayer

Son, ask God to help you walk like Jesus in every way, not only in the honorable way Jesus treated women but also in the way Jesus kept His focus on His Father's purpose for His life. Thank God for the plan He has laid out for your life, and ask Him to reveal it more clearly so that your focus might be strong.

Dad, give your son a hug and pray for him, committing your life and resources to God's purpose in your son's life.

are you ready for your number to be called?

As we close this book, we want to welcome you to the world of men and to your second half of play. We're glad God chose you for our team, and we're expecting great things from you. As veterans of this ol' game, however, we throw down the gauntlet by saying this: We challenge you to be different.

Different can mean a lot of things. My nephew Nick is different. He hasn't had a real haircut in about five months, as close as I can figure. After two months, I began calling him David Cassidy after a shaggy-headed singer in a seventies television sitcom called *The Partridge Family.* But after three *more* months with nothing more than a trim or two, I didn't know *what* to call him.

But you'd like him. If you knocked on his door, he might just answer with a two-foot-long, lime-green iguana perched atop his head. He loves snowboarding and paint-balling more than soccer and girls. He loves off-roading in the mud on his ATV. He loves "thrifting"—pawing through countless thrift shops in a ceaseless quest for odd, offbeat retro-fashion looks. He's got a penchant for leisure suits and polyester pants from the seventies, if that tells you anything. Nick's not your run-of-the-mill guy, but that makes him very special to me. I love every unique part of Nick, and I look forward to seeing him every chance I get.

But he's something special in another important way—he loves God and isn't afraid to show you. Nick is one of the kindest, gentlest, loving young men I know, filled with patience and goodness. In fact, if he were a tree (come to think of it, that bush atop his head *does* remind me of a tree), then Nick's branches would be laden with fruit, which reminds me of this verse from Scripture:

> But the fruit of the Spirit is love, joy, peace, patience, kindness, goodness, faithfulness, gentleness and self-control.... Those who belong to Christ Jesus have crucified the sinful nature with its passions and desires. Since we live by the Spirit, let us keep in step with the Spirit. (Galatians 5:22-25)

The Holy Spirit wants you to bear this fruit too. As you seek your identity, go ahead and be different. You are becoming a young man now, and what better time to go for it? But while you're at it, be different in another way. Bear the Spirit's fruit in your life abundantly and defend God's character with a spine of steel. Obey Him with all your heart.

You're growing up in some very special times. Your generation is the first to grow up with computers and the Internet, just as your parents were the first generation to grow up with television. You have a wonderful future ahead of you.

But these are special times in another way—times when the idea of sexual purity seems radical. These days are a lot like the days of Ezekiel:

> Her priests do violence to my law and profane my holy things; they do not distinguish between the holy and the common; they teach that there is no difference between the unclean and the clean. (Ezekiel 22:26)

Today, the sexual lines have been so blurred that few people know what's right or wrong, holy or profane. The great news is that God is looking for special people in these special times. His eyes are looking throughout the whole earth for young men through whom He can show His power—just like He did in the days of wicked King Ahab, when He needed someone with a steel spine to stand up to evil in *those* special times. God found that man in Elijah, who was ready to represent God before the king.

Today, God is looking for young men with the spine to stand up for Him. In light of that, we'd like to leave you with the following challenges:

- We challenge you to live without premarital sex.
- We challenge you to keep clean with regard to what media you're watching (television, movies, and the Internet).
- We challenge you to not ridicule your friends who are trying to walk closer to God.
- We challenge you to let the girls in your life know that you care more about their hearts than their bodies.
- We challenge you to be a real man...today!

To stand shoulder to shoulder with the other real Christian men in this world, you should start thinking about what kinds of practical things you can do to strengthen that spiritual spine of yours for the battles to come. Developing a few spiritual habits, like reading your Bible and praying regularly, would be a good start. By regularly, I mean ten or fifteen minutes a day. Ask your dad to help you set up a plan. Reading the Bible and talking to God are like doing spiritual push-ups and sit-ups. You'll grow strong in the Lord, that's for sure.

As you read God's Word, you'll become acquainted with what God has to say about what's wrong and what's right when measured by His standards of sexual purity. We've taught you a bunch of His thoughts in this book already, but if you are anything like my kids, you'll be amazed to hear it straight from God's mouth in His own words.

We would encourage you to memorize a few of the scriptures we've emphasized in this book, because memorizing Scripture can be incredibly powerful. In Psalm 119:9 and 11, God's Word says, "How can a young man keep his way pure? By living according to your word.... I have hidden your word in my heart that I might not sin against you."

And since memorization works so well for young guys, it couldn't hurt the grizzled, old veteran of these purity wars to memorize a few with you. Go ahead and ask your dad to join up with you.

Besides memorizing some verses, reading from Proverbs regularly, or bowing your head and lifting up your prayer requests, you can also sing to God. Yes, sing, right out loud! You can sing some of those great worship songs you hear in church or sing along as you listen to CDs by Michael W. Smith or Rebecca St. James. Listen to these worship songs, learn their lyrics, and sing them back to God. Singing is a great way to say "I love you" to the Creator of the universe.

I've made it a habit to sing to the Lord before I read my Bible in the morning. I go to the basement with my CD player where I can be alone with Jesus to sing to Him. Some of my favorite love songs to Him are "You're the One That I Love" and "Your Love Is Amazing." It's also a good idea to start chasing God now before your friends—not you, of course—start chasing girls. You need that intimacy in your life now. He's the Creator of the universe, and He's *for* you.

Intimacy with God is where it is at, my young friend. As you search for your identity, find it in God. Seek Him.

And don't fake it, pal. Don't stop short at just *seeming* to be Christian to those around you. Go and *be* a Christian in every way.

If you do, you'll become a young man to be reckoned with. But best of all, you'll like who you'll become.

And that's priceless.

THE FINISH LINE

All right. We've come to the end of the book, and you're to be commended for making it this far. I hope that what we've covered in *Preparing Your Son for Every Man's Battle* has sparked some great discussions with your dad, and I hope you've asked him questions as you went along.

Now would be a good time to ask your dad any of those tough questions that you were too embarrassed to ask before. Go ahead. He's waiting to hear from you.

You know, in the first half of this book—the part your father was supposed to read before he went through your book with you—we told him that he would be handing off the ball of truth to you as you go through adolescence and become a young man. We urged your father not to fumble away his chance.

Now you're in the huddle, and your number has just been called. As soon as the ball is snapped, your father is going to turn and hand you the ball of truth and watch you hit the O-line. God can open holes you wouldn't believe, and we're confident that you'll successfully run for daylight.

Go for it, my young friend. As ESPN's Chris Berman would say, you…
COULD…GO…ALL…THE…WAY!

> Discussion: Go back to the beginning and read through your
> highlighted phrases. Discuss them together.

Optional Discussion Questions

1. Ask your son, "What are you doing now to build your spiritual life?"
2. Tell your son what you are doing to build your spiritual life, including what things have worked best in strengthening you throughout your life.
3. Worship the Lord together before bed every night this week, singing a chorus from a favorite song, just the two of you. At the end of the week, talk about what you felt when you did this together.

Closing Scripture

I will sing of your love and justice;
  to you, O LORD, I will sing praise.
I will be careful to lead a blameless life—

I will walk in my house
  with blameless heart.
I will set before my eyes
  no vile thing. (Psalm 101:1-3)

Closing Prayer

Dad, give your son a smile and thank him for keeping his commitment to going through this book with you. Ask God to root the truths firmly in his heart that he might run normally all the days of his life.

Son, thank your father for keeping his commitment to complete this book with you. Ask God to reward your dad's faithfulness by transforming both of you, keeping each of you in perfect unity and purity.

about the authors

STEPHEN ARTERBURN is founder and chairman of New Life Ministries and host of the nationally syndicated radio show, *New Life Live!* heard across the United States and on XM and Sirius satellite. Founder of the Women of Faith Conferences, he is a best-selling author and co-author of over seventy books including the Every Man and Every Woman series and his most recent book, *Being Christian*. He has been nominated for numerous writing awards and won three Gold Medallion awards for writing excellence, carries degrees from Baylor University and the University of North Texas, and obtained two honorary doctorate degrees. Steve resides with his family in Laguna Beach, California.

FRED STOEKER is a best-selling author of several books, including *Tactics* and *Hero*, the president of Living True Ministries, and a popular conference speaker who challenges men to become sexually pure, to reconnect in true intimate relationships with their wives, and to train their sons to become godly men. A graduate of Stanford University, Fred lives in Des Moines, Iowa, with his wife, Brenda, and their children.

MIKE YORKEY, a writer living in Encinitas, California, has collaborated with Fred Stoeker on all his books for the Every Man series.

now available
on DVD
and on video

every young man's battle

Hosted by:
coauthor Steve Arterburn

Includes:

- Interviews with coauthor *Fred Stoeker*

- Segments from *Dr. James Dobson's* interview with Ted Bundy

- *Dramas*

- Music from recording artist *downhere*

- Special Guests:
  Former NFL great *William White*
  Retired Colonel *Tom Schmidt*
  (former assistant to Colin Powell)

- Filmed at a variety of locations including
  Gettysburg Battlefields

A video presentation by Guardian Studios
in partnership with Vision Word Productions.

To order call
1-800-New-Life
(1-800-639-5433)

VHS $19.95 (plus S&H)
DVD $24.95 (plus S&H)

every man's battle
workshops

from New Life Ministries

New Life Ministries receives hundreds of calls every month from Christian men who are struggling to stay pure in the midst of daily challenges to their sexual integrity and from pastors who are looking for guidance in how to keep fragile marriages from falling apart all around them.

As part of our commitment to equip individuals to win these battles, New Life Ministries has developed biblically based workshops directly geared to answer these needs. These workshops are held several times per year around the country.

- Our workshops **for men** are structured to equip men with the tools necessary to maintain sexual integrity and enjoy healthy, productive relationships.

- Our workshops **for church leaders** are targeted to help pastors and men's ministry leaders develop programs to help families being attacked by this destructive addiction.

Some comments from previous workshop attendees:

"An awesome, life-changing experience. Awesome teaching, teacher, content and program." —DAVE

"God has truly worked a great work in me since the EMB workshop. I am fully confident that with God's help, I will be restored in my ministry position. Thank you for your concern. I realize that this is a battle, but I now have the weapons of warfare as mentioned in Ephesians 6:10, and I am using them to gain victory!" —KEN

"It's great to have a workshop you can confidently recommend to anyone without hesitation, knowing that it is truly life changing. Your labors are not in vain!" —DR. BRAD STENBERG, Pasadena, CA

If sexual temptation is threatening your marriage or your church, please call **1-800-NEW-LIFE** to speak with one of our specialists.